PASS KEY

TO THE

GED

High School Equivalency Examination

Third Edition

Murray Rockowitz, Ph.D.
Former Chairman, Board of Examiners,
New York City Board of Education
Former Chairman, English Department,
Charles Evans Hughes High School, New York City

Samuel C. Brownstein
Former Chairman, Biology Department,
Wingate High School, Brooklyn, New York

Max Peters
Former Chairman, Mathematics Department,
Wingate High School, Brooklyn, New York

Ira K. Wolf, Ph.D.
Teacher of Mathematics,
Benjamin N. Cardozo High School, Bayside, New York

Johanna M. Bolton
Instructor, Adult High School Program
Daytona Beach Community College, Daytona Beach, Florida

Barron's Educational Series, Inc.

All inquiries should be addressed to:
Barron's Educational Series, Inc.
250 Wireless Boulevard
Hauppauge, New York 11788
http://www.barronseduc.com

Library of Congress Catalog Card No. 98-38864

International Standard Book No. 0-7641-0457-8

Library of Congress Cataloging-in-Publication Data
Rockowitz, Murray.
   Barron's pass key to the GED high school equivalency exam / by
Murray Rockowitz, Samuel C. Brownstein, and Max Peters. —3rd ed.
          p.   cm.
   ISBN 0-7641-0457-8
   1. General educational development tests—Study guides. 2. High
school equivalency examinations—Study guides. I. Brownstein,
Samuel C., 1909- . II. Peters, Max, 1906- . III. Title.
LB3060.33.G45R625   1998
373.12'62—dc20   98-38864
                                                         CIP

PRINTED IN THE UNITED STATES OF AMERICA
9 8 7 6 5 4 3

CONTENTS

PREFACE

Barron's PASS KEY TO THE GED is a shorter version of *Barron's How to Prepare for the High School Equivalency Examination,* which has helped over a million people like you obtain a high school equivalency diploma.

In today's tough job market, the key that opens the door to opportunity is a high school diploma. Without it, you can't get a good Civil Service position, a specialized course in the Armed Forces, admission to a good technical school, or a chance to become an apprentice in a good company.

This compact guide contains materials that will prepare you for the key areas of the test: correctness and effectiveness of expression (sentence structure, usage, punctuation, capitalization, and spelling); interpretation of reading materials in the social studies, natural sciences, literature and the arts; and general mathematical ability (with more than a hundred examples, which are carefully explained).

Keep this convenient book handy for study on the train as you go to work, or when you wait in the doctor's or dentist's office. Make every minute count. And, if after using this brief version, you feel you need more review and practice, turn to the complete edition of *Barron's How to Prepare for the High School Equivalency Examination,* the widely used, comprehensive guide with almost 800 pages of carefully prepared materials to help you achieve your two most important goals—a high school equivalency diploma and a good job.

ACKNOWLEDGMENTS

The authors gratefully acknowledge the kindness of all organizations concerned with the granting of permission to reprint passages, charts, graphs.

The copyright holders and publishers of quoted materials are listed below.

Pages 69–70, Passage from Arthur H. Doerr and J.L. Guernsey, *Principles of Geography – Physical and Cultural,* Second Edition Revised. Copyright © 1975 Barron's Educational Series, Inc.

Page 79, Pie Graph from *Annual Energy Review.* Copyright © 1995 *Energy Information Review.*

Page 81, Line Graph adapted from Klose and Lader, *College Review: United States History,* Vol. 2. Copyright © 1994 Barron's Educational Series, Inc.

Pages 156–157, Article from *Investor's Business Daily,* December 1, 1997.

Page 275, Practice Examination, Graph for Questions 39–40: Frederick S. Mattson, reprinted by permission of CDM and Associates, Arlington, Virginia.

Page 284, Practice Examination, Cartoon for Questions 62–63: from *The Times Union,* July 1991.

Page 310, Practice Examination, Passage for Questions 11–15: Excerpt from ALL GOD'S CHILDREN NEED TRAVELING SHOES by Maya Angelou, Copyright © 1986 by Maya Angelou. Reprinted by permission of Random House, Inc.

Page 313, Practice Examination, Poem for Questions 21–25: from "Elegy for Jane" by Theodore Roethke, Copyright © 1950 by Theodore Roethke, in COLLECTED POEMS OF THEODORE ROETHKE, Reprinted by permission of Doubleday & Co., Inc.

Page 315, Practice Examination, Passage for items 26–30; from *A Raisin in the Sun,* by Lorraine Hansberry, Copyright © 1958, 1959

viii   **ACKNOWLEDGMENTS**

by Robert Nemiroff as Executor of the Estate of Lorraine Hansberry. Reprinted by permission of Random House, Inc.

Page 317, Practice Examination, Passage for Questions 31–35: from "Memoirs of Chief Red Fox." Copyright © McGraw-Hill 1997.

1

THE GED HIGH SCHOOL EQUIVALENCY EXAMINATION

THE IMPORTANCE OF THE GED EXAMINATION

The General Education Development or GED Examination offers anyone who has not completed his or her high school diploma a way to earn a High School Equivalency Certificate. This is the equivalent of a high school diploma, and it is necessary for those who want to continue their educations in college or another career-oriented program. Having a high school diploma today is also very important if you want a good job.

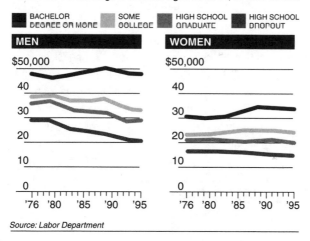

EDUCATION PAYS

Median annual earnings of workers aged 25 to 64, in 1995 dollars.

BACHELOR DEGREE OR MORE | SOME COLLEGE | HIGH SCHOOL GRADUATE | HIGH SCHOOL DROPOUT

Source: Labor Department

Study these graphs briefly. Note that the black line indicates the average annual earnings of high school graduates aged 25 to 64. The bottom gray line represents the average annual earnings of high school dropouts of similar age. Compare the two lines for 1995. You see that high school graduates earned much more than high school dropouts. Men earned nearly $10,000 a year more; women earned over $5,000 a year more. Over

1

the span of years from age 25 to age 64, a male high school graduate earns about $400,000 more than a high school dropout; the woman graduate earns over $200,000 more. It pays to have a high school diploma.

THE FIVE GED TEST AREAS

The GED Examination is divided into five tests:
1. Writing Skills
2. Social Studies
3. Science
4. Literature and the Arts
5. Mathematics

The five tests are designed to measure the knowledge and skills that a student should have acquired after four years in high school. One important thing about the tests is that, even though the questions may involve a specific area of study such as science, you don't have to memorize specific facts, details, dates, or even exact definitions. Much of this information is given to you in the test itself. You have to be able to read and understand the material that is presented and then to answer questions about it.

With the exception of the essay part of the Writing Skills test, all of the questions in the GED Examination are multiple-choice. You will be given a brief statement, short passage, map, table, or diagram, and then you will have to answer one or more multiple-choice questions about this material. This book will help you learn how to analyze and use information presented in these various ways.

COMMONLY ASKED QUESTIONS ABOUT THE GED TESTS

1. *Who can take the GED tests?* Adults who meet the eligibility requirements established by their state, territorial, or provincial departments of education can take the GED tests.
2. *Where are the GED tests given?* The address of your state, territorial, or provincial administrator can be obtained from your local high school. Write to that office for the location of the GED testing center nearest your home.

TIMETABLE OF A HIGH SCHOOL EQUIVALENCY EXAMINATION
Total: 7 hours, 35 minutes

	Section	Time Allowed*	Number of Test Items*	Description
Test 1	The Writing Skills Test Part I	75 min.	55	Sentence Structure (35%) Usage (35%) Mechanics (spelling, punctuation, capitalization) (30%)
	Part II	45 min.		Essay on a given topic
Test 2	The Social Studies Test	85 min.	64	History (25%) Economics (20%) Geography (15%) Political Science (20%) Behavioral Sciences (20%)
Test 3	The Science Test	95 min.	66	Biology (50%) Earth Science Chemistry } 50% Physics
Test 4	The Interpreting Literature and the Arts Test	65 min.	45	Popular Literature (50%) Classical Literature (25%) Commentary About Literature and the Arts (25%)
Test 5	The Mathematics Test	90 min.	56	Arithmetic (50%) Algebra (30%) Geometry (20%)

*Note: Format and timing are subject to change.

3. *What score is required to earn a High School Equivalency Diploma?* The standard score requirements vary for each state, territory, or province. You will find that in some states a candidate must earn a minimum score of 40 on each of the five test areas or a minimum average score of 45 for the five tests. The majority of states require a minimum average score of 45 and no individual test score below 35 or 40.

4. ***What types of questions are on the GED tests?*** Part II of the Writing Skills test requires a written essay. For the other test questions, you will be given information in the form of a written passage, graph, diagram, map, or table, and asked to answer one or more multiple-choice questions based on the information presented. Five answer choices are given for each question.

5. ***How can experience outside the classroom help me pass the GED tests?*** Many people worry about the difficulty of taking the GED Examination, especially if they've been out of school for a long time. What you should realize is that learning continues after you leave school. You read newspapers and follow political events; you travel and talk to many different people; you listen to the radio, watch television, and go to the movies. All of these experiences are forms of learning and add to your educational background.

6. ***Why are maturity and motivation strong assets?*** More mature students have experiences that will help them visualize or understand situations that may be involved in a problem on the GED Examination. Also, older students understand the need for good study habits and have the self-discipline to work regularly in this book. With the mature decision to study for the GED tests, half the battle is over. Many educators know that motivation, the desire to learn, is the first step toward success.

7. ***When are you ready to take the GED Examination?*** After reviewing and doing the practice exercises, take the practice tests in Unit VIII, and score your results. If your scores are in the category Good or Excellent, you are probably ready to walk into the examination room with confidence. If, however, you did not attain such scores, do not apply for the GED Examination until you have studied further. Concentrate on the areas in which you are weak.

ORGANIZING YOUR PLAN OF STUDY

SOME STUDY HINTS

Educators agree that, for learning to be efficient, certain steps must be followed. As a mature person, you will probably appreciate the value of carefully following these ten tips for successful study.

1. **Physical conditions.** Find a quiet place. Tolerate no distraction— noise or music. Do not work in an overheated room.

2. **Timing.** You will learn faster and remember longer if you study in several short sessions rather than in one long session. Do not attempt to study for an entire weekend. Fatigue will set in after a few hours. It is wiser to spend some time each day rather than to "cram" your work into one or two days.

3. **Schedule for study.** A study schedule must be workable, realistic, practical, and, above all, suited to you and your other obligations. Decide which days and hours you can spare for study. Make a schedule, and stick to it.

4. **Using odd moments.** Put spare time and wasted moments to work. Riding on the bus or train may be a good time to memorize troublesome spelling words and to study rules of grammar or definitions of unfamiliar terms.

5. **Efficiency.** Most people find that learning occurs faster in the early part of the day. Perhaps you can work into your schedule some time for study before your day's work begins or on weekend mornings. Certainly you should not schedule study in the later hours of the evening.

6. **Review periods.** On certain days, plan to review. Take stock of yourself in these study periods. This review will serve at least two purposes. It will definitely reinforce the learning, and the gratification of knowing that you have acquired new material will stimulate you to learn more.

7. **Writing while you learn.** Wherever possible, write what you are studying. Spelling can best be learned by writing. Get into the habit of writing down key ideas of the passages you read. This writing will focus attention on your learning, will help you avoid distractions that may cause your mind to wander, and will provide an opportunity to check up on yourself. Also, educators believe that the more senses employed while studying, the more effective the learning will be.

8. **Reading.** The best way to improve reading comprehension is by practicing reading. You will find that a great part of the test involves the interpretation of reading material. Read your newspaper very carefully. Make it a habit to read the editorials. If possible, engage a member of your family or a friend in frequent discussions of the ideas presented in your newspaper. Of course, this book has specific

reading exercises on the various phases of the test. But remember: there is no substitute for general reading.

9. **The dictionary.** The most important single book, in addition to this one, that can help you prepare for the High School Equivalency Examination is the dictionary. It is important to have one nearby as you study. A suggested inexpensive dictionary is the pocket-size paperback edition of *Webster's New World Dictionary of the American Language*.

10. **S Q 3R.** A popular way to remember the five important steps needed to study effectively is the S Q 3R method.

- S stands for survey. You examine the material to be learned to get a general idea of the content.
- Q stands for question. You turn the topic, the title of the section you are studying, into a question or questions. For example, if the title of the section is "Drawing Conclusions," you turn it into a challenging question: "How do I draw conclusions from what I read?"
- The first of the three R's stands for read. You use the reading skills that are taught in this book, such as locating the main idea, finding details, reading critically, detecting propaganda, determining cause and effect, and comparing and contrasting ideas.
- The second R stands for recite. You close the book and speak aloud from memory. Include especially the main ideas you have located and any name, word, or fact you find difficult to remember.
- The third R stands for review, which literally means to "view" or see again. You look over your notes, the lines you have highlighted, or the outline you have made. Do this again until you are sure you have mastered the material, for example, spelling words that trouble you or a rule of punctuation you find hard to remember.

This is a summary of the S Q 3R method of study:

S urvey
Q uestion
R ead
R ecite
R eview

BEFORE THE TEST DATE

1. **Practice reading and writing.** Besides using the material in this book, spend more time reading. Read the local newspaper and some magazines. Also practice writing. Write letters to friends and relatives. Instead of using the telephone, use your pen.

2. **Don't rush to take the tests.** Don't be in too big a hurry to apply for the GED Examination. First be sure that you are prepared by taking the exercises and tests in this book. Even though most states will let you retake the tests after a waiting period, a notice that you failed the first time is unpleasant and may even discourage you from trying again. Instead of rushing into the examination and trusting to good fortune for a passing grade, it's better to wait until you know that you're ready. Also, don't procrastinate and cram all your study into the last few days. This rarely works. It's much better to set a realistic study schedule that gives you enough time to prepare.

3. **Know what to expect.** By the time you finish the preparation material in this book, you will be familiar with all the kinds of questions you will encounter on the GED tests. The exercises and practice test questions in this book are very similar to the actual test questions. Knowing what to expect will relieve some of your anxiety about taking the exam.

4. **Be relaxed.** It's a good idea to relax the evening before you take the GED Examination. A good night's sleep will help you to think logically; you'll be well rested and alert. Also, do not eat a heavy meal, which will make you feel dull and sleepy, before you take the test.

TACTICS AND STRATEGIES IN THE EXAMINATION ROOM

1. **Allow plenty of time to get to the test site.** Taking a test is pressure enough. You don't need the extra tension that comes from worrying about whether you will get there on time.

2. **Read all directions and questions carefully.** Answer the question given, not one you expected. Look for key words, such as *except*, *exactly*, and *not*. Carefully examine tables, graphs, and diagrams so you don't miss important information.

3. **Don't expect trick questions.** A straightforward presentation is used in all test sections.

4. **When you have difficulty finding an answer, eliminate choices that are definitely wrong.** Then consider the remaining choices.

5. **Don't let one or two challenging questions upset you.** Some questions are definitely harder than others. Remember you do not have to get 100 percent on this examination. No one does.

6. **Don't get bogged down on any one question.** If a question is taking too much time, circle it and make a guess. Then, if you have time at the end of the examination, go back and review the circled questions.

7. **Change answers only if you have a good reason for doing so.** Don't change your answer on a hunch or a whim. Most often the first judgment that you make is correct.

8. **Check answer order frequently.** Make sure you are putting your answers in the right spaces.

9. **Use your time wisely.** After taking the practice tests in this book, you will be familiar with the proper pace needed to complete each test.

10. **Be careful not to make stray pencil marks on the answer sheet.** These may interfere with the rating of your performance. If you wish to change an answer, be sure to erase your first mark completely. The rating machine will automatically mark an answer wrong if more than one choice is made. Also, do not fold or crease the answer sheet.

11. **Answer all questions, even if you have to guess.** Your score will be determined by the number of correct answers; no points are deducted for wrong answers. For this reason it is better to guess at an answer than to not respond at all. Of course, wherever possible, eliminate as many wrong answers as you can before guessing. Every answer you eliminate improves your chance of guessing correctly.

12. **Remain as calm as possible.** If you consider yourself a person who "goes to pieces" on tests, cheer up! Psychologists claim that more than 90 percent of us think we don't perform well on tests *of any kind*. Nobody likes tests. But more than 80 percent of the people who have taken the High School Equivalency tests in the New York area, for example, have passed them. They must be doing something right. And so can you—with the right attitude and careful preparation.

2

WRITING SKILLS, PART I

SENTENCE STRUCTURE

A sentence is the basic means of communicating an idea.

A sentence may be defined as a group of words having a subject and a predicate and expressing a complete thought. Each sentence should be separated from the one that follows it by some form of end punctuation such as a period, a question mark, or an exclamation point.

RUN-ON SENTENCES

In one important error, you may fail to separate two or more sentences by using the proper punctuation. Instead, you may either use no punctuation at all or incorrectly use a comma. The general term for this group of errors is the *run-on sentence* or, if a comma is incorrectly used, the *comma splice*.

This type can result from an incorrectly used or omitted conjunction or adverb.

EXAMPLE
Wrong:
Joe was elected class president *x* he is very popular.

Correct:
Joe was elected class president *because* he is very popular.

SENTENCE FRAGMENTS

In another important error, you may fail to complete the sentence. (You will remember that a sentence is defined as a group of words having a subject and a predicate and expressing a complete thought.) In that kind of error, called a *sentence fragment*, either the subject is left out, so that a predicate is left standing by itself (e.g., "Wish you were here.") or a part of the predicate is broken off from the sentence and made to stand by itself (e.g., "Walking down the street.").

EXAMPLE

Wrong:

Am having a wonderful time. Wish you were here.

Correct:

I am having a wonderful time. I wish you were here.

In each case, without the subject it is impossible to know *who* is doing the action indicated in the predicate.

PARALLEL STRUCTURE

A major error in structure is failure to keep elements of the sentence that perform the *same purpose* in the *same form*. This is called an error in parallel structure.

Here is an example of such an error.

Wrong:

Joe likes *swimming*, *fishing*, and, if he has the time, *to take* a long walk.

The sentence tells us three things Joe likes. They are related to us by words that are the objects of the verb *likes*, and they serve the same purpose. But are their forms alike? Let us line them up vertically.

Joe likes   swimming
             fishing
             to take a long walk

No, they are not. *Swimming* and *fishing* are gerunds (verbs used, in the *-ing* form, as nouns). *To take*, however, is an infinitive. Words having the same function should have the same form. Then, the sentence has parallel structure. The sentence should read:

Joe likes   swimming
             fishing
             taking a long walk

Correct:

Joe likes *swimming*, *fishing*, and, if he has the time, *taking a long walk*.

MISPLACED MODIFIERS

A modifier is a word or a group of words that help describe another word or group of words by giving a more exact meaning. The modifier may be an adjective (a *big* house) or an adverb (walk *slowly*), an adjective clause (the man *who came to dinner*) or an adjective phrase (Jeanie *with the light brown hair*), an adverbial clause (he arrived *when the clock struck twelve*) or an adverbial phrase (he arrived *on time*). Very often, confusion in meaning takes place when a modifier is used incorrectly.

A modifier that is misplaced in a sentence may cause confusion in meaning.

EXAMPLE
Wrong:
Fred cut himself while shaving *badly*.

The word *badly* is a misplaced modifier. It is an adverb that modifies the meaning of the verb *cut* and, therefore, should be placed where there is no doubt about what it modifies. (It certainly isn't intended to modify *shaving*.)

Correct:
Fred cut himself *badly* while shaving.

The meaning is completely changed by the placement of the modifier. Now the sentence means what the writer intended to say.

Dangling Modifiers

In the case of the *dangling modifier*, the problem is that there is no word or words to which the modifier clearly refers.

EXAMPLE
Wrong:
Standing on the corner, *the car* passed me by.

It is important to note that merely turning the incorrect sentence around will not keep the modifier from dangling.

Wrong:
The *car* passed me by, *standing* on the corner.

The sentence has to be rewritten to read:

Correct:
While I was *standing* on the corner, the car passed me by.

Standing is now part of the verb in the subordinate clause and is no longer dangling.

USAGE

AGREEMENT
Subject and Verb

A common error is failure to provide agreement between subject and verb. The basic rule is:

> THE VERB MUST AGREE WITH ITS SUBJECT
> IN *NUMBER* AND IN *PERSON*.

EXAMPLE   *Joe*, despite the fact that he was a newcomer, *was* elected president.
[*Joe* is still the subject—singular.]

EXAMPLE   *Joe*, together with all his friends, *was* welcomed warmly.
[*Joe* is still the subject—singular.]

EXAMPLE   A *box* of chocolates is on the table.
[*Box*, the subject, is singular.]

Most of the time, *pronouns* will be involved in this type of error. Some pronouns that can cause confusion are:

Singular Pronouns		Singular or Plural Pronouns
anybody	neither	any
anyone	nobody	all
each	no one	more
either	one	most
everybody	somebody	none
everyone	someone	some

However, *compound subjects* may also be involved. When a subject has more than one part and the parts are connected by *and* or by a word or groups of words similar in meaning to *and*, it is considered a *compound subject* and is plural. A compound subject can consist of more than one group of words, more than one phrase, or more than one clause.

EXAMPLE

Joe *and* his friend *are* here.

To study hard, to play hard, to enjoy life are desirable aims.

Her outstanding contribution to school athletics, her service as class officer, and her excellent scholastic record qualify her for the position of president.

EXCEPTION

A compound subject that consists of two singular subjects connected by *either...or*, or *neither...nor* is considered a singular subject.

EXAMPLE

Neither Joe nor his friend *is* here.

Note: Agreement is always with the number of the part of the subject nearest the verb.

EXAMPLE   Neither Joe nor I *am* voting for Frank.

Sometimes the subject comes after the verb. It is still the subject and may be singular or plural.

EXAMPLE

Pasted in the upper right-hand corner of the envelope were two ten-cent stamps.
[*Stamps* is the subject, even though it is the last word in the sentence. The verb is plural because the subject, *stamps*, is plural.]

EXAMPLE

There are many ways to show you care.

Pronoun and Antecedent

> ### A Pronoun must agree with its Antecedent in *number*, *gender*, and *person*.
>
> **Number**
>
> If the antecedent is singular, the pronoun replacing it is singular.
>
> > **EXAMPLE**   Joe does *his* homework.
> > [The pronoun *his* takes the place of Joe. *Joe* is singular (one person); therefore, the pronoun is singular]
>
> **Gender**
>
> If the antecedent is masculine, the pronoun replacing it is masculine. If the antecedent is feminine, the pronoun replacing it is feminine.
>
> > **EXAMPLE**   Susan does *her* homework.
>
> **Person**
>
> Note above that both *Joe* and *Susan* are in the third person. Therefore, the pronouns replacing each must be in the third person—*his*, *her*.

> **EXAMPLE**   *Joe and* his *friend* brought *their* books.

> **EXAMPLE**   *Either* Kathy *or* the boys should explain *their* reasons.

Some Special Problems

1. PRONOUNS THAT APPEAR TO BE PLURAL BUT ARE, IN FACT, SINGULAR

Some pronouns appear to refer to more than one person, but they never refer to more than one person *at a time*. Others may be either singular or plural.

Singular Pronouns		Singular or Plural Pronouns
anybody	neither	any
anyone	nobody	all
each	no one	more
either	one	most
everybody	somebody	none
everyone	someone	some

The following sentence may sound a little strange to you, but it is correct.

EXAMPLE

Every student must do *his* homework every day.

2. PRONOUNS THAT REFER TO NOUNS THAT APPEAR TO BE PLURAL BUT ARE SINGULAR IN FORM

These pronouns require a verb in the singular.

EXAMPLE

The team continued its winning streak.

3. PRONOUNS WITH INDEFINITE ANTECEDENTS

The antecedent must be clear or the sentence rephrased.

EXAMPLE

Wrong:

Frank told Joe to take *his* books to school.

[To whom does *his* refer—to Frank or to Joe? The sentence must be rewritten to clear up this confusion.]

Correct:

Frank told Joe to take Frank's books to school for him.

or better

Frank said to Joe: "Take my books to school for me."

Practice

1. Will everyone who has the right answer raise their hands?
2. Every participant must do his best.
3. The mother told her daughter to take her laundry to the laundromat.
4. One of my friends who went to school with me lost his mother.
5. Either the workers or the foreman are expected to attend.

Answers

1. Will everyone who has the right answer raise his hand?
2. Correct.
3. The mother told her daughter, "Take my laundry to the laundromat."
4. Correct.
5. Either the workers or the foreman is expected to attend.

Practice in Agreement
In each sentence, five parts are underlined and numbered. Where there is an error in agreement, choose the number of the underlined part that contains the error. If there is no error, choose answer 5. <u>No sentence contains more than one error</u>. These are included in the sentence correction type of multiple-choice item.

1. Luis, accompanied by <u>his</u> friend <u>are</u> waiting to see whether
        (1)   (2)
   you and <u>I</u> <u>are</u> joining them. <u>No error</u>
        (3)(4)   (5)

2. <u>There</u>, Mr. Chairman, <u>is</u> all the reports that the committee prepared
   (1)   (2)
   in <u>its</u> work as well as the notes <u>that</u> were taken. <u>No error</u>
      (3)   (4)   (5)

3. <u>There's</u> several ways for the city to solve <u>its</u> fiscal problems,
   (1)   (2)
   but <u>one</u> of them is not to lose <u>its</u> integrity. <u>No error</u>
       (3)   (4)   (5)

4. News from abroad <u>is</u> that each country is supporting <u>its</u> own policies
                    (1)   (2)
   despite the fact that <u>ours</u> <u>are</u> superior to theirs. <u>No error</u>
                        (3) (4)   (5)

5. Let everyone who <u>agrees</u> raise <u>his</u> hand so that neither George nor
   (1)   (2)
   I <u>am</u> in doubt about what the majority opinion <u>is</u>. <u>No error</u>
     (3)   (4)   (5)

6. Margaret asked Rosa to take <u>her</u> clothes to the cleaners and to make
                               (1)
   certain that <u>none</u> of <u>them</u> <u>were</u> in need of repair. <u>No error</u>
                (2)   (3)   (4)   (5)

7. Watching <u>our</u> game <u>were</u> Fred and his father and his mother, together
             (1)   (2)
   with <u>their</u> other children and <u>their</u> neighbors. <u>No error</u>
        (3)   (4) (5)

8. <u>Each</u> American must ask <u>himself</u>: "<u>Don't</u> it matter if we pollute <u>our</u>
   (1)   (2)   (3)   (4)
   environment?" <u>No error</u>
                 (5)

9. "Neither I nor they are attending the game," we said to its promoter.
        (1)   (2) (3)   (4)
No error
(5)

10. Everyone gave her opinion that a blue and white suit was the best
      (1)   (2)   (3)
choice for Liz to wear although there were exceptions. No error
                            (4)   (5)

Answer Key

1. **2**	3. **1**	5. **5**	7. **5**	9. **5**
2. **2**	4. **5**	6. **1**	8. **3**	10. **5**

What's Your Score?

        _____right,   _____wrong
      Excellent   9–10
      Good   8
      Fair   7

If you scored lower, restudy this section, concentrating on the rules and examples.

Answer Analysis

1. **2** Luis, the subject of the sentence, is singular, so the verb should be singular: *is* instead of *are*.
2. **2** The subject of the sentence, *reports*, follows the verb. Since the subject is plural, the verb should be plural: *are*, not *is*.
3. **1** The subject is *ways*, which follows the verb. The verb must be plural to agree with the plural subject. *There's* should be *There are*.
4. **5** No error.
5. **5** No error.
6. **1** The antecedent of *her* is not clear. Is it Margaret or Rosa? Depending on the answer, *her* should be changed to *Margaret's* or *Rosa's*.
7. **5** No error.
8. **3** The correct form of the third person singular of the verb *do* is *does*. *Doesn't it...* is correct.
9. **5** No error.
10. **5** No error.

CASE OF NOUNS AND PRONOUNS

Nouns

Only in the *possessive case* do the forms of most nouns change.

Nominative Case

> **EXAMPLE** *Frank* hit Joe.
> [*Frank* is the subject.]

Objective Case

> **EXAMPLES** Joe hit *Frank*.
> [*Frank* is the object.]
>
> Ellen ate the *salad*.
> [*Salad* is the object.]

Possessive Case

> **EXAMPLE** Cesar's friend went away.
> [A noun requires an apostrophe to indicate possession.]

Pronouns

Nearly all pronouns have different forms in the nominative, objective, and possessive cases. Only the pronoun forms *you* and *it* do NOT change when the case changes from *nominative* to *objective* or vice versa.

BASIC RULES FOR THE CASE OF PRONOUNS
Nominative

1. The subject of a verb (a noun or a pronoun) is in the nominative case. This is true whether the subject is singular or compound.

   EXAMPLE *Wrong:* Me and Frank are good friends.
   Correct: Frank and *I* are good friends.

2. A predicate pronoun, whether singular or plural, is in the nominative case.

   EXAMPLES
   They thought that the visitor was *he*.
   Frank and Joe knocked on the door. "It is they," Sue said.

---

3. Pronouns in apposition with nouns in the nominative case are also in the nominative case.

EXAMPLE

The two *contestants*, *she* and *I*, were tied for first place.

Objective

4. The object of a verb (a noun or pronoun) is in the objective case. This is true whether the object is singular or compound.

EXAMPLE

They applauded *him* and *her*.
Did they face Frank and *us* in the contest?

5. The object of a proposition is in the objective case. This is true whether the object is singular or compound.

EXAMPLES

Everyone but *her* did the homework.
Between *you* and *me*, Sue is my best friend.

6. Pronouns in apposition with nouns in the objective case are also in the objective case.

EXAMPLES

They gave the prizes to the *winners*, *her* and *me*.
For us *amateurs*, it is fun to watch professionals perform.

7. The subject of an infinitive is in the objective case; the same is true for the object of an infinitive.

EXAMPLES

We asked *him* to go.
We wanted him to ask *them* to come along.

Possessive

8. Pronouns in the possessive case, unlike nouns in the possessive case, *never* have an apostrophe.

EXAMPLES

The dog wagged *its* tail.
We have met the enemy and they are *ours*.
She has *hers*; they have *theirs*.

VERBS

The *verb*, the part of the sentence that indicates the action carried out by the subject, *also indicates* when the action was carried out. It does so by its tense.

Tense

Verb: to live	
Present tense:	live
Past tense:	lived
Future tense:	shall live
Present perfect tense:	have lived

Examples of the use of tense:
    Note the way in which the rest of each sentence is affected.

Present tense:	I *live* in New York *now.*
Past tense:	I *lived* in New York *last year.*
Future tense:	I *shall live* in New York *next year.*
Present perfect tense:	I *have lived* in New York for *five years.*

Verb Forms

The principal parts of *to live, to see, to do,* and *to lie* are:

Verb	Past	Past Participle
live	lived	lived
see	saw	seen
do	did	done
lie	lay	lain

    Many of the difficulties you have with verbs involve the irregular verbs. These change form in either the past or the past participle or in both. The most frequent error is the use of the wrong part of the verb, most often the past participle for the simple past.

EXAMPLES	*Wrong:*	*Wrong:*
	I seen him do it.	I done it.
	Correct:	*Correct:*
	I *saw* him do it.	I *did* it.

Frequently Used Irregular Verbs

Verb	Past Tense	Present Perfect Tense
be	I was	I have been
bring	I brought	I have brought
drink	I drank	I have drunk
eat	I ate	I have eaten
get	I got	I have got *or* gotten
go	I went	I have gone
have	I had	I have had
lay	I laid (place)	I have laid
lie	I lay (recline)	I have lain
run	I ran	I have run
speak	I spoke	I have spoken
swim	I swam	I have swum
take	I took	I have taken
throw	I threw	I have thrown
write	I wrote	I have written

What is the proper sequence of tenses for verbs in the main and dependent clauses of a complex sentence?

This can vary, but some common sequences follow.

VERB SEQUENCES

Main Clause	Dependent Clause
Present tense: I *gain* weight	**Present tense:** when I *eat* too much.
Present tense: I *believe*	**Past tense:** that he *studied* for the examination.
Past tense: The audience *applauded*	**Past tense:** when the soloist *finished*.
Past tense: I *played* my first concert	**Past perfect tense:** after *I had studied* piano for three years.

Note: The action of the dependent clause (the studying) took place *before* the action in the main clause.

Future tense: I *shall leave*	**Present tense:** when he *comes*.

ADJECTIVES AND ADVERBS

An **adjective** is used to describe a noun or pronoun.

EXAMPLE
He wore a *dark* hat.

An **adverb** is used to modify a verb, an adjective, or another adverb.

EXAMPLE
He played *very poorly*.
[*Poorly* modifies *played; very* modifies *poorly*.]

USE OF A VERB THAT DESCRIBES A CONDITION, NOT AN ACTION

If the verb is not used as an action verb, or if the verb describes a condition, then an *adjective rather than an adverb* must follow it.

EXAMPLES
He looks *sick*.
[*Sick* describes *he*.]

I feel *good*.
[Good describes *I*.]

Some Special Problems
ADJECTIVES INDICATE THE DEGREE TO WHICH THEY DESCRIBE NOUNS

Degree is indicated in one of two ways:

* the adverb *more* or *most* is placed before the adjective;
* The suffix *-er* or *-est* is added to the adjective.

EXAMPLES
He was *more quiet* than she.
He was *quieter* than she.
He was the *most friendly* person there.
He was the *friendliest* person there.

Never use a negative adverb
and a negative adjective in the same sentence

EXAMPLE
Wrong:
He does*n't* do *no* work.
[A negative adverb—*n't [not]* and a negative adjective—*no*]

Correct:
He doesn't do *any* work.

CAPITALIZATION

BASIC RULES OF CAPITALIZATION
1. Capitalize the first word of a sentence.

    EXAMPLE
    We went to the theater.

2. Capitalize the first word of a direct quotation.

    EXAMPLE
    He said, "Don't give up."

3. Capitalize the first word of a line of poetry.

    EXAMPLE
    "Poems are made by fools like me . . ."

4. Capitalize proper nouns (names of specific persons, places, or things).

    EXAMPLES
    Winston Churchill; Mr. James Jones; New York City; Main Street; City Hall

5. Capitalize proper adjectives (adjectives formed from proper nouns).

    EXAMPLES
    American; Shakespearean

---

6. Capitalize names of specific organizations or institutions.

   EXAMPLES
   Sousa Junior High School; Columbia University; American Red Cross; Federal Bureau of Investigation

7. Capitalize days of the week, months of the year, and holidays. (*Note:* Do not capitalize seasons, e.g., winter.)

   EXAMPLES
   Sunday; June; Thanksgiving

8. Capitalize languages. (Note: These are the *only* school subjects that are capitalized.)

   EXAMPLES
   French; Hebrew
   I study English, Spanish, biology, mathematics, and social studies.

9. Capitalize races and religions.

   EXAMPLES
   Hindu; Christian

10. Capitalize references to the Deity and to the titles of holy books.

    EXAMPLES
    the Almighty; the Old Testament; the Koran

11. Capitalize titles of people when they are followed by a name, being careful to capitalize both the title and the name. (*Note:* If a specific person is meant, the name may, at times, be omitted.)

    EXAMPLES
    President Bill Clinton; Dr. Schweitzer; Her Majesty the Queen

12. Capitalize titles of works of literature, art, and music.

    EXAMPLES
    War and Peace (note that articles, short prepositions, and conjunctions such as *and* are not capitalized in titles); *American Gothic*; *Beethoven's Fifth Symphony*

13. The pronoun *I* is capitalized at all times.

    EXAMPLES
    I walked one mile south to the school.

14. Sections of the country are capitalized, but directions are not.

EXAMPLES
I lived in the South for five years.
We traveled south.

15. Capitalize specific places and addresses, but do not capitalize the second half of a hyphenated number.

EXAMPLE
Times Square; 25 Main Street; 65 West Thirty-third Street.

PUNCTUATION

BASIC RULES OF PUNCTUATION
The Period is used after

1. a sentence that makes a statement;

CXAMPLE
He arrived on time.

2. a sentence that gives a command;

EXAMPLE
Sit up straight.

3. some abbreviations and contractions.

EXAMPLES
Mr., lb., a.m., etc.

The Question Mark is used after a sentence that asks a question.

EXAMPLE
Did you like the game?

The Exclamation Point is used after a sentence that emphasizes a command or that conveys strong feeling.

EXAMPLES
Stop writing immediately!
What a pleasant surprise!

The Comma *is*

1. used to separate a word or words that indicate the person to whom a remark is addressed;

    EXAMPLES
    John, please come here.
    You may come, little friend, if you like.

2. used to separate a word or words that are in apposition with a noun; that is, add information about the noun;

    EXAMPLE
    Nancy, my secretary and receptionist, is very efficient.

3. used to set off expressions or phrases that are inserted in the sentence and that interrupt the normal word order;

    EXAMPLES
    Notre Dame, in my opinion, will win the championship.
    Joan, on the other hand, disagrees with us;

    Note: The next two rules (4 and 5) do not apply to short introductory phrases and clauses and short independent clauses.

4. used after introductory phrases and clauses, particularly when they are long or when the meaning may be temporarily confused if the comma is omitted;

    EXAMPLES
    When the dog jumped up, Darryl's parents became frightened.
    After a long but exciting trip through the Alps, Amy returned tired but happy.
    Springing into action, the police caught the bandit.

5. used to separate independent clauses of a compound sentence joined by a conjunction such as *and, but, for, nor, or, so,* or *yet;*

    EXAMPLE
    Joe decided to attend the game, but I remained at home.
       but
    Joe returned but I remained.

6. used to separate items in a series;

EXAMPLES

The box contained books, toys, games, and tools.

Jason, Meghan, and Sarah are going to the office today.

[If the comma is omitted after "Meghan," it might seem that Jason was being told that Meghan and Sarah were going to the office.]

For breakfast he had juice, ham and eggs, and coffee.

7. used before the text of a quotation; in a divided quotation, commas are used to set off the speaker;

EXAMPLES

The teacher said, "Return to your seats."

"Return to your seats," said the teacher, "so we may continue the lesson."

8. used to set off clauses and phrases that are not essential to the meaning of the sentence *(No commas are needed if the clause or phrase is essential to the meaning intended by the speaker or writer.)*;

EXAMPLE

Jan, who was seated beside me, left early.

[Note that the clause "who was seated beside me" is not essential to the sentence, which, without it, would read, "Jan left early."]

    but

The students who studied hard passed the test.

[The clause "who studied hard" is essential since only the students who studied hard passed. Without this clause the meaning intended by the writer—that students who did not study hard failed—would not be clear to the reader.]

The comma also has a number of uses that are the result of custom:

9. after the salutation in a friendly letter;

EXAMPLE

Dear Dad,

10. after the complimentary close in all letters;

EXAMPLE
Very truly yours,

11. between the day of the month and the year in writing a date;

EXAMPLE
May 24, 1919

12. between the city and the state in writing an address;

EXAMPLE
Brooklyn, New York 11201
Note: **Do NOT** use a comma
—between a subject and its verb when the verb immediately follows the subject;

EXAMPLE
The boys on the team celebrated their victory.
—to separate parts of a compound predicate.

EXAMPLE
They enjoyed a good dinner and saw a play.

The Semicolon *is used to*
1. separate independent clauses in a sentence; either a semicolon or a comma may be used when the clauses are short;

EXAMPLE
I came; I saw; I conquered. (*or* I came, I saw, I conquered.)

2. separate items in a series when these items contain commas;

EXAMPLE
The guests included William H. Rehnquist, Chief Justice of the United States; Madeleine Albright, Secretary of State; and Newt Gingrich, Speaker of the House.

The Colon *is used*
1. to introduce a series or a list of items;

EXAMPLE
These items were included on the shopping list: fruit, vegetables, meat, fish, and ice cream.

2. before a restatement, an illustration, or an explanation of the main idea of the sentence;

EXAMPLE

I have but one rule of conduct: do unto others as you would be done by.

3. after the salutation of a business letter;

EXAMPLE

Dear Sir:

The Apostrophe is used to

1. indicate possession;
   a. In general, to make a singular noun possessive, add an apostrophe and *s ('s)* to words not ending in *s*.

EXAMPLE

boy's hat

   b. To make a plural noun possessive, add an apostrophe if the noun ends in *s*. If it does not end in *s*, add an apostrophe and *s*.

EXAMPLES

ladies' hats

men's coats

2. indicate that one or more letters have been omitted in a contraction;

EXAMPLE

He didn't come.

3. indicate the plural of letters or numbers;

EXAMPLE

There are 4 *s*'s in Mississippi

Note: Before adding the apostrophe to make the possessive, first form the plural of the noun;

EXAMPLE

child—children—children's

—Do *not* break up a word by using the apostrophe. The apostrophe can be added only at the end of a word.

EXAMPLE *Wrong:* ladie's hats   *Correct:* ladies' hats

Parentheses are used to enclose any words that explain or add to an idea or ideas contained in a sentence. Parentheses are always used in pairs (that is, one opens and the other closes the included word or words).

EXAMPLE

Frank Jones (author of *Ideas that Work*) has written many best sellers.

Quotation Marks are used to

1. indicate the titles of works that are part of a book; (*Note:* The title of a whole book is underlined to indicate that the title should be italicized in print.)

   EXAMPLES

   I particularly enjoyed Chapter 3, "Your Pet as a Companion."
   "Trees" is a poem by Joyce Kilmer.

2. set off a direct quotation of the speaker or the writer. (*Note:* Only the speaker's or writer's exact wording may be used.) Indirect quotations, quotations that do not use the exact words of the speaker or writer, do *not* require quotation marks.

   EXAMPLES

   Nathan Hale said: "I regret that I have but one life to give for my country."
   The boy said that he would be late.
       but
   The boy said, "I will be late."
   Note: In almost every case, the comma and the period are enclosed within the quotation marks.

SPELLING

Modern educational research has made the job of becoming a good speller a lot easier than it used to be. We now know which words are used most frequently in print. In fact, thorough mastery of the words on the following lists will enable you to spell correctly approximately *two thirds* of the words you use in writing.

The Basic 100

The first list contains 100 basic words that you should know thoroughly.

ache	done	making	there
again	don't	many	they
always	early	meant	though
among	easy	minute	through
answer	enough	much	tired
any	every	none	tonight
been	February	often	too
beginning	forty	once	trouble
believe	friend	piece	truly
blue	grammar	raise	Tuesday
break	guess	read	two
built	half	ready	used
business	having	said	very
busy	hear	Saturday	wear
buy	heard	says	Wednesday
can't	here	seems	week
choose	hoarse	separate	where
color	hour	shoes	whether
coming	instead	since	which
cough	just	some	whole
could	knew	straight	women
country	know	sugar	won't
dear	laid	sure	would
doctor	loose	tear	write
does	lose	their	writing

How do you go about studying this list?

One way involves the following steps.

1. Fold a sheet of paper into three parts, holding the paper sideways.
2. Fold the left third of the paper over so that it covers the center part.
3. Look at the word, noticing the difficult spot or spots. Say it aloud carefully.

4. Look at the word again, spelling it aloud by syllables. We'll help you with the problem of dividing words into syllables later on.
5. Spell the word aloud by syllables again, without looking at it this time.
6. Look at the word a third time, copying the letters on the folded part of the paper while you say them aloud by syllables.
7. Turn the fold back, this time writing the letters on the right-hand third of the paper while you again say them aloud by syllables.
8. Fold the left third of the paper over again so that you can compare the word you originally copied with the word you wrote from memory. If it is spelled correctly, turn the fold back and write the word twice more on the central third of the paper, being careful to spell the word aloud by syllables each time. If you made an error, the word will require more study, particularly of the letter or syllable you misspelled.
9. Master this list before turning to the next list. This second word list contains 200 words that are somewhat more difficult than the basic 100, but that are still rated "Easy" by those who test spelling ability. The letters or parts of the words that cause difficulty are underlined.

200 Often Used Easy Words

absence	aroused	changing	crowd
accept	arrival	chief	curtain
accident	article	children	customer
address	asked	choice	
adjourn	athletic	chosen	decided
advice	attacked	climbed	delivery
advise	attention	cloth	destroy
airplane	author	clothes	determine
allowed		cloud	device
almost	because	coarse	dictator
already	before	collar	didn't
altogether	brakes	common	different
American	breathe	conceal	dining
amount		confident	discussed
annual	careful	conquer	divided
anxious	carrying	corner	doesn't
around	certain	course	dropped

due	hundred	past	strictly
dying	hungry	perform	striking
	hurrying	perhaps	studying
earliest		permanent	succeed
easily	interesting	planning	success
effect	invitation	politics	summer
eighth	its	possible	surely
eliminate	it's	presence	surround
English		probably	
entirely	jealous	prominent	terrible
envelope		promptly	than
etc.	ladies	proved	they're
everybody	later	purpose	thorough
evidently	latter		those
excellent	led	quarter	threw
expense	library	quiet	together
experience	losing	quite	toward
extremely	lying	quizzes	tries
			twelfth
fatigue	magazine	realize	
formerly	merely	really	until
forth	minutes	receipt	unusual
forward	movable	received	useful
fourteen		recognize	
fourth	neither	reference	varied
future	nevertheless		
	nickel	safety	wasn't
generally	niece	salary	weather
genius	ninety	sandwich	weird
gentlemen	ninth	scarcely	welfare
good-bye		secretary	whose
guard	o'clock	sentence	wonderful
	officer	shining	wouldn't
handful	operate	shriek	written
handle	owing	speech	
handsome		stopped	you're
hasn't	paid	stories	yours
height	partner	strength	
hoping	passed	stretched	

Most Frequently Made Errors

Over sixty percent of all spelling errors are caused by either <u>leaving out a letter</u> that belongs in a word or <u>substituting one letter for another</u> (usually because of incorrect pronunciation of the word).

An example of a word misspelled because of a letter left out is *recognize*. Many students mispronounce the word by leaving out the "g"; they also, therefore, leave out the "g" when they spell the word.

An example of a word misspelled because one letter is substituted for another is *congratulations*. Many students mispronounce the word by substituting the voiced "d" sound for the unvoiced "t" sound; they also, therefore, substitute a "d" for the "t" when they spell the word.

Other words that are misspelled because of the omission or substitution of letters are:

accident<u>a</u>lly	envi<u>ro</u>nment	lib<u>r</u>ary	su<u>r</u>prise
arc<u>t</u>ic	e<u>s</u>cape	par<u>t</u>ner	temp<u>era</u>ture
can<u>di</u>date	Feb<u>r</u>uary	pos<u>t</u>pone	tra<u>g</u>edy
choc<u>o</u>late	gover<u>n</u>ment	pre<u>j</u>udice	tremen<u>d</u>ous
di<u>ph</u>theria	lab<u>o</u>ratory	prob<u>ab</u>ly	us<u>u</u>ally

Over twenty percent of all errors are caused by either <u>adding letters to a word</u> or <u>reversing two letters within the word.</u>

An example of a word to which a letter is added is *equipment*. Some people incorrectly pronounce the word with a *t* after the *p*. As a result, they add a *t* to the word when they spell it.

An example of a reversal of letters within the word is the simple word *doesn't*. Very often, the letters *e* and *s* are reversed and the student spells the word incorrectly—"dosen't."

Other words that are misspelled because of the addition or reversal of letters are:

aspara<u>gus</u>	*(not "gras")*
athletics	*(no e after the th)*
barbarous	*(no i after the second bar)*
chimney	*(no i after the m)*
disastrous	*(no e after the t)*
hun<u>dred</u>	*(not "derd")*

in<u>tro</u>duce	*(not* "ter"*)*
lightning	*(no e* after the *t)*
mischievous	*(no i* after the *v)*
mo<u>dern</u>	*(not* "dren"*)*
<u>per</u>cent	*(not* "pre"*)*
<u>per</u>formance	*(not* "pre"*)*
<u>per</u>spire	*(not* "pre"*)*
<u>pro</u>duce	*(not* "per"*)*
<u>pro</u>fession	*(not* "per"*)*
<u>pro</u>nounce	*(not* "per"*)*
<u>pro</u>tect	*(not* "per"*)*
remembrance	*(no e* after the *b)*
sec<u>re</u>tary	*(not* "er"*)*
umbrella	*(no e* after the *b)*

The next most common error is the confusion of two words having the <u>same pronunciation</u> but <u>different spellings and meanings</u>. These are called *homonyms.* In this humorous sentence—"A doctor must have lots of patients (patience)"—there is no way of our knowing which word the speaker means if the sentence is spoken. Therefore, we don't know how to spell the word. The words *patients* and *patience* are homonyms.

Forty of the most frequently used groups of homonyms follow. Be certain to check the meaning of each word in each group so that you can figure out the spelling from the meaning of the word as it is used in a sentence.

air; ere; heir	hole; whole	sew; so; sow
ate; eight	hour; our	stationary;
blew; blue	knew; new	stationery
bough; bow	know; no	steal; steel
brake; break	lead; led	straight; strait
buy; by	mail; male	some; sum
cent; scent; sent	meat; meet	son; sun
coarse; course	pail; pale	their; there; they're
for; four	pair; pare; pear	threw; through
forth; fourth	peace; piece	to; too; two
grate; great	principal; principle	way; weigh
groan; grown	read; red	wood; would
hear; here	right; write	your; you're
him; hymn	road; rode	

How to Become a Good Speller

There are three things you can do to help eliminate the frequently made errors and to equip yourself with the skills you will need to become a good speller.

Learn how to syllabicate. Knowing how to syllabicate—divide a word into syllables—will help you avoid many kinds of errors. This skill is particularly helpful with words of more than average length. Here are some simple rules that will help you to syllabicate properly.

RULES ON HOW TO SYLLABICATE

1. When a word has more than one vowel sound, it is broken into parts or syllables.

   EXAMPLES
   strength   *strength*   [one syllable]
   metal   *me/tal*   [two syllables]

2. Every syllable contains a sounded vowel or a pair of vowels sounded as one vowel (digraph).

   EXAMPLES
   going   *go/ing*   [sounded vowel in each syllable]
   breakout   *break/out*   [pairs of vowels sounded as one vowel in each syllable]

3. Sometimes a sounded vowel forms a syllable by itself.

   EXAMPLE
   again   *a/gain*

4. Double consonants usually are separated.

   EXAMPLES
   mitten   *mit/ten*
   possesses   *pos/ses/ses*

5. A consonant between two vowels usually is joined to the vowel that follows it.

   EXAMPLES
   local   *lo/cal*   **final**   *fi/nal*

---

6. When the suffix "ed" is added to a word ending in "d" or "t," it forms a separate syllable.

EXAMPLE
added   *add/ed*

Applying these rules to the words listed earlier will help you avoid many of the common types of errors, particularly in the omission and addition of letters.

EXAMPLES
ath / le / tics
chim / ney
um / brel / la
ac / ci / den / tal / ly

Learn the correct pronunciation of the word you must spell. Mispronunciation is known to be one of the most common causes of misspelling. Your best ally in learning the pronunciation of a word is the dictionary. Knowing the correct pronunciation will help you attack successfully such words as:

EXAMPLES
Feb / ru / a / ry
[The first *r* is often not pronounced.]

gov / ern / ment
[The first *n* is often not pronounced.]

choc / o / late
[The second *o* is often not pronounced.]

Learn the most helpful spelling rules, and know how to apply them.

BASIC RULES OF SPELLING
1. Plurals of most nouns are formed by adding *s* to the singulars.

EXAMPLE
house, hous*es*

2. When the noun ends in *s*, *x*, *ch*, or *sh*, the plural generally is formed by adding "*es*."

EXAMPLES
gas, gas*es*
box, box*es*
witch, witch*es*
dish, dish*es*

3. a. The plural of a noun ending in *y* preceded by a consonant is formed by changing *y* to *i* and adding *es*.

EXAMPLE
lady, lad*ies*

b. The plural of a noun ending in *y* preceded by a vowel does not change *y* to *i* EXCEPT for words ending in *quy*.

EXAMPLES
toy, toy*s*
but
soliloquy, soliloqu*ies*

4. a. A word that ends in *y* preceded by a consonant usually changes *y* to *i* before a suffix unless the suffix begins with *i*.

EXAMPLE
beauty, beaut*iful*

b. A word that ends in *y* preceded by a vowel usually keeps the *y* when a suffix is added.

EXAMPLE
coy, coy*er*

5. a. A word that ends in silent *e* generally keeps the *e* when a suffix beginning with a consonant is added.

EXAMPLE
care, care*ful*

b. A word that ends in silent *e* generally drops the *e* when a suffix beginning with a vowel is added.

EXAMPLES
believe, believ*able*
move, mov*ing*

6. **Exceptions to Rule 5.**
   Words ending in *ce* and *ge* keep the letter *e* before *able* and *ous*.

   EXAMPLES
   notice, notic*eable*
   change, chang*eable*
   courage, courag*eous*

7. A one-syllable word that ends in one consonant following a short vowel generally doubles the consonant before a suffix that begins with a vowel.

   EXAMPLES
   big, big*gest*
   thin, thin*ner*

8. A word of more than one syllable that ends in one consonant following one short vowel generally doubles the final consonant before a suffix beginning with a vowel *if* the accent is on the last syllable.

   EXAMPLES
   omít, omit $\boxed{t}$ *ed*
   regrét, regret $\boxed{t}$ *ing*
   allót, allot $\boxed{t}$ *ed*

9. The letter "i" is generally used before "e" except after "c."

   EXAMPLES
   bel*ie*ve, rec*ei*ve
   There are many exceptions, as:
   either
   neither
   neighborhood
   weigh
   leisure

10. An apostrophe is used to show that a letter has been omitted in a contraction.

    EXAMPLES
    it is, it's
    they are, they're

11. An abbreviation is always followed by a period.

EXAMPLE
etc.

12. Nouns of Latin origin ending
—in *us* become *i* in the plural,

EXAMPLE
rad*ius*, rad*ii*
—in *a* become *ae* in the plural,

EXAMPLE
formul*a*, formul*ae*
—in *um* become *a* in the plural,

EXAMPLE
medi*um*, medi*a*
—in *is* become *es* in the plural,

EXAMPLE
ax*is*, ax*es*

13. The suffix *ful* is spelled with a single *l*.

EXAMPLES
help*ful*
tablespoon*ful*

(*Note:* The word *full* itself is the only exception.)

ADDITIONAL WRITING SKILLS

CORRECT USE OF WORDS

Here are thirty pairs of words that are frequently confused and misused. Study the distinctions between the words in each pair.

Accept, Except
Aggravate, Irritate
Already, All Ready
Altogether, All Together
Among, Between
Amount, Number
Around, About
As, Like
Beat, Bet
Beside, Besides
Borrow, Lend
Both, Each
Bring, Take
Can, May
Fewer, Less

Hanged, Hung
Imply, Infer
In, Into
Latest, Last
Learn, Teach
Myself, Me
Pour, Spill
Precede, Proceed
Principal, Principle
Quite, Quiet
Raise, Rise
Rob, Steal
Set, Sit
Stand, Stay
Stationary, Stationery

FREQUENT ERRORS IN WORD USE

1. **DON'T USE** the expression *being that*. Instead, use a conjunction such as *because* or *since*.

   Wrong: Being that he was first, he won the prize.
   Correct: *Since* he was first, he won the prize.

2. **DON'T USE** the expression *could of, should of,* or *would of*. Instead, use the correct expression (with *have*) for which any of these aural distortions is an incorrect substitute.

   Wrong: He could of been the winner if he had tried.
   Correct: He *could have* been the winner if he had tried.

3. **DON'T USE** the expression *different than*. Instead, use *different from*.

   Wrong: Playing baseball is different than playing softball.
   Correct: Playing baseball is *different from* playing softball.

4.   **DON'T USE** incorrect prepositions.

>   *Wrong:*   May I borrow a dollar off you?
>   *Correct:*   May I borrow a dollar *from* you?
>
>   *Wrong:*   Come over our house for a party.
>   *Correct:*   Come *to* our house for a party.

5.   **DON'T USE** *don't* in the third person singular. Use *doesn't*, which is the contraction of *does not*.

>   *Wrong:*   He don't belong here.
>   *Correct:*   He *doesn't* belong here.

6.   **DON'T USE** any article after the expression *kind of* or *sort of*.

>   *Wrong:*   He's not the kind of a person I like.
>   *Correct:*   He's not the *kind of* person I like.

7.   **DON'T USE** the expression *the reason is because*. Use *the reason is that* since the words *reason* and *because* have similar meanings; a *reason* is indeed a cause.

>   *Wrong:*   The *reason* he left is because he did not get a raise.
>   *Correct:*   The *reason* he left *is that* he did not get a raise.

8.   **DON'T USE** *who's* when you mean *whose*. *Whose* should be used to show possession. *Who's* is a contraction of *who is*.

>   *Wrong:*   I know who's book this is.
>   *Correct:*   I know *whose* book this is.

3

WRITING SKILLS, PART II

THE ESSAY TEST

The essential skills in writing are:
1. Writing effective, interesting, and varied sentences;
2. Writing effective paragraphs;
3. Putting these together in planning, writing, and revising your essay.

To write effective sentences:
1. Use personal pronouns (I, you, we, your) where possible;
2. Prefer using active verbs to passive verbs, not "The examination was passed by me," but "I passed the examination."
3. Use conversation when appropriate. In a 200-word essay, you may be able to use a single exchange of words.

To write varied sentences:
1. Vary the types of sentences (simple, compound, complex);
2. Vary the purpose of the sentences (ask a question, give a command, use an exclamation point where appropriate;
3. Vary sentence length. Use a short one for emphasis.

To write effective paragraphs:
1. Have a clearly stated topic sentence;
2. Develop it by details, by illustration and example, by defining or explaining an idea, by comparison (likes) or contrast (differences), or by reasons and proof;
3. Vary the sentences in the paragraph. Vary the purpose and length of sentences;
4. Vary paragraph length. A one-sentence paragraph can emphasize an important point.
5. Organize the paragraph to emphasize the important idea, at the beginning and then developing it, or at the end leading up to it.

THE ESSAY: EXAMPLES AND PRACTICE

Opening the test booklet, you see, under Writing Skills, Part II, the following essay topic:

Television plays a very important part in American life. As an entertainment and educational medium, it has brought the world into the average home. It has its advantages and disadvantages.

Write an essay of about 200 words giving your views on television, indicating its positive effects, its negative effects, or both. Support your views by giving specific examples.

This topic requires you *to present your opinion and defend it.* How do you go about doing this?

Before You Begin

Note the following important facts:

1. The essay must be *about 200 words,* or a minimum of 25 lines for the average writer.
2. You are allowed 45 minutes to write the essay.
3. You must write your essay legibly in ink, on the answer sheet provided.

Read the instructions carefully. You will learn additional important information, including advice on how to take the test.

Essentially there are three major steps:

1. Planning the essay
2. Writing the essay
3. Revising the essay

You are advised to (1) plan carefully, (2) write your essay, and (3) revise your essay to improve what you have written before handing in your paper.

Finally, you are told how your essay will be rated. Two evaluators will read it, judging how clearly you express your opinions, how well you support your opinions by examples and/or arguments, and how effectively and correctly you write.

Planning the Essay

The first step is to

1. *Allot your time.* Remembering that you have a 45-minute maximum, allow the following amounts of time:
   1. For reading the instructions: 3 minutes
   2. For reading the topic and planning the outline: 7 minutes
   3. For writing the 200-word essay: 20–25 minutes
   4. For reading and revising the essay: 5–10 minutes

   These limits are not compulsory, but they will prevent you from failing to finish your essay (and be penalized) or from handing in a paper containing errors you did not have time to correct.

2. *Plan your essay.* It is essential to read the topic carefully and to write on the given topic. *Your essay will receive a failing grade if you write on a topic different from the one you are given.*

   Let us return to our sample topic: television. Reread the topic carefully, noting on your scrap paper what is required. You are asked to do two things: *give your opinions and support them by specific examples and proof.* You are given a choice of the aspects of television on which you will write: *its good points, its bad points, or both.* You must plan your essay accordingly.

   Think through the topic, briefly jotting down your ideas. Your notes might look like this.

TV is entertaining.
Too much violence
Public TV is educational.
Sitcoms
Informative news programs
Cost of programs
Reruns waste time.
Overdone game shows
"Sesame Street"
Baseball, football, and other sports

   To organize your notes into an *outline* or *plan,* combine ideas that belong together and eliminate those that don't fit in.

   The notes *TV is entertaining, Public TV is educational, Informative news programs, "Sesame Street,"* and *Baseball, football, and other sports* might be positive examples of programming. *Too much violence, Reruns waste time,* and *Overdone game shows* are negative aspects of programming. *Cost of programs* is irrelevant to the other notes, so drop it.

After you have gathered related ideas from your notes, combine them into a paragraph that has a suitable topic sentence. Simple sentences like "Television has many good points" and "Television has its bad points" can serve as headings under which to put your related notes.

Warning: Notes are just that—notes. Your outline or plan should be *written in full sentences* so you can go directly from the outline into your essay. A sample plan from the notes looks like this.

Sample Plan

1. Television affects the lives of all Americans. It has its good points and its bad points. *(Restatement of the given topic can serve as a topic sentence.* You have chosen to deal with the positive *and* negative aspects of television.)

2. Television has many good points.
   a. There are educational programs on public TV.
   b. There are informative news programs.
   c. There are entertaining comedies, adventures, and mysteries.
   d. There are exciting sports events.

3. Television also has its bad points.
   a. It often portrays violence.
   b. Its situations are unrealistic.
   c. Its programs are often a waste of time.

4. Despite its good/bad points, television enriches/impoverishes our lives. (You may choose either conclusion to *serve as a summary sentence.*)

Writing the Essay

This plan can easily be expanded into an essay of about 200 words. All you need to do is:

1. ***Give more reasons.*** Television brings good movies into the home; it provides excellent programs for children; it features important sports

events. Or, negatively, there are too many and too annoying commercials; there are too many reruns of movies; its dramas are tasteless.

2. **Give more examples.** Under 2 of the Sample Plan above, you can give examples of nature programs (National Geographic specials), politics (election coverage), theater (Shakespeare), and music (Metropolitan Opera).

Here is a sample essay in which you present your opinion and defend it.

Television: A Force for Good or Evil

Television affects the lives of all Americans. It has its good points and its bad points.

Television programming has much to recommend it. It features excellent educational programs on public television as well as on certain commercial stations. Well-known programs include "Masterpiece Theater," which presents dramas, the National Geographic specials featuring natural history, "Great Performances" of music and ballet, and educational children's programs such as "Sesame Street." News programs keep us well informed. Nightly newscasts include international and local news, and programs like "Meet the Press" bring us face to face with newsmakers. Entertainment is provided by comedies such as "Friends," dramas such as "ER," and quiz shows such as "Jeopardy." On many sports specials, the television viewer has a front seat.

Unfortunately, however, television programming also has a negative side. It often portrays violence in its ugliest forms. Viewing is often a waste of time when tasteless dramas, overdone reruns of sitcoms, and poor movies are presented. Viewers may be frustrated and envious when they see game-show participants win huge prizes.

(There are two possible endings depending on your own feelings.)

Despite its bad points, television can be a powerful force for enriching our lives, since its faults can be improved if the public insists.

OR

Despite its good points, television's weaknesses make this medium an evil influence on the viewing public. The American public would be better off without it.

Writing A Superior Essay

Although this sample essay would receive a good grade, the reasons and examples deal only with programming. Television, however, has deeper effects on American life. *If you treat these less obvious but more important aspects of the topic, you will get a superior grade.*

Television affects the use of our leisure time. If we watch television as *spectators,* we cannot be *participants* in other activities. We have less time for reading, less time for physical activity, and less time for conversation and other socialization. These are some of the negative sociological effects of television.

On the other hand, television can have deeper positive effects. Those who must endure long periods of forced inactivity, such as shut-ins or the frail elderly, have, because of television, an entertaining and sometimes constructive way to use their time. Furthermore, viewers can experience many things that they cannot know firsthand, such as faraway places, underwater and space exploration, and scientific discoveries.

These kinds of reasons are more mature than discussions dealing merely with programming. Therefore, this kind of essay will receive a higher grade.

Explanatory Topics

Another kind of topic you might be given is an explanatory topic. This requires you to explain something. There are four major kinds of explanatory topics and we shall analyze each of these in turn. One might be a *process* (example, How to Prepare a Budget); another might be a *term to be defined* (example, Being a Good Citizen). Still another might be a *comparison,* explaining similarities (example, Big Cities Are All Alike), or differences, explaining *a contrast* (example, Urban and Suburban Ways of Life). Finally, the topic might call for *classification* (example, The Basic Four of a Good Diet).

1. ***Explaining a process.*** This involves a series of steps, each of which is a part of a total process. These steps must be presented in order, so that an exact sequence is followed. For the explanation to be clear, each paragraph must be developed in a definite time sequence.

2. *Defining a term.* The best way to write an essay that defines a term is to list the parts that make up the concept being defined and to give an example of each. For example, good citizenship may be explained by a number of behaviors that, taken together, make up a definition.

3. *Making a comparison or a contrast.* In a *comparison,* you discuss the similarities in two or more items.

In making a *contrast* between two ideas or objects, use the same plan, but point out the differences.

ADDITIONAL ESSAYS

Study the following essay carefully. Note that each one is based on the arguments listed after it. Note also how each paragraph supports the opinion presented.

> Affirmative action is the use of racial, ethnic, or gender preference in allocating economic and social benefits: job hiring and promotion, admission to schools, and establishment of seniority.
>
> Some regard affirmative action as necessary because of historical discrimination. Others believe that it is undesirable because it results in reverse discrimination.
>
> Write a composition of about 200 words in which you present your view on this issue, giving reasons and examples to support your position.

For affirmative action

For many generations, large numbers of Americans have suffered discrimination in many forms. People of color have not been hired because of race, and certain ethnic groups have been excluded from social benefits. Educational and job opportunities for women have been limited. Discrimination against the elderly continues to be widespread. Minorities and women do not have access in many instances to higher, better paid positions.

As a result, in the competition for jobs and admission to good schools, minorities, women, and the elderly are at a disadvantage.

Affirmative action is needed to compensate for this discrimination, which has led to illiteracy, poverty, and general second-class citizenship. Under affirmative action, minorities and women receive preference in hiring and in promotion. Places are set aside by colleges and professional schools for preferential admission. Compensatory programs provide additional training to level the field of competition. Scholarships help promising minority students and women who lack money for college or other training. Also, since past discrimination did not allow certain groups to gain seniority in the workplace, seniority is waived when firings are necessary.

All these benefits can be achieved by federal and state legislation and, if necessary, by court order.

Only by affirmative action programs can historical wrongs be righted and equality of opportunity provided for these long-suffering citizens.

Against affirmative action

Although in the past America has provided unequal opportunity to many of its citizens, affirmative action programs are not the way to remedy this situation.

Reverse discrimination results when racial and gender preferences determine who is to be hired. Qualified members of majorities are passed over in favor of minority-group members for available jobs. Women are favored over equally qualified men. In most instances, the individuals who were passed over were in no way responsible for the discrimination of the past. Instead of merit, race or gender has been substituted as the criterion for hiring. When this happens, quotas, that is, fixed numbers of jobs set aside for minorities, limit job opportunities for other, more qualified applicants.

Affirmative action hurts the U.S. economy. In many cases, to make jobs available to minorities, less qualified, less productive applicants are hired.

In addition, affirmative action often has a negative effect on the people who supposedly benefit from it because they feel that they did not achieve their goals on their own merits. As a result, minority-group members are split, with the qualified, who do not need preference, on one side and the less qualified, who need help, on the other.

For these reasons, affirmative action programs are unwise.

Revising the Essay

You read the directions and the topic carefully; you planned what you would say; you have written your essay. You may think you are finished, but in reality you are not.

It is essential that you read the essay you have written, revising it where necessary. You will recall that you left 5 to 10 minutes for revision when you planned your time.

What do you look for when you read your essay?

Checklist for Revision

Content

1. Are your ideas pertinent to the topic?
2. Are they clearly stated?
3. Are they properly organized?
4. Are they logically developed? Have you used the proper connecting and transitional words?
5. Is the purpose of your essay achieved? If you had to make a judgment, did you do so? Explain a process? Did you define a term? Did you make a comparison or contrast?

Organization

1. Does each paragraph have a good topic sentence?
2. Is each key idea developed in a separate paragraph?
3. Does each paragraph conclude with a clear summary sentence?

Correctness (Review Writing Skills Part I Unit)

1. Is your essay free of sentence errors (run-on sentences and sentence fragments)?
2. Are agreement, case of pronouns, and verb forms correct?
3. Have you punctuated and capitalized correctly?
4. Have you chosen your words with proper usage in mind?
5. Have you spelled them correctly?

Only after you have read and revised your essay can you feel you have completed the Writing Skills, Part II test. Don't hesitate to make changes or corrections on your paper. As long as *your writing is legible*, neatness is not a factor.

4

SOCIAL STUDIES

READING AND INTERPRETING SOCIAL STUDIES MATERIALS

HOW TO READ POLITICAL SCIENCE, HISTORY, ECONOMICS, GEOGRAPHY, AND BEHAVIORAL SCIENCE PASSAGES

Reading in the social studies requires a number of skills that are common to all reading materials. When you read in any subject, you want to identify the *main ideas* of the writer. So, too, in social studies you need to get at the key thoughts being expressed.

Locating the Main Idea

If you read too slowly, you may miss the main point because you have gotten too involved in details. It is important, therefore, that you first read the selection through to the end rather quickly *before* you turn to the questions.

Where do you look for the main idea? Most often you will find it in the topic sentence, usually the first sentence in the passage. Sometimes, however, the writer will withhold the main idea until the last sentence, building up to it throughout the entire selection. At other times, the writer will include both a main idea and an important secondary (or subordinate) idea.

To train yourself in **locating the main idea,** ask yourself the same questions that will be asked of you on the examination.
1. What is the main idea of the passage?
2. What is the best title for the passage?
3. If I were choosing a suitable headline for the article in a newspaper, what headline would I choose?
4. What is the *topic sentence* of this paragraph or paragraphs; *that is, the sentence that includes the ideas contained in all the other sentences?*

Finding Details

After you have determined the main idea, the next step is to *locate the facts supporting the main idea or details* that flow from the main idea. If, for example, the main idea of a passage is that democracy is the best form of government, the author will undoubtedly provide facts or reasons to support this statement or include facts that show the superiority of democracy to other forms of government. If the main idea is a general conclusion that many persons with physical disabilities have overcome them and become famous, details would probably include such examples as Helen Keller and Franklin D. Roosevelt.

How do you locate a detail? You go back to the selection a second or third time to dig it out of the passage. It most frequently will come in the middle or toward the end of the selection. Sometimes clues in the passage steer you to the detail or fact in question. Clues for locating details may read:

An example is...

One reason is...

An argument in support of (or against)...is...

A reason for...is...

To train yourself in **locating details,** ask yourself these questions:
1.   What examples are given to illustrate the main point?
2.   What reasons are offered to support the author's position?
3.   What arguments for or against a proposal does the author present?
4.   When, where, how did something happen?
5.   What did someone do?
6.   Why did he or she do it?

To find the proper detail, it will be necessary for you to *learn how to skim,* that is, to read rapidly to locate the piece of information you are seeking. You can do this only if you know specifically what you need to find in a given selection and limit your reading to finding only that fact.

Determining Organization

Note the manner in which the writer organizes his or her material. This will help you to follow the author's thoughts effectively. The writer may organize his or her material chronologically, that is, in the order in which a series of events happened. Alternatively, the writer may organize the material logically by presenting the arguments *for* a position in one paragraph and the arguments against in another. Or the writer may present his or her ideas in the order of their importance, with the most important ideas first. This, in fact, is the way a newspaper article is written— "from the top down"—in case the reader doesn't have time to finish it all.

If you can determine the organization of a passage, you can zero in on the relationship between the main parts of a passage.

Clues to Finding the Relationship between the Main Parts of a Passage

Sequence of ideas is indicated by such words as:

first	next	finally
second	further	

Additional ideas are indicated by such words as:

and	furthermore	likewise
besides	also	in addition

Opposing or contrasting ideas are indicated by such words as:

on the other hand	but	yet
however	still	although

Drawing Conclusions

Another step involves *drawing conclusions from the material presented.* Conclusions are often indicated by such words as:

thus	accordingly	consequently
therefore	so	as a result

Sometimes, however, the author does not draw the conclusion, but leaves it to you, the reader, to do so. You infer the conclusion from the materials presented; you draw the inference as a result of details you have noted and the relationships you have determined (time sequence, logical order, cause-and-effect, among others). Thus, if an author indicates that a given president vetoed many bills, you might infer that the president and the Congress differed in their thinking about legislation, perhaps because the Congress was controlled by a political party different from that of the president.

To train yourself to **make inferences** properly in order to draw a conclusion, ask yourself these questions:

1. What do I think will happen next? (inference or prediction as to the outcome)
2. Putting these arguments together, what conclusion can I reach?
3. If one result was caused by something, will a similar effect take place in another situation where the same cause is operating?
4. What is the writer suggesting, rather than saying outright?

Reading Critically

In addition to drawing conclusions and making inferences, it is essential in social sciences that you react to what you have read. Often you must judge the material you are reading, not merely understand it. Historians, political scientists, economists, sociologists, and anthropologists often present one side of the story, their side, but there is almost always another side. In other words, they may "slant" the material to suit their bias by including only facts and arguments favorable to their own view and omitting everything else. It is essential for you to *read critically*. Do *not* accept everything that is written just because it appears in print.

You must develop the habit of challenging the author by raising questions, judging the completeness and truth of the information presented, and distinguishing fact from opinion.

A *statement of fact* is one that can be proved true by consulting a reliable source of information such as an encyclopedia, an almanac, or an official government document. Here is an example.

EXAMPLE

The federal government spends billions of dollars each year helping states with aid to needy persons: needy through unemployment, disability, or family problems.

This statement can be verified by consulting the official federal budget.

A *statement of opinion or belief* is one that expresses the feelings, thoughts, or beliefs of a person or persons, and that cannot be proved to be true by reference to any reliable source at the present time.

EXAMPLE

It is believed that by the year 2000, population will have outstripped food production and starvation will be widespread.

This is a prediction in the form of a statement or belief attributed to an unidentified source ("It is believed...") that cannot be proved until the year 2000. It is possible that others may have their own beliefs. In any case, the statement is definitely not a fact.

Note that certain words are clues to statements of opinion.

Words That Are Clues to Statements of Opinion

claim	probably
boliovo	poooibly
think	might
consider	should (have)
will be	could (have)
likely	ought

Words That Probably Reflect Opinion Rather Than Fact

better	undesirable
worse	necessary
desirable	unnecessary

REMEMBER: Always apply the test, "Can this statement be proved by reference to a reliable source?"

It is important to distinguish fact from opinion in the printed word when writers unconsciously allow their opinions or biases to enter into their writing. It is even more important to do so when a writer slants his or her material deliberately.

You can read critically if you ask yourself the following questions:
1. Why is the author writing this selection?
2. What is the author trying to get me, the reader, to believe?
3. Is the author presenting a balanced or one-sided view of the situation?
4. Is the author omitting essential information?
5. Is the author appealing to my mind or to my emotions and prejudices?
6. Does the author have some hidden reason for writing what he or she writes?
7. Is the author accurate? Or does he or she deal in half-truths?
8. Does the author use words with specific agreed-upon meanings, or does he or she use words that are "loaded" because they have special meanings?

Detecting Propaganda and Propaganda Techniques

When writers deliberately spread ideas or opinions to benefit themselves or institutions to which they belong or to damage opponents or opposing institutions, they are engaging in propaganda. A propagandist tries to influence your thinking or behavior and to turn your opinions and actions in a certain direction. He or she uses words that appeal to your emotions— your fears, your loves, your hates—rather than to your reason, to your ability to think clearly, in order, ultimately, to make you do things in a way you never ordinarily would do.

Seven common techniques in propaganda are:

1. *Name-calling.* The writer tries to influence you by attaching a bad name to an individual, group, nation, race, policy, practice, or belief.

   EXAMPLE

   It would be wise to pay no attention to that loony liberal (or retarded reactionary, depending upon the writer's point of view).

   Certain names are loaded with emotional overtones: Fascist, Red, Nazi, Commie. You must note carefully in what way and for what purpose these terms are used. Name-calling is a common propaganda technique.

2. *Glittering generalities.* The writer attaches "good" names to people and policies, in the hope that you will accept them without really looking into the facts.

EXAMPLE

> The writer appeals to our emotions by using such "good" terms as *forward-looking, peace-loving, straight-shooting,* and *idealistic.*

We all love progress, peace, honesty, and idealism so we tend to accept rather than challenge. Always ask the questions "why" and "how" when "good" terms are applied to people and policies.

3. **Transfer.** The writer tries to use the approval and prestige of something or some institution we respect to get us to accept something else in which he or she is interested.

EXAMPLE

> Most Americans are law-abiding and respect their police officers. One who writes on behalf of an athletic league supported by the local police will try to get you to transfer your approval of the police to the athletic league he or she is sponsoring.

Always examine the person or institution receiving the transfer on its own merits rather than on the merits of the original institution you love and respect.

4. *Testimonial.* Advertisements on television and radio make wide use of testimonials. A top athlete endorses a breakfast cereal. A beautiful actress recommends a cosmetic cream. An ex-senator testifies to the value of a credit card. A testimonial is a recommendation made by someone on behalf of a person, a product, or an institution.

But is the athlete an expert on nutrition? Is the actress an expert on skin care? Is the politician an expert on personal money management? REMEMBER: these people are being paid to make these testimonials. You must ask yourself whether the person making the testimonial is expert enough to do so before you believe what you read or hear.

More subtle is newspaper reporting that is based on *indirect* testimonials.

EXAMPLES

> Official circles report...; It was learned from a senior government official...: A reliable source stated...

> Always ask *which* circles, *which* official, *which* source. Be careful of any information that comes from a high *unidentified* source.

5. *Card-stacking.* The writer attempts to get you to see only one side of a particular issue. To do so, he or she will use half-truths and omit the other side of the argument. Examples occur frequently in "authorized" biographies that present a person's life in glowing terms, including all the good qualities while omitting or toning down the poor ones. When reading about an issue, always note whether both sides have been discussed or whether the cards have been stacked by the writer on one side of the issue only.

6. *Bandwagon.* The writer tries to make you go along with the crowd. Since most people like to follow the trend, they will respond favorably to such statements as "Nine out of ten Americans prefer..." or "...sells more... than all other companies put together." In politics, the bandwagon technique is often seen in action in national political conventions. "Join the swing to...."

> The bandwagon-approach writer does not want you to think clearly for yourself. You should always ask *why* you should join the others, and not do so because your emotions have gotten the better of you.

REMEMBER:

A critical reader

- does not believe everything he or she reads simply because it is in print;
- accepts as true only statements that can be proved or that are made by reliable authorities;
- separates fact from opinion, recognizes emotional language and bias, and is aware of slanting by omission.

Determining Cause and Effect

A reading skill frequently used in social studies involves determining the relationship between events. Events rarely occur in isolation. They are generally the result of other events that happened earlier.

EXAMPLE

The Japanese bombed Pearl Harbor on December 7, 1941. The United States then declared war on Japan.

The bombing of Pearl Harbor was the cause; the declaration of war was the result or effect of the bombing. Always try, when reading of an event, to determine its cause or causes. *Here is a question involving cause and effect:*

Question

1. President Franklin D. Roosevelt's New Deal policy led to numerous government agencies, created in an effort to combat the effects of the Great Depression. One major result of this policy was to
    (1) weaken the power of the chief executive
    (2) strengthen the policy of laissez-faire
    (3) increase the power of the federal government
    (4) expand the importance of states' rights
    (5) lessen the need for judicial review

Answer and Analysis

The question asks for a result of President Franklin D. Roosevelt's New Deal policy. The opposite results occurred from those listed as Choices 1, 4, and 5; that is, the New Deal strengthened the power of the chief executive; weakened the importance of states' rights, and increased the need for judicial review. Choice 2, the policy of laissez-faire, provides for little or no interference by government in the affairs of business, clearly an incorrect response. Only Choice 3 is correct because the New Deal program called for executive action to advance economic recovery and social welfare.

Comparing and Contrasting Ideas and Organizations

Another frequently needed skill in social studies reading involves the ability to compare and contrast institutions and events. You may be asked to compare American democracy with French democracy, contrast democracy with communism, compare the platforms of the Republicans and Democrats, or contrast the role of women in the eighteenth century with their role in the twentieth.

Question

1. The careers of Theodore Roosevelt and Franklin D. Roosevelt were similar because each man
   (1) was an outstanding military leader before becoming president
   (2) led the cause for international peace, but involved the United States in a war
   (3) succeeded to the presidency upon the death of the preceding president
   (4) believed in a strong presidency and acted accordingly
   (5) represented the same political party

Answer and Analysis

You are asked to compare the careers of two American presidents. Franklin D. Roosevelt was not an outstanding military leader before becoming president. Theodore Roosevelt did not involve the United States in a war. Franklin D. Roosevelt did not succeed to the presidency upon the death of the preceding president. Theodore Roosevelt was a Republican; Franklin D. Roosevelt, a Democrat. Thus Choices 1, 2, 3, and 5 are incorrect. Choice 4 is correct because both Roosevelts were strong presidents: Theodore Roosevelt was a trust buster, had a Square Deal policy, and pursued an expansionist foreign policy; Franklin D. Roosevelt carried out New Deal policies and a Good Neighbor policy with Latin America, and he led the nation for most of World War II.

Learning Social Studies Vocabulary and Deriving Meaning from Context

In social studies as in science, vocabulary is of critical importance. Words found in social studies may

- represent complicated ideas, such as *nationalism, referendum, mercantilism;*
- imply a whole set of ideas, such as *feudalism, militarism, bimetallism;*
- have meanings specific to the social studies although they have other meanings as well, such as *Axis, act, shop;*
- come from foreign languages, such as *apartheid, junta, laissez-faire;*
- have meanings that go beyond the usual ones, such as *dove, plank, scab.*

Try to derive the correct meaning from the *context*—the words with which the term appears in a sentence.

You can **check your understanding of the meaning of the vocabulary** in a given selection by asking yourself:

1. What is the key word in the sentence (paragraph, selection)?
2. What is the meaning of the word in *this* sentence (context)?
3. What is the exact meaning (denotation) of the word in this selection?
4. What is the extended meaning (connotation) of the word in this selection? (What does it *suggest* as well as say?)
5. What is the effect of a given word on me?
6. What is the special meaning of this word in social studies?

Political Science

There are the following four key committees at a political convention.

- The *Credentials Committee.* This group decides who is an official dologato ontitlod to votc.
- The permanent *Organization Committee,* which picks the convention's officers, including the chairperson. This official decides who can speak at the convention and who cannot.
- The *Rules Committee,* which makes the rules by which the convention and the party organization are run.
- The *Resolutions and Platform Committee,* which writes the party platform. Usually, a convention lasts about four days. Typically, a temporary convention chairperson opens the convention with a *keynote address,* which is meant to set the tone of the convention— and quite frequently does. The real business of the day, however, goes on behind the podium, where the Credentials Committee settles disputes over *delegate credentials.*

On the second day the *party platform* is read, debated, and usually voted upon. A *permanent chairperson* is installed, and the convention is asked to approve the reports of its major committees.

On the third day actual *nominations* for presidential candidates are taken. States are called alphabetically at the Republican Convention, by lottery at the Democratic. Each state may nominate one candidate, second a nomination already made, yield (surrender the floor to another state), or pass. After each nomination there is usually a loud demonstration for the nominee.

Balloting begins only after nominations have been closed. A *simple majority*—one more than half the votes—is all that is needed to win. Every Republican presidential candidate since 1948 and every Democratic one since 1952 has won on the first ballot. If no one wins a simple majority on the first ballot, the vote is taken again until a candidate is picked.

By the fourth day a *presidential nominee* has usually emerged. He, in turn, addresses party leaders and tells them whom he prefers for *vice president.* Usually he gets his way.

Finally, the two candidates make their *acceptance speeches,* go through a few ceremonial events, and the *convention ends.*

1. The main idea of the above selection is
    (1) choosing a president and vice president
    (2) four key committees
    (3) how Republican and Democratic conventions differ
    (4) conventions: American political dramas
    (5) how conventions are organized and run
2. The vice-presidential candidate is chosen by the
    (1) party leaders
    (2) roll-call vote
    (3) Rules Committee
    (4) permanent convention chairman
    (5) presidential nominee
3. In the next convention, it is most likely that the party candidates will be nominated by
    (1) simple majority on the second ballot
    (2) plurality on the second ballot
    (3) two-thirds vote on the first ballot
    (4) simple majority on the first ballot
    (5) plurality on the first ballot
4. The INCORRECTLY paired group below is
    (1) Organization Committee—convention chairperson
    (2) permanent chairperson—keynote address
    (3) nominees—acceptance speeches
    (4) states—nominations
    (5) simple majority—choice of nominee

5. One difference between Republican and Democratic conventions is the way in which
   (1) committees are organized
   (2) convention chairpersons are chosen
   (3) nominations for presidential candidates are made
   (4) balloting takes place
   (5) party platforms are decided

6. The writer of this selection has organized the passage
   (1) logically
   (2) psychologically
   (3) chronologically
   (4) argumentatively
   (5) critically

Answer Key

1. **5**   2. **5**   3. **4**   4. **2**   5. **3**   6. **3**

History

The United States is often considered a young nation, but in fact it is next to the oldest continuous government in the world. The reason is that its people have always been willing to accommodate themselves to change. We have been dedicated to equality, but have been willing to realize it by flexible means. In the European sense of the term, America's political parties are not parties at all, because they do not divide over basic beliefs. Neither wishes to overturn or replace the existing political and economic order; they merely desire to alter it at slower or faster rates of speed.

One of our proudest achievements has been the creation of a system of controlled capitalism that yields the highest living standards on earth, and has made possible a society as nearly classless as man has ever known. The profit system as it has developed in America shares its benefits with all parts of society: capital, labor, and the consuming masses. Yet even this was the result of trial and error. Unprincipled businessmen had first to be restrained by government, and by the growing power of organized labor, before they came to learn that they must serve the general good in pursuing their own economic interests. Now labor is feeling the restraint.

Even our creed of democracy is not fixed and unchangeable. Thus the statesmen of the early republic, though they strongly believed in private enterprise, chose to make the post office a government monopoly and to give the schools to public ownership. Since then, government has broadened its activities in many ways. Americans hold with Lincoln that "the legitimate object of government is to do for a community of people whatever they need to have done but cannot do at all, or cannot do so well for themselves, in their separate and individual capacities."

1. The main quality of the United States stressed in this passage is its
   (1) youth
   (2) equality
   (3) high living standards
   (4) profit system
   (5) flexibility
2. The widely held belief about the United States with which the passage mentions disagreement concerns American
   (1) political parties
   (2) capitalism
   (3) private enterprise
   (4) labor
   (5) public ownership
3. All of the following are characteristic of the United States, according to the passage, EXCEPT a
   (1) dedication to equality
   (2) classless society
   (3) belief in democracy
   (4) profit system
   (5) controlled capitalism
4. An agency that performs a function of which Lincoln, according to his quoted words, would most approve is the
   (1) U.S. Office of Education
   (2) U.S. Chamber of Commerce
   (3) National Guard
   (4) Public Service Commission
   (5) Federal Aviation Administration
5. The creation of the U.S. government post office monopoly is cited as an example of a
   (1) replacement of the existing economic order
   (2) restraint of unprincipled businesspersons

(3) control of organized labor
(4) flexible view of private enterprise
(5) system of shared profits

6. According to the passage, which of the following statements is true?
   (1) Our political parties agree on goals but not on methods.
   (2) Business has a larger share of profits than labor.
   (3) Government has tended to restrict its role in American life.
   (4) Americans are conservative where change is required.
   (5) Americans have kept their democratic beliefs intact.
7. The author's view of change in America is
   (1) critical
   (2) cautious
   (3) favorable
   (4) qualified
   (5) unclear

Answer Key

1. 5   2. 1   3. 2   4 5   5. 4   6. 1   7. 3

Economics

Could the United States fall into the depths of another Great Depression?

Economists can't say for sure. Most feel, however, that past depressions have taught us how to avoid economic disaster.

We've learned, for example, of the need for:

- *Government regulation of the stock market.* The Securities Act of 1933 made stock dealings less of a shell game by bringing them out into the open. The Securities Exchange Act of 1934 set up the Securities and Exchange Commission (S.E.C.), which acts as a sort of official consumer watchdog group. One of its jobs is to warn the investing public against the sort of crazy speculating that preceded the 1929 crash.
- *A permanent Council of Economic Advisers to take the economy's pulse for the government.* The Employment Act of 1946 created the Council of Economic Advisers. Its recommendations in 1949, 1958, 1969, and 1985, observers feel, helped keep the recessions of these years from becoming depressions.

- *A Federal Deposit Insurance Corporation (F.D.I.C.) to promise government backing of bank deposits.* The F.D.I.C. insures certain bank deposits. Such insurance has so far prevented the type of bank runs—panic withdrawals—that forced thousands of banks to close their doors in the early 1930s.
- *A federal relief system for jobless people.* State and local governments struggled to provide relief for the poor in the early years of the Great Depression. For the most part, they failed. They, too, ran out of money.

The New Deal introduced Social Security, a government pension plan. Government insurance followed for workers who are laid off or can't work because of injuries. Veterans' benefits and public assistance (welfare) are two other forms of government help in which Washington became involved during the 1930s.

These *transfer funds,* as they are called, don't merely help the recipients. In the long run, they help the whole economy by giving people buying power. This buying power helps keep up the demand for bonds. Thus, it helps keep factories open and factory workers employed.

For these and other reasons, many economists believe that we are now in better control of the U.S. economy, which, in the 1990s, is one of the strongest in the world.

1. The selection emphasizes
   (1) the effects of the Great Depression
   (2) the contributions of the New Deal
   (3) the strength of the U.S. economy
   (4) ways to avoid economic disaster
   (5) the role of people's buying power
2. All of the following are associated with the New Deal EXCEPT
   (1) Social Security
   (2) Council of Economic Advisers
   (3) veterans' benefits
   (4) welfare
   (5) unemployment insurance
3. All of the following were characteristics of the Great Depression that economists sought to correct EXCEPT
   (1) stock market speculation
   (2) bank failures

(3) unemployment

(4) soaring inflation

(5) poverty

4. The federal government stepped in where state and local govern-
    ments failed in

(1) regulating the stock market

(2) backing bank deposits

(3) providing relief for the jobless

(4) providing veterans' benefits

(5) introducing Social Security

5. Which of the following statements is NOT true?

(1) The United States avoided depressions in each decade following
     the Great Depression.

(2) Bank panics have been avoided since the Great Depression.

(3) The Securities and Exchange Commission alerts investors to the
     kind of stock market activity that preceded the Great Depression.

(4) Transfer funds help the unemployed.

(5) We have learned how to prevent another Great Depression.

6. We can conclude from the author's presentation that he sees another
    Great Depression as

(1) inevitable

(2) likely

(3) unlikely

(4) impossible

(5) predictable

Answer Key

1. **4**   2. **2**   3. **4**   4. **3**   5. **5**   6. **3**

Geography

Geography may be subdivided into several areas of study.

Physical Geography In the study of physical (natural) geography, stress
is laid upon the natural elements of man's environment. These include
topography, soils, earth materials, earth-sun relationships, surface and
underground water, weather and climate, and native plant and animal life.
Physical geography must also include the impact of man on his physical
environment as well as those influences omnipresent in nature.

Cultural Geography In cultural geography emphasis is placed upon the study of observable features resulting from man's occupation of the earth. These features include population distribution and settlement, cities, buildings, roads, airfields, factories, railroads, farm and field patterns, communication facilities, and many other examples of man's work. Cultural geography is one of the very significant fields of geographic inquiry.

Economic Geography In economic geography, the relationship between man's efforts to gain a living and the earth's surface on which they are conducted are correlated. In order to study how man makes a living, the distribution of materials, production, institutions, and human traits and customs are analyzed.

Regional Geography In regional geography the basic concern is with the salient characteristics of areas. Emphasis is placed upon patterns and elements of the natural environment and their relationships to human activities. By using the regional technique in studying geographic phenomena, what otherwise might be a bewildering array of facts is brought into focus as an organized, cohesive pattern.

Systematic Geography It is also feasible to study the geography of a small area or the entire surface of the earth in systematic fashion. Settlement, climates, soils, landforms, minerals, water, or crops, among others, may be observed, described, analyzed, and explained. Research in systematic geography has proved to be very valuable.

1. This passage describes geography's
    (1) growth
    (2) scope
    (3) importance
    (4) role in the social sciences
    (5) principles
2. The difference among the five areas of geography described is one of
    (1) method
    (2) importance
    (3) emphasis
    (4) recency
    (5) objectivity
3. A student interested in the influence of a geographical feature of a region on available jobs would study
    (1) physical geography
    (2) cultural geography

(3) economic geography

(4) regional geography

(5) systematic geography

4. A meteorologist would likely be most interested in

(1) physical geography

(2) cultural geography

(3) economic geography

(4) regional geography

(5) systematic geography

5. An urban sociologist would probably study

(1) physical geography

(2) cultural geography

(3) economic geography

(4) regional geography

(5) systematic geography

6. A person studying the problems of the Middle East will use the approach found in

(1) physical geography

(2) cultural geography

(3) economic geography

(4) regional geography

(5) systematic geography

7. A conservationist studying the effects of such human activities as strip mining and land erosion would turn to

(1) physical geography

(2) cultural geography

(3) economic geography

(4) regional geography

(5) systematic geography

8. That aspect of geography that seeks to study in a planned and orderly way the geography of a small area is

(1) physical geography

(2) cultural geography

(3) economic geography

(4) regional geography

(5) systematic geography

Answer Key

1. **2**   2. **3**   3. **3**   4. **1**   5. **2**   6. **4**   7. **1**   8. **5**

Behavioral Sciences

PASSAGE 1

Onta, a youth in his middle teens, was led away from his parents by one of the tribal elders. He was taken to a hut on the other side of the village. There he and several other young men went through the ceremony. After they were bound together in a large circle, the chief quizzed each boy on the tribal traditions they had all studied. Then, each had to pass through a line of elders, head covered with ash from a nearby fire. Finally, after two more hours of religious chanting, the binding was cut; and each youth was formally received into the tribe as a man, having left childhood behind forever.

David, a youth in his middle teens, was led away from his parents by one of the officials dressed in a dark uniform. He was taken to a room somewhere on the other side of the building. There he and several other young men began the examination. Seated in neat rows they underwent the examination under the stern eye of another official. Later they were required to manipulate a giant machine under the watchful eye of still another official. Finally, after waiting at home for a period of up to several weeks, they were welcomed into the community of their brothers.

Onta and David are fictional people, but their rites of passage are not. A rite of passage is a ceremony, usually formal and dictated by custom. It formally marks a person's transition from one stage to another: from childhood to maturity, from being single to being married, from life to death.

Onta's trial is fairly common (there are many variations) among so-called primitive people. Sometimes called a puberty rite, it is usually held around the time a young person achieves sexual maturity. Passing through the rite means that, in his society, Onta is officially a man.

But the practice is hardly limited to primitive tribes. All kinds of rituals, including rites of passage, are common to people everywhere. The Jewish Bar Mitzvah, a religious rite performed when a boy turns 13, is a proclamation that the youth has passed into manhood.

Rites can change, of course, according to the time and temper of the society. In David's case, if you hadn't already guessed, the rite is something vital to great numbers of young people in the United States today.

In a way, David too finally became a member of the tribe after passing through the *rite* of passage: completing his examination, and receiving his driver's license. In motor-minded America, a male teenager who can't pass his driver's test is probably under the same kind of scorn as an Indian boy who flunked his test of manhood.

Getting a driver's license is a popular rite of passage. There are others, some of them regional, some even local. Are there special rites of passage in your community?

One of the first to identify "rites of passage" was a French anthropologist named Arnold van Gennep. Gennep divided rites of passage into three stages: separation, transition, and incorporation. He found that each stage is present in rites everywhere in the world.

"Among the majority of peoples, in all sorts of ceremonies, identical rites are performed for identical purposes....

"Their position may vary, depending on whether the occasion is birth or death, initiation or marriage, but the differences lie only in matter of detail. The underlying arrangement is always the same."

1. This selection deals mainly with
   (1) Onta and David
   (2) rites of passage
   (3) getting a driver's license
   (4) the views of Arnold van Gennep
   (5) the Jewish Bar Mitzvah
2. All of the following are rites of passage referred to in the article EXCEPT
   (1) birth
   (2) initiation
   (3) marriage
   (4) parenthood
   (5) death
3. The author
   (1) deals only with the experiences of Onta and David
   (2) stresses the many differences in rites throughout the world
   (3) points out the essential similarity of rites throughout the world
   (4) emphasizes the unchanging nature of certain rites
   (5) feels that rites are unimportant rituals that must be observed
4. Onta's trial at puberty is an example, as a rite of passage, of
   (1) separation
   (2) separation and transition
   (3) transition
   (4) transition and incorporation
   (5) incorporation

5. Puberty rites are associated in this article with
   (1) proclamations
   (2) driver's licenses
   (3) tribal traditions
   (4) life and death
   (5) religious rites
6. All of the following are true of rites of passage EXCEPT that they
   (1) are milestones on the road of life
   (2) mark the end of a stage of life
   (3) mark the beginning of a stage of life
   (4) are fictional
   (5) are common to people everywhere

Answer Key

1. **2**   2. **4**   3. **3**   4. **4**   5. **2**   6. **4**

Tables

The ability to read tables is an important skill because tables are the most common means of presenting data in the social studies.

What is a table? It is an arrangement of figures, usually in one or more columns, which is intended to show some relationship between the figures. In political science, a table may show the growth of the number of eligible voters in national elections. In economics, a table may show the annual incomes of various groups within the population of a country. A table may also show the relationship between two factors, for example, between the amounts of education of various groups as related to their annual incomes.

Just how do you read a table? First you read the title of the table to determine just what figures are being presented. The title is usually at the top of the column or columns of figures. Let us use the following table as a typical illustration.

First note the title of the table: Sizes, Populations, and Densities of the World's Largest Nations and Regions.

Now, look at the headings of the columns in the table. Six headings are given: Country, Size, Population 1968, Population 1990, People per Square Mile 1968, People per Square Mile 1990.

Next, locate the columns to which each heading is related. In the first column, the different countries or areas of the world are listed. The next column gives their sizes in square miles. The next two columns list population figures for 1968 and 1990, and the last two give the numbers of people per square mile for the same two dates.

Having identified the title, the column headings, and the columns to which they relate, you are now in a position to *locate facts.*

**SIZES, POPULATIONS, AND DENSITIES
OF THE WORLD'S LARGEST NATIONS AND REGIONS**

1	2	3	4	5	6
		Population (U.N. Estimate)		Peuple per Square Mile	
Country	Size (sq. mi.)	1968	1990	1968	1990
USSR*	8,600,000	238,000,000	290,122,000	28	33.5
Canada	3,850,000	21,000,000	26,620,000	5	7.5
China	3,700,000	730,000,000	1,133,000,000	197	306.7
United States	3,600,000	200,000,000	251,394,000	57	68.3
Brazil	3,300,000	88,000,000	150,000,000	27	45.8
India	1,200,000	534,000,000	853,373,000	437	698.0
		Other Areas			
Japan	143,000	101,000,000	123,692,000	706	848.0
Southeast Asia	1,692,000	270,000,000	447,000,000	159	262.9
Middle East	3,784,000	261,000,000	306,400,000	69	81.0
Africa— south of the Sahara	8,600,000	254,000,000	500,000,000	30	62.2

Note the great increase of population in the 22 years that separate the two sets of figures. Scientists estimate that the earth's present population will double in the next 50 years.
*Note that "USSR" refers to all the former republics of the former Soviet Union.

Questions

1. What is the size of the United States?
2. What was the population of India in 1968? What is the U.N. estimate of the population of India in 1990?
3. What was the number of people per square mile in Japan in 1990?
4. What country's population grew to over 1 billion between 1968 and 1990?

Answers

1. **3,600,000 square miles**   3. **848.0**
2. **534,000,000**   **853,373,000**   4. **China**

Answer Analysis

1. The second column from the left lists sizes. Put your finger at the top of that column, and move it down until you locate the figure on a line with United States—3,600,000.
2. Locate the column for population in 1968. Put your finger at the top of the column, and move it down to the figure on a line with India—534,000,000. Do the same for 1990.
3. Locate the column for people per square mile in 1990. Find the number on a line with Japan—848.0.
4. To answer this question, you have to locate two populations, one in 1968 and one in 1990. You also must locate a figure that is over 1 billion. Scan both columns of population figures. Only one is over 1 billion, that of China in 1990. In the column to the immediate left for 1968, the figure for China's population is 730,000,000, so that figure grew to 1,133,000 in 1990.

Now you are ready to *find relationships between facts.* This type of question requires you to locate one figure and then relate it to at least one other figure.

Questions

1. What is the basic trend of the world's population?
2. What is the basic trend in the number of people per square mile?
3. From 1968 to 1990, what country or area had the smallest increase in population?
4. In what country or area did the number of people per square mile double?

Answers and Analysis

1. Compare column 4 (pop. 1990) with column 3 (pop. 1968). In every instance, the population in 1990 is greater. The conclusion can be reached that population is increasing all over the world.
2. Compare column 6 (people per square mile—1990) with column 5 (people per square mile—1968). The conclusion can be reached that the number of people per square mile is increasing all over the world.

3. Subtracting the figures in column 3 (pop. 1968) from those in column 4 (pop. 1990), it is apparent that Canada had the smallest increase, 5,620,000, in population.

4. Comparing the figures in columns 5 and 6 for people per square mile in 1968 and 1990, it is clear that in Africa—south of the Sahara the number of people per square mile more than doubled, from 30 to 62.2.

Now you can proceed to the most difficult skill of all—*inferring conclusions from the facts presented.* Sometimes you can draw a conclusion from the table alone. Other times, you must add facts from your general knowledge.

Questions

1. What conclusion can you draw from Japan's population figures?
2. What conclusion can you draw about the population in Africa—south of the Sahara?
3. What major problem may exist for Canada's population?
4. What common problems may China, India, and Japan experience?

Answers and Analysis

1. Japan has the most crowded population in the world, with attendant problems of housing, health, and transportation among others.
2. The half-billion population of Africa—south of the Sahara is spread over 8,600,000 square miles. This fact will result in problems of distribution of goods and services to the countries of the area.
3. A similar problem exists for Canada, with the added possibility that adequate manpower may not be available.
4. The high population density in each country suggests potential difficulty in providing food, shelter, and other essential services to the inhabitants.

Summary of How to Read a Table
1. Note the title.
2. Look at the column headings.
3. Locate the column to which the other columns are related.
4. Locate facts.
5. Find relationships between facts.
6. Infer conclusions from the facts presented.

Graphs

The Circle (Pie) Graph

Tables, as you have just seen, are composed of columns of figures selected to show the relationship between facts that the social studies writer considers important. Very often, the author will present these same facts in another way so that you can visualize them more readily and draw conclusions more easily. The writer does this by means of a graph.

Let us look at the following set of facts arranged in a table. They concern the principal religions of the world in the year 1991.

Principal Religions of the World, 1991			
Buddhist	6%	No religion	21%
Christian	33%	Other	1%
Hindu	13%	Para-religions	8%
Islam	18%		

Looking at these facts in table form, you find it hard to draw any ready conclusions. But when you see them in the form of a circle (pie) graph, you are able to immediately visualize the relationships that exist between them.

PRINCIPAL RELIGIONS OF THE WORLD, 1991

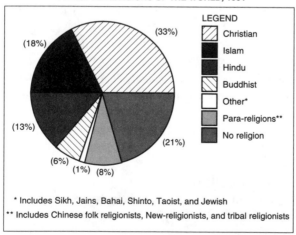

LEGEND
- Christian
- Islam
- Hindu
- Buddhist
- Other*
- Para-religions**
- No religion

(18%) (33%) (13%) (6%) (1%) (8%) (21%)

* Includes Sikh, Jains, Bahai, Shinto, Taoist, and Jewish
** Includes Chinese folk religionists, New-religionists, and tribal religionists

Now use this graph to answer the following questions.

Questions

1. Which religion has the most followers?
2. Which of the individually named religions has the fewest followers?
3. Which two religions account for more than half of the world's population?
4. Which proportion of the world's people do not practice a religion?

Answers

1. **Christian**
2. **Buddhist**
3. **Islam and Christianity**
4. **21%**

Answer Analysis

The answers almost leap up at you from the circle graph. The Christian religion has by far the largest slice of the circle; all of the religions combined under "Other" are hardly visible. By visually combining the various slices of the pie, you can see that the Christian and Islamic religions account for just over half of the total pie. By referring to the legend and then back to the pie, you can see that a large slice of the pie represents people who practice no religion. Just by inspection, you can estimate the number at around one-fifth or 20% of the total. The actual figure (21%) is provided.

The circle graph can also help you to compare visually two sets of facts. Here are a circle graph and a graph of another type (the bar graph).

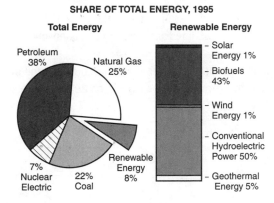

SHARE OF TOTAL ENERGY, 1995

Total Energy

Petroleum 38%
Natural Gas 25%
7% Nuclear Electric
22% Coal
Renewable Energy 8%

Renewable Energy

– Solar Energy 1%
– Biofuels 43%
– Wind Energy 1%
– Conventional Hydroelectric Power 50%
– Geothermal Energy 5%

Note the title—Share of Total Energy, 1995
Note the unit used—percent of 100
Note the date—1995

Note the major categories—petroleum, natural gas, renewable energy, coal, nuclear electric

Study both graphs carefully and answer the following questions.

Questions

1. What are the most important sources of energy?
2. To reduce our dependence on oil imports, the use of which sources would have to be increased?
3. What percent of total energy does conventional hydroelectric power contribute?

Answers and Analysis

1. **Three sources—petroleum, natural gas, and coal—amount to 70% of total energy.**
2. **The percents of the other sources—natural gas, coal, renewable energy, and nuclear electric—would have to be increased from their current total of 62%.**
3. **The circle graph tells you that renewable energy contributes 8% of the total energy consumed. Now look at the bar graph. Conventional hydroelectric power contributes half of renewal energy, or 4% of total energy.**

The Line Graph

This common type of graph shows relationships between facts by plotting points on a coordinate plane (two lines are involved) and connecting them with straight lines.

As an example, let us construct a line graph based on the following data about world population growth between 1650 and 2000 (estimated).

Year	World Population in Millions
1650	550
1750	725
1850	1175
1900	1600
1950	2490
1993	5554
2000 (est.)	6500

To construct the graph, draw a horizontal line and, perpendicular to it, a vertical line. Let:

- the horizontal line (technically known as the *abscissa*) represents the period of years from 1650 to 2000 (est.);
- the vertical line (technically known as the *ordinate*) represents world population.

To plot the line graph, start with the first line of data—year 1650, world population 550 million. Go up the ordinate 550, and place a dot there. Then find the next date, 1750, on the abscissa and go up the ordinate and place a dot opposite 725. Next find the date 1850 on the horizontal line and go up to a point opposite 1175. Place a dot there. Continue to do the same thing for each year on the table. Then draw a straight line from dot to dot to complete the graph.

What can you tell or visualize from this line graph?

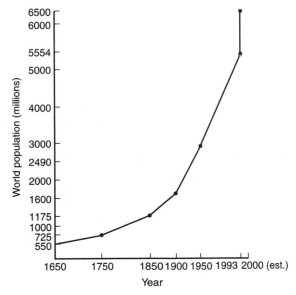

Questions

1. What is the trend of the world population?
2. What was the world population in 1900?
3. In what 50-year period was the increase the greatest?
4. In the period covered by the graph, approximately how many times did the population grow?

Answers

1. **The trend is sharply upward.**
2. **1600 million**
3. **1950–2000 (est.)**
4. **About 12 times, from 550 million to 6500 million**

Answer Analysis

1. The plotted line always trends upward, with the slant becoming steeper in recent decades to indicate accelerating population growth.
2. First find the year 1900 on the abscissa. Then move your finger straight up to the point in line with the ordinate indicating the population. The number is 1600 million.
3. The growth is greatest where the line is steepest—between 1950 and 2000 (est.).
4. The population grew from 550 million to 6500 million, or about 12 times.

The Bar Graph

A bar graph is very much like the line graph we just studied. There is the same visual presentation of one set of facts in relation to another set. There is the same horizontal line (abscissa) representing one set of facts. The same vertical line (ordinate) represents the other set.

For a bar graph, however, you do not put a dot at the point that represents one fact in relation to another, nor do you connect those points by lines. Instead, you make bars of equal width and of heights that indicate the relationship. Thus you could change the line graph you just studied to a bar graph by making a bar for each point identified.

The bar graph that is set out below is entitled "Aging Societies." It gives the percentages of population 65 and over for five countries at four different times, one past and three projected. It also indicates by small pie

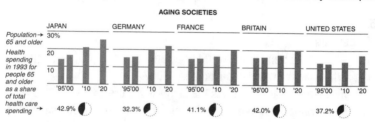

AGING SOCIETIES

Source: Organization of Economic Cooperation and Development

graphs the percentages of health spending in 1993, in each country, for people 65 and over as a share of total health care spending.

Use these graphs to answer the following practice questions.

Questions

1. In what country will the government have to spend the most in the year 2020 for health care for the aging?
   (1) Japan
   (2) Germany
   (3) France
   (4) Britain
   (5) United States

2. Which country will have the greatest population under 65 in 2020?
   (1) Japan
   (2) Germany
   (3) France
   (4) Britain
   (5) United States

3. Which countries have the most similar aging characteristics?
   (1) Japan and Germany
   (2) Germany and France
   (3) France and Britain
   (4) Britain and the United States
   (5) Japan and the United States

4. Which country will have the least stable growth of population over 65 for the rest of this century?
   (1) Japan
   (2) Germany
   (3) France
   (4) Britain
   (5) United States

5. What country was the least responsive to the health-care needs of its aging population in 1993?
   (1) Japan
   (2) Germany
   (3) France
   (4) Britain
   (5) United States

Answer Key

1. **1**   2. **5**   3. **3**   4. **1**   5. **2**

Answer Analysis

1. **1** In 2020, 25% of the population of Japan will be 65 or older, at least 4% more than any other country in the graph.
2. **5** In 2020, the United States will be the only country with an over-65 population below 20%.
3. **3** For France and Britain, percents are nearly identical for 1995, 2000, and 2010. The two countries will have the identical percent of population 65 or older in 2020, and in 1995 differed by less than 1% in percent of health care spending for the elderly as a share of total health-care spending.
4. **1** Japan will have an increase in population over 65. The other countries will remain at the same level.
5. **2** The pie graphs show that Germany spent least, approximately 9 to 10% less than France and Britain, for similar numbers of elderly.

Maps

A map is a visual representation of all or part of the surface of the earth. A map may or may not include a number of aids to help you visualize the surface it is depicting. It will always include a *title.* If the map uses

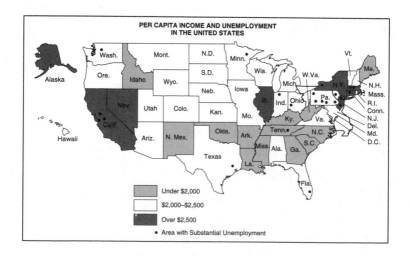

symbols, it will always include a *legend* (or key) to give the meaning of those symbols. It may also include:

- latitude and longitude to indicate direction and help you to find a specific location;
- a scale of miles to indicate what distance on the map equals a specific distance in miles on land;
- a grid, or square, usually identified by a set of letters on one axis (vertical or horizontal) and a set of numbers on the other, so that a place can be found in, for example, a grid identified as F 3 or H 7;
- relief or differences in height of land, shown by lines.

The two most important aids that you must learn to use in order to read a map are its *title* and its *legend* (or key). The map above is in many respects typical of the maps you will encounter. The following questions will sharpen your skills in map reading.

Questions
1. What is the *title* of the map?
2. What three indications make up the *legend*?
3. What does • mean?
4. What is the average per capita income of the population of the state of New York?
5. What is the average per capita income of the population of the state of New Mexico?
6. What is the average per capita income of the population of the state of Iowa?
7. Which state has a larger per capita income, Alaska or Hawaii?

Answers and Analysis
1. The title of the map is "Per Capita Income and Unemployment in the United States." See the heading above the map.
2. The dark gray areas indicate per capita income over $2,500; the white areas indicate per capita income between $2,000 and $2,500; the light gray areas indicate per capita income under $2,000.
3. The • indicates an area with substantial unemployment.
4. Since New York is a dark gray area, its per capita income is over $2,500.

5. Since New Mexico is a light gray area, its per capita income is under $2,000.
6. Since Iowa is a white area, its per capita income is between $2,000 and $2,500.
7. Since Alaska is a dark gray area (per capita income over $2,500) and Hawaii is a white area (per capita income between $2,000 and $2,500), Alaska has a larger per capita income than Hawaii.

Additional Questions

1. Per capita income in Maine is most nearly equal to per capita income in
    (1) Washington
    (2) Idaho
    (3) Utah
    (4) Nevada
    (5) Missouri
2. Which generalization is best supported by the map?
    (1) All New England states have per capita incomes of over $2,000.
    (2) All states along the Atlantic seaboard have a high per capita income.
    (3) All southern states have incomes below $2,000.
    (4) All states along the Pacific coast have per capita incomes of $2,000 or over.
    (5) Most states have per capita incomes over $2,500.
3. According to the map, in which state is unemployment a major problem?
    (1) Pennsylvania
    (2) Florida
    (3) Alabama
    (4) Texas
    (5) Washington
4. Which state has both a per capita income of between $2,000 and $2,500, and an area with substantial unemployment?
    (1) Kansas
    (2) Ohio
    (3) Kentucky
    (4) Mississippi
    (5) California

5. Which state has a high per capita income and substantial unemployment?
   (1) Florida
   (2) Louisiana
   (3) Minnesota
   (4) California
   (5) Nevada

6. Unemployment is less of a problem in Indiana than in
   (1) Massachusetts
   (2) Tennessee
   (3) Mississippi
   (4) Louisiana
   (5) Arizona

7. Which conclusion concerning the state of Tennessee is supported by the map?
   (1) It is larger than Montana and richer than Mississippi.
   (2) It has more unemployment than Georgia and was richer than Kentucky.
   (3) It is as rich as Arkansas and poorer than Nevada
   (4) It had less unemployment than Oklahoma and more unemployment than Georgia.
   (5) It is smaller than Minnesota and richer than Illinois.

Answer Key

1. **2**   2. **4**   3. **1**   4. **2**   5. **4**   6. **1**   7. **3**

Answer Analysis

1. **2**   The answer is Choice 2 since both states are light gray areas, with per capita incomes under $2,000.

2. **4**   Choice 4 is correct. California had a per capita income of over $2,500; Washington and Oregon had incomes between $2,000 and $2,500; all have incomes of $2,000 or over per capita. Choice 1 is incorrect since Maine has an income of less than $2,000. Choice 2 is wrong since three states—North Carolina, South Carolina, and Georgia—have incomes lower than $2,000. Choice 3 is incorrect since Texas, Florida, and Virginia have incomes above $2,000. Choice 5 is incorrect; only 10 states have per capita incomes over $2,500.

3. **1**   On the map, Pennsylvania has six dotted areas with substantial unemployment; Florida, Washington, and Texas have one each and Alabama has none. Choice 1 is correct.

4. **2**   You have to find a white area with a dot. Only Ohio, Choice 2, fits these criteria.

5. **4**   You have to find a dark gray area with several dots. Only California, Choice 4, fits this description.

6. **1**   You need to locate a state with more than one dot since Indiana has one such dot. The correct answer is Choice 1, Massachusetts, which has two dots.

7. **3**   The map compares Tennessee with other states with regard to per capita income and unemployment. Choice 1 is wrong since Montana is larger. Choice 2 is wrong since Tennessee is not richer than Kentucky but the same. Choice 4 is wrong since Tennessee has more unemployment than both Oklahoma and Georgia. Choice 5 is incorrect since Tennessee is poorer than Illinois. Choice 3 is correct; both Tennessee and Arkansas have per capita incomes of less than $2,000, while Nevada has a per capita income of over $2,500.

BASICS IN INTERPRETING POLITICAL CARTOONS

Political cartoons, as a distinct art form, first became important in the second half of the nineteenth century.

1. They are important because most cartoons deal with a single important issue, usually an election campaign issue, questions of peace or war, or corruption in government.

2. The cartoonist frequently uses an exaggerated likeness, or caricature, of some well-known person or institution, for example, Uncle Sam, as the main focus of attention. Or he or she may use or create a familiar symbol to represent an important idea; a dove for peace, a tiger for Tammany Hall.

3. Reading is kept to a minimum so that the appeal is largely visual. A few words at most are used to drive home an idea, so the visual appeal of the political cartoon is universal. Boss Tweed pointed out that, even if his followers could not read, they could "look at the d——n pictures." Thus the cartoonist presents an issue in simplified form, stripped of all relatively unimportant details, in a way that his readers can understand.

4. The cartoonist graphically presents his or her own point of view or that of a newspaper or magazine. The cartoonist is usually openly anticorruption or antiwar, and portrays the object of his or her criticism in the ugliest manner possible.

Because of the visually appealing use of a caricature and/or a symbol focusing critically on a single important issue, the political cartoon is a powerful means of shaping public opinion. Its appeal to the emotions is difficult to equal, and its influence continues to the present day.

How, then, do you interpret a political cartoon when you encounter it on the High School Equivalency Examination?

Here are a few suggestions:

Step 1. *Identify the caricatures or symbols used in the cartoon.* For historical cartoons, you may need some social studies background. In contemporary cartoons, the caricatures and symbols are easier to identify.

Step 2. *Identify the issue being exposed or criticized by the cartoonist.*

Step 3. *Determine the point of view being expressed by the cartoonist.*

Now look at this cartoon, study it, and try to answer the questions based on it.

Questions

1. What issue is the subject of this cartoon?
2. What do the elephant and the donkey represent?
3. What is each trying to do?
4. What point of view is the cartoonist expressing?

Answers and Analysis

1. The issue is campaign-funding abuse, as indicated on the cookie jar.
2. The elephant is the traditional symbol of the Republican party; the donkey, of the Democratic party.
3. Each has a hand in the cookie jar and is trying to extract money for the campaign.
4. The cartoonist finds both parties at fault even though he portrays the equally guilty Republicans expressing disapproval of the Democrats.

PRACTICE WITH CARTOONS

1. The main purpose of Mike Thompson's cartoon is to
   (1) portray the conflict between Republicans and Democrats
   (2) show the superiority of the Republicans over the Democrats
   (3) show the superiority of the Democrats over the Republicans
   (4) show that Republicans and Democrats are both at fault in campaign fund-raising
   (5) show that Democrats do not feel guilty about their campaign fund-raising
2. The cartoonist achieves his purpose by
   (1) exaggerating the conduct of both parties
   (2) arousing our sympathy for both parties
   (3) portraying the humor of the conduct of both parties
   (4) favoring Republicans over Democrats
   (5) showing the irony of the Republicans' conduct

Answer Key

1. **4**   2. **5**

Answer Analysis

1. **4** Choice 4 is correct because the cartoonist indicates that both parties have their hands in the cookie jar and are guilty of campaign

fund-raising abuses. Neither party is superior to the other, nor does either feel guilty.

2. **5** The irony arises from the fact that each party has a hand in the jar, yet the Republican elephant is faulting the Democratic donkey for an abuse of which both are equally guilty.

HANDLING SOCIAL STUDIES SKILLS QUESTIONS

The Social Studies test no longer tests your ability to recall information such as dates, isolated facts, or events. It now emphasizes higher level skills. It does so by testing your ability to understand the written word or graphics, to analyze and apply the given information and ideas, and to evaluate the accuracy of the information and the conclusions based on it.

COMPREHENSION ITEMS

Twenty percent of the test, or about 13 items, require you to understand the meaning and purpose of written material, passages or quotations, and information contained in maps, graphs, tables, and political cartoons. These items test your ability to restate information, summarize ideas, and identify incorrectly stated ideas. The question will usually include a quotation and be followed by the words "This most nearly means" or "The best explanation of this statement is" or "The author believes or suggests."

EXAMPLE

A CODE

Never DO, BE, or SUFFER anything in soul or body, less or more, but what tends to the glory of God.

Resolved, never to lose one moment of time; but improve it the most profitable way I possibly can.

Resolved, to think much, on all occasions, of my own dying, and of the common circumstances which attend death.

Resolved, to maintain the strictest temperance in eating and drinking.

Questions

1. The author of the code believes that people should be mainly concerned with
   (1) monetary issues
   (2) luxuries
   (3) patriotism
   (4) spiritual matters
   (5) politics

Answer and Analysis

The passage reflects the ideas of Puritanism, a code that stresses spiritual concerns.

You can answer this question correctly if you read the passage carefully and decide what is being emphasized. Then, look for the answer that identifies that emphasis. In this question, the emphasis is on living for the glory of God, concern for one's manner of dying, and discipline in such material concerns as eating and drinking. The spiritual is stressed. Indeed, you can answer the question even if you do not know it is the Puritan Code that is being quoted. The correct choice is 4.

APPLICATION ITEMS

Thirty percent of the test, or about 19 items, require you to use information and ideas in a situation other than that indicated to you in the question. Applying information and ideas is a high-level skill because you must not only understand the general content, but also be able to transfer it to the context of a particular situation. In other words, you must go from the general information you are given to a specific case.

EXAMPLE

The principle of judicial review provides for the judiciary to determine the constitutionality of both state and federal laws.

Question

1. Which action best illustrates the principle of judicial review?
   (1) Congress enacts civil rights legislation.
   (2) The Senate approves appointment of federal judges.

(3) An act of Congress is struck down by the Supreme Court.

(4) The states refuse to cooperate with the federal authorities in crime control.

(5) Congress overrides a presidential veto.

Answer and Analysis

The principle of judicial review means the power of the U.S. Supreme Court to rule on the constitutionality of acts of Congress, state legislatures, executive officers, and lower courts. The only choice that involves a court action is Choice 3, a specific application of this principle to an act of Congress. You must apply the principle of judicial or court reexamination to an act of Congress.

The purpose of another form of question or item on the High School Equivalency Examination Social Studies Test is to test your ability to apply given information that defines ideas in historical documents, divisions of subject matter in the social studies, systems of government, economics, psychology, and groups of basic concepts in the five areas of the social studies. You will have to

1. understand information that is presented in defined categories, usually five in number;
2. relate a situation, action, or event to those categories;
3. arrive at an application of the information in the categories to the given situation, action, or event.

An illustration will make this clear. In this example, the information presented in defined categories is the central idea of each of five articles of the Bill of Rights, the first ten amendments to the Constitution.

EXAMPLE

The first ten amendments to the Constitution make up the Bill of Rights ratified by Congress in 1791. Parts of five of the amendments read as follows:

(A) Article 1—Congress shall make no law...abridging the freedom of speech or of the press.

(B) Article 2—The right of the people to keep and bear arms shall not be infringed.

   (C) Article 5—No person...shall be compelled in any criminal case to be a witness against himself, nor be deprived of life, liberty, or property, without due process of law.

   (D) Article 7—The right to trial by jury shall be preserved.

   (E) Article 8—Excessive bail shall not be required...nor cruel and unusual punishments inflicted.

The questions that follow deal with three ways in which the given information can be used by three individuals in three different situations.

Questions

Indicate the amendment (article) most likely to be cited in support of his or her position by

1. an opponent of capital punishment
   (1) Article 1
   (2) Article 2
   (3) Article 5
   (4) Article 7
   (5) Article 8

2. a member of the National Rifle Association
   (1) Article 1
   (2) Article 2
   (3) Article 5
   (4) Article 7
   (5) Article 8

3. a person accused of a criminal act who is testifying at his or her trial
   (1) Article 1
   (2) Article 2
   (3) Article 5
   (4) Article 7
   (5) Article 8

Answers and Analysis

You must apply the categorized information to each situation.

The correct answer to question 1 is Choice 5. An opponent of capital punishment will cite Article 8's prohibition against cruel and unusual punishment.

The correct answer to question 2 is Choice 2. A member of the National Rifle Association will cite Article 2, "The right of the people to keep and bear arms shall not be infringed."

The correct answer to question 3 is Choice 3. The person on trial might "take the Fifth," citing the provision of Article 5 that "no person...shall be compelled in any criminal case to be a witness against himself."

Try another item set in this format.

EXAMPLE

Psychology is the science of behavior and of human thought processes. There are a number of closely interrelated branches of human psychology.

(A) Social psychology investigates the effect of the group on the behavior of the individual.

(B) Applied psychology puts to practical use the discoveries and theories of psychology as in industrial psychology.

(C) Clinical psychology diagnoses and treats mental disorders and mental illnesses.

(D) Comparative psychology deals with different behavioral organizations of animals including human beings.

(E) Physiological psychology attempts to understand the effects of body functions on human behavior.

Questions

Each of the following describes a proposed study. Indicate which branch of psychology is most clearly involved.

1. A company wants to study the effects of music piped into a factory where workers are on an assembly line.
    (1) Social psychology
    (2) Applied psychology
    (3) Clinical psychology
    (4) Comparative psychology
    (5) Physiological psychology

2. A drug rehabilitation center wants to study the role of peer pressure on a teenager in a drug prevention program.
    (1) Social psychology
    (2) Applied psychology
    (3) Clinical psychology
    (4) Comparative psychology
    (5) Physiological psychology
3. A grant is available for a study of schizophrenia, a disorder characterized by hallucinations and delusions.
    (1) Social psychology
    (2) Applied psychology
    (3) Clinical psychology
    (4) Comparative psychology
    (5) Physiological psychology

Answers and Analysis

The correct answer to question 1 is Choice 2. Applied psychology puts the findings of industrial psychologists to practical use, in this case for people who work on an assembly line.

The correct answer to question 2 is Choice 1. Social psychologists are concerned with the effects of groups, in this case teenagers, who put pressure on their peers to use drugs.

The correct answer to question 3 is Choice 3. Clinical psychologists would apply for the grant because of their interest in schizophrenia, a mental disorder.

ANALYSIS ITEMS

Thirty percent of the test, or about 19 items, requires you to break down information into its parts to determine their interrelationships. These items involve the ability to identify cause-and-effect relationships, separate fact from opinion, separate conclusions from supporting statements, and show that you can recognize assumptions on which conclusions are based.

Question

1. Democracy may be defined as government by the people directly or through representatives chosen in free elections. Which quotation from the Declaration of Independence best describes the fundamental principle of democracy in the United States?

(1) "imposing taxes on us without our consent"
(2) "governments long established should not be changed for light and transient causes"
(3) "depriving us, in many cases, of the benefits of trial by jury"
(4) "deriving their just powers from the consent of the governed"
(5) "quartering large bodies of armed troops among us"

Answer and Analysis

Not only must you understand the meaning of each possible answer, but you must analyze it to determine which is a *fundamental* principle of government in the United States. First you must understand; then you must analyze.

You have to go through all of the following steps:

Choice 1: imposing taxes without consent—meaning taxation without representation

Choice 2: governments long established should not be changed for light causes—meaning change in government must be for good reason

Choice 3: benefits of trial by jury—meaning the right to trial by jury

Choice 4: deriving powers from consent of the governed—meaning the government gets its power from those it governs, the people

Choice 5: quartering armed troops—meaning compulsion to keep soldiers in homes

Now the test of a *fundamental* principle of government in the United States must be applied to each.

Choice 1 is not fundamental; it is a grievance.

Choice 2 refers not to the government of the United States, but to changing governments in general.

Choice 3, trial by jury, is an important right, but it is not as fundamental as Choice 4, which states that the U.S. government is a democracy in which the people rule through their elected representatives. This is an absolutely fundamental principle.

Choice 4 is the only correct interpretation that can be made.

Choice 5 refers to unauthorized quartering of soldiers—important, but not fundamental.

EVALUATION ITEMS

Twenty percent of the test, or about 13 items, is the most difficult. You must make judgments about the soundness or accuracy of information. These questions test your ability to determine whether facts are adequately documented or proved, whether they are appropriately used to support conclusions, and whether they are used correctly or incorrectly in the presentation of opinions or arguments.

Question
1. Which statement is an opinion rather than a fact?
    (1) France was involved in the Vietnam conflict before the United States entered it.
    (2) There are tensions between mainland China and Taiwan.
    (3) Peace will be achieved by regional agreements throughout the world.
    (4) Great Britain has become a full member of the European Common Market.
    (5) The United States is a member of the North Atlantic Treaty Organization.

Answer and Analysis
Five statements are presented. Four are facts that can be proved or verified by evidence—that France was involved in Vietnam; that mainland China and Taiwan have tensions; that Great Britain is a member of the European Common Market; that the United States is a member of the North Atlantic Treaty Organization. Choice 3, peace will be achieved by regional agreements throughout the world, is an opinion or a hypothesis—not a fact—and it remains to be proved.

PRACTICE WITH SOCIAL STUDIES SKILLS QUESTIONS

Comprehension
1. During the last 150 years, immigrants were attracted to the United States because manpower needs increased. This occurred when the United States was experiencing periods of

(1) economic expansion
(2) economic depression
(3) war
(4) political change
(5) stability

2. "The privilege to be involved and to conduct a business in any manner that one pleases is not guaranteed by the Constitution. The right to engage in certain businesses may be subject to various conditions. Laws regulating businesses have been found to be valid. We find no justification to reject the state law under question."

Which is best illustrated by the passage?
(1) residual powers
(2) legislative consent
(3) judicial review
(4) executive order
(5) executive privilege

3. Which is a basic assumption of the graduated income tax?
(1) The ability to pay increases as wealth increases.
(2) Each wage earner should contribute to the government the same percentage of his or her income.
(3) The middle class should bear the burden of financing the government.
(4) Citizens should pay the costs of government services in proportion to their use of such services.
(5) Taxes on the wealthy should not be too great.

4. "In a sense the people of the Third World were forced to help pay for the Industrial Revolution in the West."

Which statement most clearly supports this viewpoint?
(1) The colonizing powers encouraged industries in their colonies.
(2) Western nations depended upon raw materials from their colonies.
(3) Financial centers of the world blocked investments in these new nations.
(4) The Third World is now experiencing an Industrial Revolution.
(5) The Third World supplied most of the manpower needed by the West.

5. "Public opinion is of major significance in social control."

The author of this statement most probably means that
(1) the influence of public opinion on government leaders is very limited
(2) problem solving is simplified when public opinion is not known
(3) public opinion may be predicted accurately, especially in the time of national crisis
(4) government officials must pay attention to public opinion in the formulation of policies
(5) polls provide little help to lawmakers

Analysis

THE BUSINESS CYCLE

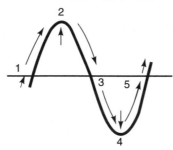

6. If economic indicators place the economy at a point on the cycle between 1 and 2, then the Council of Economic Advisers would most likely suggest which action to the president?
(1) planned deficit spending
(2) increasing income tax rates
(3) lowering interest rates
(4) increasing government expenditures
(5) encouraging higher wages

7. "The showpieces are, with rare exceptions, the industries dominated by a handful of large firms. The foreign visitor, brought to the United States...visits the same firms as do the attorneys of the Department of Justice in their search for monopolies."

The best explanation of this seemingly contradictory behavior is that
(1) only the largest corporations will allow foreign visitors to inspect their factories
(2) both State and Justice Department officials oppose the development of monopolies
(3) the developing countries of the world are interested only in large corporations
(4) the largest corporations often pioneer in research and production methods
(5) small firms do not welcome foreign investment

8. "Why, by interweaving our destiny with that of any part of Europe, entangle our peace and prosperity in the tolls of European ambition, rivalship, interest, humor, or caprice?"

Which action by the United States best reflects the philosophy expressed in this quotation?
(1) passage of legislation restricting immigration
(2) rejection of the Treaty of Versailles
(3) enactment of the Lend-Lease Act
(4) approval of the United Nations Charter
(5) membership in the North Atlantic Treaty Organization

9. "If a nation expects to be ignorant and free, in a state of civilization, it expects what never was and never will be."

Which idea is most strongly supported by this statement?
(1) the government's right to tax
(2) universal suffrage
(3) a strong central government
(4) compulsory education
(5) abolition of slavery

10. "Ours is a country where people...can attain to the most elevated positions or acquire a large amount of wealth...according to their talents, prudence, and personal exertions."

This quotation most clearly supports the idea that
(1) upward social mobility and the work ethic are closely related
(2) economic collectivism is part of American life
(3) regulated capitalism reflects private initiative
(4) the United States has a centrally controlled economic system
(5) the U.S. economic system favors the wealthy

Application

11. Which is the most valid statement concerning the problem of balancing human wants with limited resources?
    (1) It exists only in societies with a free enterprise economy.
    (2) It has been solved in nations with strong governmental controls over economic activity.
    (3) It has become less of a problem with the advancements in technology.
    (4) It exists in all societies, no matter what the economic system.
    (5) It will be solved by the year 2000.

12. A "strict constructionist," one who would permit the federal government to exercise only those powers specifically granted by the U.S. Constitution, would favor which of the following actions?
    (1) the institution of programs for social reform
    (2) annexation of territory by the United States
    (3) bypassing constitutional restraints
    (4) limiting the power of the federal government
    (5) increasing the power of the states

A basic principle of the U.S. Constitution is the division of governmental power in the executive, the legislative, and the judicial branches. Legislative powers are vested in Congress; judicial powers, in the Supreme Court and federal court system; executive powers, in the president and his governmental machinery. Thus, a system of checks and balances exists among the three branches of government.

Each of the following is an example of the system of checks and balances in operation. Identify the one branch that is checking the other by choosing the appropriate response.

13. Congress overrides a presidential veto.
    (1) the executive checks the legislative
    (2) the executive balances the judicial
    (3) the judicial balances the legislative
    (4) the legislative checks the executive
    (5) the legislative checks the judicial

14. The Senate refuses to confirm a presidential nominee for an ambassadorship.
    (1) the executive checks the legislative
    (2) the executive balances the judicial

(3) the judicial balances the legislative

(4) the legislative checks the executive

(5) the legislative checks the judicial

15. The president nominates a Supreme Court justice.

    (1) the executive checks the legislative

    (2) the executive balances the judicial

    (3) the judicial balances the legislative

    (4) the legislative checks the executive

    (5) the legislative checks the judicial

Evaluation

16. Which statement would be most *difficult* to prove?

    (1) Japan's emperors have reigned but have seldom ruled.

    (2) The workers of the United States are better workers than those of Japan.

    (3) In the post-World War II period, the United States was the source of much cultural borrowing by the Japanese.

    (4) Japanese technology in the 1970s was more advanced than it was in the 1940s.

    (5) The cost of living in Japan has been rising ever since World War II.

17. Which statement would be most *difficult* to prove?

    (1) Popular ideas of third parties in the United States tend to be adopted by the major political parties.

    (2) The Articles of Confederation rendered more authority to the state government than to the federal government.

    (3) The Sherman Antitrust Act was used to reduce the effectiveness of labor unions.

    (4) World War II was necessary in order to end the Great Depression.

    (5) The right to vote has been extended in the twentieth century.

18. Which information about country *X* would be most useful to the head of a government establishing a foreign policy toward country *X*?

    (1) an analysis of the national resources and goals of country *X*

    (2) a file containing the major public statements made by the leaders of country *X* concerning their nation's foreign policies

    (3) an analysis by religious leaders of the major religious groups and beliefs of the people of country *X*

(4) a newspaper report summarizing the treaties and international agreements of country *X*

(5) knowledge of the party to which leaders of country *X* belong

19. Which statement expresses an opinion rather than a fact?

(1) The United States did not join the League of Nations.

(2) At one time, the United States was on the gold standard.

(3) President Franklin D. Roosevelt made unnecessary concessions to the Russians at Yalta.

(4) The Oregon Dispute was settled by extending the 49th parallel to the Pacific Ocean.

(5) The United States is a member of NATO.

20. "The privilege to be involved and to conduct a business in any manner that one pleases is not guaranteed by the Constitution. The right to engage in certain businesses may be subject to various conditions. Laws regulating businesses have been found to be valid. We find no justification to reject the state law under question."

Which concept would most likely be REJECTED by the author of this passage?

(1) laissez-faire

(2) welfare

(3) competition

(4) profit motive

(5) antitrust legislation

Answer Key

1. **1**	4. **2**	7. **4**	10. **1**	13. **4**	16. **2**	19. **3**
2. **3**	5. **4**	8. **2**	11. **4**	14. **4**	17. **4**	20. **1**
3. **1**	6. **2**	9. **4**	12. **4**	15. **2**	18. **1**	

5

SCIENCE

READING AND INTERPRETING SCIENCE QUESTIONS

There are several types of questions on the Science test, and each calls for a specific plan of attack.

SINGLE-ITEM QUESTIONS

In this type, a short paragraph of one or two sentences is followed by a single question. Your first task in dealing with this kind of question is to identify the main idea or ideas presented, and the best way to do this is to start by reading the paragraph and the question quickly, without stopping to be sure you understand every point. This will give you some sense of the content of the question and of the kind of information you will need to answer it. Fix in your mind the main idea of the paragraph.

Next, reread the question carefully. You may be able to select the correct answer at once. If you have any doubt, go back to the paragraph and reread it carefully, searching for the answer to the question.

Practice this technique on the following question:

Question

Growing plants will not develop their green color, caused by the chlorophyll in their leaves, unless they have both sunlight and the necessary genetic system.

If a seedling growing in dim light turns out to be colorless, what could be done to find out why?

1. Give it a new set of genes.
2. Add chlorophyll to the soil.
3. Graft it onto a green plant.
4. Move it into the sunlight.
5. Add fertilizer to the soil.

Answer and Analysis

A quick reading tells you that the main idea deals with the factors involved in the development of a plant's green color. Now go back to the paragraph and read it again. After rereading, you know that the crucial factors are sunlight and genes. This narrows the answer possibilities to Choices 1 and 4. Since there is no way to give the plant a new set of genes, the answer is Choice 4.

MULTIPLE-ITEM QUESTIONS BASED ON READINGS

Some questions require you to read a passage consisting of several paragraphs and then to answer a number of questions about the material. In this case, you need to study the passage carefully *before* you look at the questions. As you read, note two or three main ideas.

To find the main ideas in the passage, look for key words. These are words such as *aorta* and *nucleus* and *ecosystem* that are normally used in a scientific context. Once you have found these words, they should lead you to one of the main ideas in the passage.

EXAMPLE

The annual migration of birds is a complex process that is only partly understood. Some birds that hatch in the Arctic fly thousands of miles to South America each winter, and then return to the place where they were born. The adults make these trips separately from their offspring. The young birds, however, find their way to the correct wintering grounds even though no adult bird shows them the way. No one knows how they are able to do this.

Biologists do understand, however, that in temperate zones the urge to migrate is prompted by a change in the length of daylight. As days grow shorter in the fall, certain physical changes occur in the birds, such as degeneration of the ovaries or testes. These changes are accompanied by restlessness and the urge to fly south.

There is some evidence that birds navigate using many clues, including the earth's magnetic field, the position of the sun in the sky, visible land forms, and even the pattern of the stars at night. How they know the route, however, is a complete mystery. It can be called instinct, but that is simply a word that explains nothing.

As you read this passage through for the first time, you should identify several key words, such as *migration, degeneration, ovaries, testes, navigate, magnetic field*. Now use these words to locate the main ideas in the passage. They will probably lead you to three main ideas: (1) the changing length of daylight is the signal that prompts migration; (2) birds use a number of clues to navigate; and (3) how they know the route is completely unknown.

Once you have these main ideas firmly fixed in your mind, you are ready to read the questions. Refer to the passage as needed to find the answers.

Question

What is the most probable factor that prompts birds to migrate north in the spring?

1. depletion of the food supply during the winter
2. the disappearance of snow from the ground
3. the coming of warmer weather
4. the increase in the amount of daylight
5. the instinct to fly north

Answer and Analysis

One of the main ideas tells you that, in the fall, migration is prompted by the decreasing length of daylight. It is surely reasonable to suppose that the reverse is true in the spring, so the answer is Choice 4. It should not be necessary for you to reread the passage.

Question

What has the study of migration revealed about how birds know what route to follow?

1. Young birds learn by following their parents.
2. Birds are born with an instinct that tells them the route.
3. Birds use several different means of navigation.
4. The changing length of daylight gives birds the necessary clues.
5. So far, investigation has not given any answers to the question.

Answer and Analysis

One of the main ideas, already extracted from the passage, is Choice 5—the answer. The passage says that Choice 1 is not true, and Choice 2 offers a word, *instinct*, but not an explanation. Choices 3 and 4 are true, but irrelevant to this particular question.

QUESTIONS BASED ON GRAPHS, DIAGRAMS, AND DATA TABLES

Line Graphs

A line graph is a common way to show how something changes or to show the relationship between two or more things. This kind of graph uses two scales, one going up the left side of the graph, called the vertical axis, and another along the bottom of the graph, called the horizontal axis.

If you are given a line graph on the GED test, read it carefully. Note the title, the labels on the vertical and horizontal axes, and the legend or key if there is one. Take your time, and pay attention to all of the printed material as well as the lines and the scales. Only then will you be ready to answer questions based on the line graph.

Here is a sample for you to work on:

EXAMPLE

The graph below represents the temperatures of a white sidewalk and a black asphalt driveway on a sunny day. The surfaces are side by side, and the measurements were made during a 24-hour period.

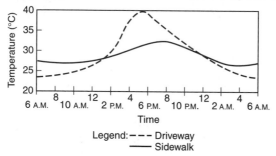

What are the features of this graph? The vertical axis represents temperatures between 20 and 40 degrees Celsius. It does not matter whether you are familiar with the Celsius scale of temperature or not. All you need to be able to do is recognize the changes and the intervals from one temperature to another.

The horizontal axis represents the time of day. It is divided into 4-hour intervals for a 12-hour period.

According to the legend, the solid line on the graph represents the temperature of the sidewalk and the dashed line represents the temperature of the driveway. Note that both temperatures increase during daylight hours and start to decrease in the late afternoon or early evening.

Now you are ready for the questions.

Question

At noon, what was the temperature of the driveway?

1. 22°C
2. 26°C
3. 28°C
4. 30°C
5. 32°C

Answer and Analysis

Noon is halfway between 10 a.m. and 2 p.m., so start by placing the point of your pencil halfway between these two points on the horizontal scale. Move it straight up until it meets the dashed line, which represents the driveway. Now move the pencil point to the left; it meets the temperature scale at 26°. The answer is Choice 2.

Question

What is the difference in the times when the two surfaces reach their maximum temperatures?

1. The driveway reaches its maximum about 4 hours before the sidewalk.
2. The sidewalk reaches its maximum about 4 hours before the driveway.
3. The driveway reaches its maximum about 2 hours before the sidewalk.
4. The sidewalk reaches its maximum about 2 hours before the driveway.
5. Both surfaces reach their maximums at the same time.

Answer and Analysis

The dashed line (driveway) peaks at about 4 p.m., halfway between 2 p.m. and 6 p.m. The solid line (sidewalk) peaks a little before 8 p.m. The difference is fairly close to 4 hours, so the answer is Choice 1.

Bar Graphs

Whereas a line graph is used to show how something changes, a bar graph is used to compare several quantities. Like a line graph, a bar graph has a vertical axis marked off as a kind of scale. The horizontal axis is used to indicate the different quantities that are being compared.

Look at a bar graph the same way you would a line graph. Read the title and the legend (if any). Then note the information given on the horizontal axis and on the vertical axis.

EXAMPLE

The following graph represents the counts of three kinds of leukocytes (white blood cells) in an animal that was administered a standard dose of a drug starting on day 4.

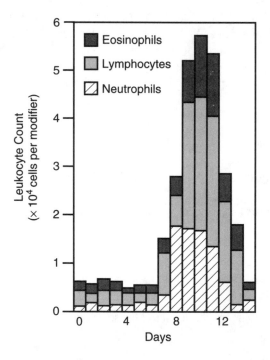

Note that the numbers of the three different kinds of leukocytes are indicated by using different patterns in the bars.

Question

How long did the medication take to produce its maximum effect?

1. 4 days
2. 7 days
3. 10 days
4. 12 days
5. 14 days

Answer and Analysis

Remember that the drug was started on day 4. The peak of leukocyte production was reached on day 10. When you subtract the three days during which no medication was given, you have the answer: 7 days, Choice 2.

Question

In regard to amount of increase, how did the three different kinds of leukocytes react to the medication?

1. All three increased in roughly the same proportion.
2. The neutrophils increased proportionally more than the others.
3. The eosinophils increased proportionally more than the others.
4. There was proportionally less increase in the eosinophils.
5. There was proportionally less increase in the lymphocytes.

Answer and Analysis

At the peak, the ratios were about 1/4 neutrophils and 1/5 eosinophils, which were not much different from the starting ratios. The answer is Choice 1.

Pie Charts

A pie chart is a circular graph in which the circle is divided into sections. Pie charts are useful when a particular item of information is a part, that is, a fraction or percentage, of a whole.

The first thing to notice on a pie chart is the labels, which tell you what the various segments represent. Each label is usually accompanied by a number that indicates what part of the whole this segment represents. Next you should note the sizes of the segments to get some idea of which are largest and which are smallest.

EXAMPLE

The pie chart below indicates the average numbers of macroscopic (large) organisms in one area.

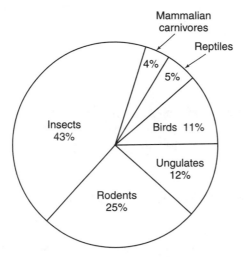

Note that insects, although physically the smallest of the animals represented, are the largest group—43%. Hoofed animals (ungulates) make up 12%.

Question

Which statement is supported by the chart?

1. Birds eat either insects or seeds.
2. Most reptiles are carnivores.
3. Eighty percent of the ecosystem consists of herbivores.
4. The ecosystem in this study was a savannah.
5. Insects are important because they are plant pollinators.

Answer and Analysis

Although Choices 1 and 2 are true statements, nothing on the chart indicates what birds or reptiles eat. Choice 4 is an excellent assumption, but nothing on the chart proves this statement conclusively. Choice 5 is partly true, but again is not supported by the chart. The best answer is Choice 3. If you know that a great many insects, ungulates (hoofed animals), and rodents eat plants, and if you add up the number represented by their portions of the chart, the total is 80%.

Diagrams

Diagrams, sometimes called graphics, show the relationships among the various parts of an object. Some parts may be inside others, be connected to others, or even be completely separate. When you see a diagram, the first things to look for are the connections between parts. Be sure to read all of the labels.

EXAMPLE

The following diagram represents the human ear. Empty spaces are shown in black.

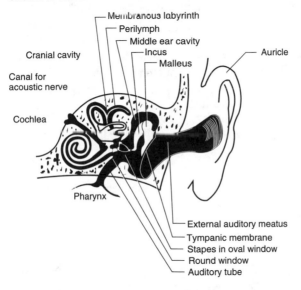

You should see at once that the external auditory meatus is an empty space separated from the middle ear cavity by the tympanic membrane. The middle ear cavity contains three bones.

Questions

The incus is inside the

1. malleus
2. middle ear cavity
3. tympanic membrane
4. round window
5. auditory tube

Answer and Analysis

The label "Incus" points to something white, a bone. The label "Middle ear cavity" indicates a black area, a cavity. The answer is Choice 2.

Data Tables

When a series of objects or situations, each having a certain value, is under consideration, a data table is used to make comparison easy. The table is in columns, each column headed by a label that tells what the column contains. If there are numerical data, the column head will also indicate the unit of measure, usually in parentheses. There are no special precautions in reading a data table; just be sure you know what the headings mean.

EXAMPLE

The following table gives the symbols, atomic numbers, and average atomic weights of the most common elements in the Earth's crust. The atomic number is the number of protons in the atom.

Element	Symbol	Atomic Number	Average Atomic Weight (daltons)
Aluminum	Al	13	27.0
Calcium	Ca	20	40.1
Carbon	C	6	12.0
Iron	Fe	26	55.8
Magnesium	Ma	12	24.3
Oxygen	O	8	16.0
Potassium	K	13	39.1
Silicon	Si	14	28.1
Sodium	Na	11	23.0

Question

How many protons are there in a molecule of magnesium oxide (MgO)?

1. 4
2. 8
3. 12
4. 16
5. 20

Answer and Analysis

Just add the 12 in magnesium to the 8 in oxygen; the answer is Choice 5.

HANDLING SCIENCE SKILLS QUESTIONS

The makers of the GED Examination try to test you for a wide range of skills. You can be asked to do something as simple as restating an idea from the passage, or something as complex as evaluating the scientific validity of an experiment. The questions are generally grouped into four levels of skill.

THE FOUR SKILLS

It is not worth your while to try to determine to which of the four levels any one question belongs, or to develop special strategies for each of the four levels. In taking the test, this sort of approach would consume valuable time and require you to use a part of your thinking ability that is best reserved for answering questions. Nevertheless, it is a good idea to become familiar with the four levels of skill that are investigated in the test.

Comprehension

Comprehension is the simplest level. What it comes down to is this: Do you understand the passage, graph, or diagram? Can you rephrase some of the information in it? Can you summarize it? Can you identify a simple implication of the information given?

Here are some examples of the simple comprehension type of question:

Question

Elements can be either mixed mechanically to form a mixture, or combined chemically to form a compound. In a mixture, the properties of each of the elements present are recognizable. A mixture is rather like a stew in which the carrots, potatoes, and tomatoes are all identifiable. In a compound, however, the original elements are no longer recognizable as themselves, and another form of matter with its own characteristics has been produced.

Which of the following is NOT a mixture?

1. iron filings in sawdust
2. sugar water
3. vegetable soup
4. fireplace ash
5. soda water

Answer and Analysis

If you understood the passage, you know that the components of a mixture remain separate and identifiable, while the components of a compound are changed into a new form of matter. The only answer in which the elements have been completely altered is Choice 4, fireplace ash, the result of burning wood. All of the other substances can be separated into their original parts.

Question

The scientific name of an animal is printed in italic type and has two parts. The first word (capitalized) is the name of the genus to which the animal belongs. The second word (lower case) is the name of its species within the genus. Here are the English and scientific names of five birds:

A. American robin, *Turdus migratorius*
B. European robin, *Erithacus rubecula*
C. European blackbird, *Turdus merula*
D. Military macaw, *Ara militaris*
E. Red-breasted blackbird, *Sturnella militaris*

Of the following pairs, which belong to the same genus?

1. A and B only
2. D and E only
3. B and C only
4. A and C only
5. C and E only

Answer and Analysis

Since the passage deals only with scientific names, you can ignore the English names. The first word of the scientific name is the same for two birds in the same genus, so the answer is Choice 4. If you understood the passage, you got the answer.

Question

When you place a solution in a test tube and then spin the test tube very rapidly in a machine called a centrifuge, the materials in the solution will separate, with the heaviest ones on the bottom and the lightest ones on top.

The following diagram represents the result of spinning a suspension of broken cells in a centrifuge. Which is the correct conclusion?

1. Ribosomes are more dense than mitochondria.
2. Nuclei are more dense than mitochondria.
3. Mitochondria and ribosomes are equal in density.
4. The cell consists of only solid components.
5. Nuclei are less dense than mitochondria.

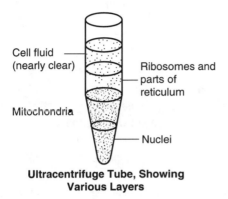

Cell fluid
(nearly clear)

Ribosomes and
parts of
reticulum

Mitochondria

Nuclei

**Ultracentrifuge Tube, Showing
Various Layers**

Answer and Analysis

The correct choice is 2 because the most dense particles settle at the bottom after spinning.

Question

The soft body feathers of a bird are useful as insulation, while the stiff feathers of the wings and tail form airfoil surfaces, like those of an airplane wing. If a new species of bird is found that has no stiff feathers, it is safe to assume that it

1. cannot fly
2. lives in a tropical country
3. migrates south in winter
4. lives mainly in the water
5. is able to run rapidly

Answer and Analysis

This question calls for you to make a simple deduction. If the stiff feathers are used in flight, a bird without them cannot fly, so the answer is Choice 1.

Question

The table below gives the densities of four kinds of materials found in the Earth:

Substance	Density (g/cm3)
Water	1.00
Petroleum	0.86
Wood chips	0.75
Sand	2.10

If a mixture of all four materials is placed in a cylinder, shaken, and allowed to stand, the materials will settle out with the most dense on the bottom. What will the cylinder look like?

1. The sand and wood chips will be mixed together on the bottom, and the water will be on top of the petroleum.
2. The sand will be on the bottom; above will be the water with the wood chips in the layer between the petroleum and the water.
3. The wood chips will form a layer above the sand on the bottom, and the water will form a layer over the petroleum.
4. The sand will be on the bottom; the petroleum will form a layer over the water, with the wood chips floating on top.
5. The water will be on the bottom, with the wood chips floating on it; the petroleum and sand will be mixed above the water.

Answer and Analysis

The materials, top to bottom, must be in the sequence of increasing density—wood chips, petroleum, water, sand—so the answer is Choice 4.

Application

If you have thoroughly understood the information provided in the passage, graph, diagram, or table, you should be able to apply what you have learned. The application questions ask you to use the general principle contained in the information, but to apply that principle to a different situation.

Here are some examples:

Question

Study the graph below, which shows the percentage distributions of the Earth's surface elevation above, and depth below, sea level.

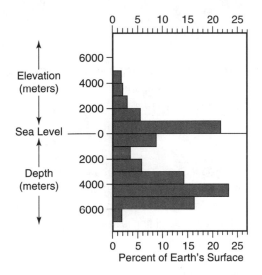

Approximately what total percentage of the Earth's surface is below sea level?

1. 30%
2. 50%
3. 70%
4. 80%
5. 90%

Answer and Analysis

There are more shaded bars below than above sea level on the graph. Adding up the lengths of all the shaded bars below sea level yields a total of about 70%. This represents the total percentage of the Earth's surface below sea level. The correct answer is Choice 3.

Question

High-energy sound waves are known to produce long-term damage to the ears, resulting in loss of ability to hear high frequencies. Which of the following individuals is most likely to have good high-frequency hearing after many years of work?

1. a rock musician
2. an aircraft mechanic
3. a riveter
4. an accountant
5. a sawmill operator

Answer and Analysis

Again, you cannot get the answer just by looking back at the information. You have to look at the list of choices to figure out who is least likely to have been exposed to loud noise. The answer is Choice 4; a pencil and a calculator are not noisy.

Question

A 20-watt fluorescent lamp produces as much light as a 100-watt incandescent bulb. The lighting in a factory is redesigned to provide the same amount of light when half of the incandescent lamps are replaced with fluorescents. What fraction of the cost of lighting is saved?

1. 10%
2. 20%
3. 25%
4. 40%
5. 80%

Answer and Analysis

A complete change to fluorescents would save 80 of every 100 watts. Since only half of the lamps are changed, the saving is half this, 40%; the answer is Choice 4.

Question

When an animal eats another that contains PCB pollutants, the PCB concentrates in the predator's liver. The following food relationships exist in a certain ecosystem:

> Big fish eat little fish.
> Little fish eat plankton.
> Wolves eat otters.
> Otters eat big fish.

If the water of a pond contains PCB, which of the following will have the greatest concentration of PCB?

1. otters
2. wolves
3. big fish
4. plankton
5. little fish

Answer and Analysis

The concentration of PCB must increase in the sequence plankton, little fish, big fish, otters, wolves, so the answer is Choice 2.

Questions

Many foods, such as bread, potatoes, and spaghetti, contain a great deal of starch. An enzyme in saliva slowly changes starch to sugar. Which of the following statements is most probably true?

1. A piece of bread held in the mouth for a long time becomes sweet.
2. Spaghetti in the mouth causes an increase in the flow of saliva.
3. If you eat a potato, the enzyme is in your saliva.
4. If you eat sugar, it can turn to starch in the mouth.
5. A cookie tastes sweet because it contains starch.

Answer and Analysis

If the saliva in the mouth changes the starch in the bread to sugar, you might expect that the bread would begin to taste sweet. Choice 1 is correct. None of the other choices is suggested by the information given.

Analysis

These questions are more complicated. To answer them, you will have to find the relationships among several different items of information. Some of these items will not be given; you will be expected to know things that are general knowledge. It is possible to identify five somewhat different kinds of skills that belong to the general category of analysis:

• Recognizing unstated assumptions
• Using several related pieces of information
• Distinguishing fact from opinion
• Distinguishing cause from effect
• Drawing conclusions from data

Here are some examples of questions requiring analysis:

Questions

A doctor discovers that a patient has blood pressure of 170/110. He tells the patient that medication, accompanied by a reducing diet and limited exercise, will bring the blood pressure down. What has the doctor assumed without actually stating it?
1. Blood pressure of 170/110 is dangerous to the health of the patient.
2. Medication can bring down blood pressure.
3. Medication will reduce the patient's weight.
4. The patient has not been exercising at all.
5. Blood pressure varies greatly in the population at large.

Answer and Analysis

Surely the doctor would not bother with the problem if he did not assume that the patient's blood pressure is too high for continued good health, so the answer is Choice 1. Choice 2 is true, but it is not unstated; the doctor told the patient that medication would work. Since there is no reason to believe that the medication is used for weight reduction, Choice 3 is wrong. Choice 4 is wrong because the prescription for limited exercise might just as easily mean that the patient has been exercising too much. Choice 5 is true, but irrelevant.

If you are asked to find an unstated assumption, do not select one that is (a) stated in the information given; (b) untrue; (c) ambiguous; or (d) irrelevant.

Question

Corals are tiny animals that obtain their energy from their close association with green algae. Fish that eat corals do not live in deep water because
1. the pressure is too great in deep water
2. the fish that live in deep water eat them
3. sunlight does not penetrate into deep water
4. there are no currents in deep water to carry nutrients to them
5. it is too cold in deep water

Answer and Analysis

This is one of the questions in which you are expected to know a few facts and to put some ideas together. You should know that green algae need sunlight to grow, and that corals use energy for growth. The answer is Choice 3. Some of the other answers may be true, but they are irrelevant.

Question

Someone sees a high waterfall on the side of a cliff and comments about it. Which of the following comments is probably based on opinion rather than fact?

1. The waterfall is about 30 meters high.
2. The valley into which it falls was carved by a glacier.
3. The rock in the mountain is a form of granite.
4. The speed of the water at the bottom of the fall is about 25 meters per second.
5. A photograph of the fall would be really beautiful.

Answer and Analysis

"Based on fact" is not the same as "factual." A statement is probably based on fact if it can be derived from one or more facts. Choices 1 and 4 could be determined by measurement or calculation—facts. Choices 2 and 3 could be determined from facts by any competent geologist. Since beauty is in the eye of the beholder, Choice 5 is an opinion.

Question

It is found that, when a stream becomes more muddy, the population of catfish increases. Three possible explanations are offered:

A. More catfish tend to make the water muddy.
B. Catfish thrive on invertebrates that live in mud.
C. Other fish cannot live in muddy water, so catfish have less competition.

Which of these explanations is (are) feasible?

1. A only
2. B only
3.. C only
4. A and B only
5. B and C only

Answer and Analysis

This question requires you to tell the difference between cause and effect. Is it possible that explanation A is true? No; the water became muddy before the catfish population increased, and a cause can never come after its effect. In both explanation B and explanation C, the water is already muddy, and both are reasonable hypotheses, so the answer is Choice 5.

This type of question can be tricky. If one event follows another, the one that occurs first may or may not be the cause of the second, even if the second invariably follows the first. The crowing of the rooster does not make the sun rise. In the example given, the sequence of the two events stated in the question establishes only that B and C are possible explanations, not that they must necessarily be true.

Question

A chemical factory manufacturing a detergent discovers that its product contains a material that is considered a biohazard. Of the following, which can be considered a conclusion based on data?

1. The amount of reactant A is twice as great as that of reactant B.
2. The temperature of the reaction is 140°C.
3. The pH of the reaction mixture is 5.4.
4. The problem can be solved by adding an alkali.
5. There is a contaminant in reactant A.

Answer and Analysis

Fact or conclusion? All the statements except Choice 4 are data, testable and presumably confirmed by measurement. Putting all the known facts together, the engineer might use his knowledge of the process to obtain an overall picture of what is happening. He can then draw the conclusion in Choice 4.

A conclusion is a general statement that is not obtained from direct observation. It comes from intelligent application of known principles to measurement data.

Evaluation

We all have our own beliefs and ideas, and most of our beliefs and general thought processes are not scientific. But then, this is how it should be. Science cannot tell you what career to choose or whom to marry, or whether to go to church on Sunday, or who to vote for, or what kind of music to listen to. What science can do, however, is provide highly reliable and accurate answers to questions.

On the GED Examination, evaluation questions test your ability to apply the rules of scientific analysis to questions. Before you can do this, though, you need to understand a little about some of the many different kinds of statements that you will encounter.

Fact or Datum

A fact (datum) is something that can be observed and proved to be true.

EXAMPLE

If you measure a piece of wood and it is precisely 8 feet long, you have established a fact. If, however, someone estimates and tells you that the piece is 8 feet long even though it has not been measured, then you have an estimation, not a fact. Another kind of statement is an opinion, as when someone remarks that the piece of wood is an attractive color. Again, you do not have a fact.

You may be asked to determine whether a statement is a valid fact. Sloppy techniques can produce a statement that looks like a fact, but which cannot be supported by evidence or by the experimental process. You will need to be able to identify such statements.

Hypothesis

A hypothesis is an educated guess, the possible answer to a question. It is a purely tentative statement that may be modified or even disproved when more information becomes available.

EXAMPLE

If you find that a type-A shrub in the sunlight grows better than another type-A shrub in the shade, you might propose the hypothesis that type-A shrubs need sunlight for optimum growth. This hypothesis can be tested by a controlled experiment. The most common mistake that people make is to accept a hypothesis as a fact without realizing the need for an experiment to provide proof.

You may have to distinguish between a fact and a hypothesis.

Conclusion

A conclusion may be the result of a controlled experiment. A hypothesis becomes a conclusion when you have tested and verified the initial statement.

EXAMPLE

If the type-A shrub really does grow better in the sunlight during a carefully designed experiment, then it is a reasonable conclusion that this particular plant should be grown in the sun.

You may be asked whether it is reasonable to draw a certain conclusion from a given set of data. You will have to be able to distinguish between a hypothesis and a conclusion.

Generalization

A generalization is a conclusion that can apply to a wide variety of situations.

EXAMPLE

Many experiments with green plants have indicated that all of them, whether a tiny alga cell or an enormous redwood tree, need some sunlight in order to live.

If you are asked whether a certain generalization is reasonable, look to see if it applies to many situations.

Value Judgment

A value judgment is an opinion based on cultural or emotional factors rather than on scientific evidence. Opinions have an important place in our lives, but they cannot be allowed to affect the process of arriving at a scientific conclusion.

EXAMPLE

A certain landowner decided that he should kill every snake on his property because he didn't like snakes. He also killed squirrels and chipmunks for the same reason—he didn't like them.

You will be asked to distinguish value judgments from scientifically valid statements.

Logical Fallacy

A fallacy is a wrong conclusion that results when you use information incorrectly. The most common logical fallacy goes by the imposing name *post hoc ergo propter hoc*, which means "followed by, therefore caused by."

EXAMPLE

I drink a glass of milk for breakfast every morning, and I always get sleepy. Does the milk make me sleepy? Maybe. Or maybe I would become sleepy even if I didn't drink the milk. The way to avoid this kind of fallacy is to perform a controlled experiment and test the possible relationship.

The examples below will give you some idea of the sorts of questions that will test your ability to evaluate scientific statements.

Question

A proposal to build a dam on a river is opposed by a group of citizens, offering various reasons. Which of the following reasons is based on a value judgment rather than scientific information?

1. The river should be preserved because it is a habitat for much beautiful wildlife.
2. The cost of the dam will be too high for the amount of electricity it produces.
3. It is not possible to dam the river at the site selected because of the surface features of the land.
4. The proposed site is on a fault, and the dam could be destroyed by an earthquake.
5. The river carries so much silt that the lake formed by it would soon fill up and render the dam useless.

Answer and Analysis

The word *beautiful* in Choice 1 is a giveaway, specifying a value judgment. Whoever makes that argument sees an esthetic value in the preservation of wildlife. All the other objections are based on arguments that can be subjected to rigid testing, using established scientific principles.

Question

The following graph shows the average growths of two groups of rats. The solid line represents a group raised under standard conditions by a supplier of laboratory animals; the dashed line, a group raised in a laboratory and treated with pituitary extract.

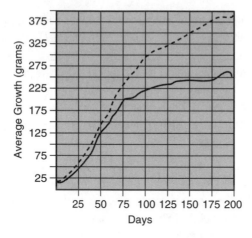

—— Average growth of 38 untreated rats (control)
- - - - Average growth of 38 rats injected with
anterior pituitary extract (experimental)

What is a proper conclusion from the experiment?
1. It is known that pituitary extract stimulates growth, and the experiment confirms it.
2. The difference between the control group and the experimental group is so clear that it can be concluded that pituitary extract stimulates growth.
3. The growths of the two groups are too similar to show that there is any difference in average growth.
4. The experiment is useless because there is no reason to believe that the same result would be obtained with human beings.
5. The experiment is inconclusive because there was no attempt to control the heredity of the animals or the conditions of their nurture.

Answer and Analysis

Whether an experiment should have some obvious use is a value judgment that is not at issue here, so Choice 4 is wrong. Choice 1 is wrong because it suggests that the outcome of the experiment was prejudiced in advance. At first this looks like a nice, neat experiment; the difference in growth is marked, and so Choice 3 is wrong. However, Choice 2 is wrong because the controls are inadequate. The rats were not necessarily of the same breed, nor were they raised in the same place. They could differ also in their hereditary endowments, their feeding, and any number of other factors. The results of this experiment could lead to a hypothesis, but not a conclusion, so the answer is Choice 5.

Question

Over the last hundred years, people have been burning more and more fossil fuel, which releases carbon dioxide into the atmosphere. This excess CO_2 is a cause of global warming, which, according to ecologists, is one of the most serious problems facing us today. Carbon dioxide in the upper atmosphere traps the Sun's heat, in much the same way that the panes of glass hold heat in a greenhouse.

Which graph best represents what most likely happens to the temperature of the Earth's atmosphere as the amount of carbon dioxide in the atmosphere increases over a period of many years?

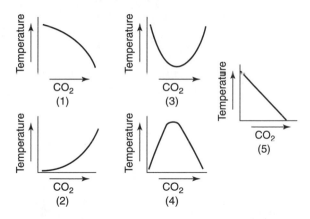

Answer and Analysis

Graph (2) shows that, as the amount of carbon dioxide increases, the average temperature of the atmosphere also increases.

6
INTERPRETING LITERATURE AND THE ARTS

BASIC READING SKILLS

Reading consists of a complex combination of skills. The writer sets forth his or her ideas using the medium of language consisting of printed words. If the writer has stated the ideas clearly, they have been well organized and well developed. You, the reader, must draw meaning from the ideas expressed on the printed page. In addition, there may be ideas that are implied rather than openly stated. For example, a woman dressed in black is described as grieving. The implication is that she has lost a loved one, even if this fact is not stated in so many words.

Reading requires the use of a number of skills so you can decode or derive from the language used the meaning intended by the writer, whether it is explicitly stated or suggested by implication.

These skills are basically three in number.

You read to find the main idea of the selection.
You find the main idea in a variety of places. It may be stated directly in the first sentence (easy to find). It may be stated in the final sentence to which the others build up (a bit harder to find). It may have to be discovered within the passage (most difficult); an example (note the underscored words) occurs in the following paragraph:

Several students were seriously injured in football games last Saturday. The week before, several more were hospitalized. Football has become a dangerous sport. The piling up of players in a scrimmage often leads to serious injury. Perhaps some rule changes would lessen the number who are hurt.

You may also find that the main idea is not directly expressed, but can only be inferred from the selection as a whole.

The plane landed at 4 P.M. As the door opened, the crowd burst into a long, noisy demonstration. The waiting mob surged against the police guard lines. Women were screaming. Teenagers were yelling for autographs or souvenirs. The visitor smiled and waved at his fans.

The main idea of the paragraph is not expressed, but it is clear that some popular hero, movie or rock star is being welcomed enthusiastically at the airport.

To find the main idea of a passage, **ask yourself any or all of these questions:**
1.   What is the *main idea* of the passage? (Why did the author write it?)
2.   What is the *topic sentence* of the paragraph or paragraphs (the sentence that the other sentences build on or flow from)?
3.   What *title* would I give this selection?

You read to find the details that explain or develop the main idea.

How do you do this? You must determine how the writer develops the main idea. He or she may give examples to illustrate that idea, or may give reasons why the statement that is the main idea is true, or may give arguments for or against a position stated as the main idea. The writer may define a complex term and give a number of aspects of a complicated belief (such as democracy). He or she may also classify a number of objects within a larger category. Finally, the writer may compare two ideas or objects (show how they are similar) or contrast them (show how they are different).

In the paragraph immediately above, you can see that the sentence "You must determine how the writer develops the main idea" *is* the main idea. Six ways in which the writer can develop the main idea follow. These are the details that actually develop the main idea of the paragraph.

To find the main details of a passage, the questions to ask yourself are these:
1.   What examples illustrate the main point?
2.   What reasons or proof support the main idea?
3.   What arguments are presented for or against the main idea?
4.   What specific qualities are offered about the idea or subject being defined?

5. Into what classifications is a larger group broken down?
6. What are the similarities and differences between two ideas or subjects being compared or contrasted?

You read to make inferences by putting together ideas that are expressed to arrive at other ideas that are not.
In other words, you draw conclusions from the information presented by the author. You do this by locating relevant details and determining their relationships (time sequence, place sequence, cause and effect).

How do you do this? You can put one fact together with a second to arrive at a third that is not stated. You can apply a given fact to a different situation. You can predict an outcome based on the facts given.

To make inferences from a passage, ask yourself the following questions:
1. From the facts presented, what conclusions can I draw?
2. What is being suggested, in addition to what is being stated?
3. What will be the effect of something that is described?
4. What will happen next (after what is being described)?
5. What applications does the principle or idea presented have?

READING POPULAR LITERATURE

The basic reading skills apply to popular and classical literature alike. Popular literature is easier to read. The content presents fewer problems since you are more likely to have shared the same experiences as the writer. Also, you are generally more familiar with the language of the writer. Since the selections are drawn from sources that you read quite frequently—newspapers and magazines, for example—they should be no more difficult than the usual materials geared to the high school graduate.

READING CLASSICAL LITERATURE

Classical literature differs from popular literature in a number of ways. The settings are certainly different because they go back at least fifty to two hundred years. Also, the style of writing is different; sentences are longer and more complicated. The vocabulary is less familiar. Some of the subject matter may be dated for today's reader. On the other hand, fine classical literature deals with the eternal emotions of love, hate, greed, loyalty, self-sacrifice, joy, fear, among others. And many themes are eternal—the relationship of man to his fellow man and woman, of man to God, of man to nature, of man to his family, of man to his country.

Reading classical literature requires patience but it can be greatly rewarding. Try to imagine the unfamiliar setting. Reread the difficult sentences. Get the meaning of the unfamiliar word from its context. Find the application to life today of the theme of the selection. Continued practice will make these worthwhile tasks easier and the literature more satisfying.

LOCATING THE MAIN IDEA

Depending upon the type of passage—poetry, fiction, essay, drama—the technique of finding the main idea may vary. In the essay, for example, the main idea may very well appear as a straightforward statement, usually expressed in the topic sentence. In this particular case, the trick is to find the topic sentence. In works of fiction, poetry, or drama, the main idea might be found in a line of dialogue or exposition, or within a long, flowing line of verse.

Prose

In reading *prose*, the main unit is the paragraph. Since all the paragraphs you will encounter on the GED examination have been chosen for their "loaded" content—that is, because they contain a number of ideas offering possibilities for questions—it is important that you learn how to locate the main idea. This, in turn, will enable you to understand many of the subordinate (less important) elements of the paragraph—all of which may also be the basis for examination questions.

The topic sentence containing the main idea is used in five standard patterns:

1. The topic sentence, expressing the main idea, may introduce the paragraph and be followed by sentences containing details that explain, exemplify, prove, or support the idea, or add interest.

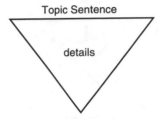

EXAMPLE

In _Alice in Wonderland,_ Lewis Carroll created a world of fantasy out of essentially real creatures, transformed into whimsy by the odd patterns of a dream. Sitting with her sister by a stream, Alice sees a rabbit; as she dozes off, the rabbit becomes larger, dons a waistcoat and a pocket watch, and acquires human speech.

2. The topic sentence may appear at the end of the paragraph, with a series of details leading to the main idea.

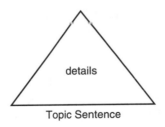

EXAMPLE

The small, darting rabbit on the riverbank becomes a huge White Rabbit, complete with waistcoat and pocket watch. The cards in a discarded deck become the Queen of Hearts and her court. The real world of Alice Liddell becomes, through the odd patterns of the dream, the fantasy world of _Alice in Wonderland._

3. The selection may begin with a broad generalization (topic sentence) followed by details that support the main idea and lead to another broad generalization that is called the "summary sentence" (conclusion).

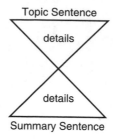

EXAMPLE

<u>The elements of the real world become, through the strange, shifting patterns of the dream, objects and creatures of curiosity and whimsy.</u> A scurrying rabbit becomes a humanized White Rabbit; a deck of cards becomes the court of the Queen of Hearts; a kitten becomes a chess Queen. In *Alice in Wonderland* reality becomes fantasy and, for a while, fantasy becomes reality.

4.   The topic sentence may appear in the body of the paragraph.

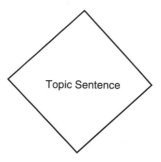

EXAMPLE

When Alice goes through the looking glass, she enters a garden where the flowers speak. In a dark forest, a fawn befriends her. <u>The dream world reverses the events of the real world.</u> The Lion and the Unicorn come off their shield and do battle. The Red Queen, originally a kitten of Alice's pet cat Dinah, gives Alice instructions in etiquette.

5.   The selection may contain *no expressed topic sentence* but consist of a series of sentences giving details and implying a central thought.

EXAMPLE

A deck of cards becomes a royal court. A kitten becomes a chess Queen. A scurrying wild creature becomes a sophisticated courtier, a White Rabbit in vest and pocket watch. A proper Victorian tea party becomes the setting for rude remarks and outrageous behavior.

Poetry

Poetry is a form of literature that is difficult to define. Dictionary definitions are very complicated. One states that a poem is a rhythmical composition, sometimes rhymed, expressing experiences, ideas, or emotions in a style more concentrated, imaginative, and powerful than that of ordinary speech or prose. Another dictionary defines poetry as writing that formulates a concentrated imaginative awareness in language chosen and arranged to create a specific emotional response through meaning, sound, and rhythm. A desk encyclopedia defines poetry as a meaningful arrangement of words into an imaginative emotional discourse, always with a strong rhythmic pattern.

All these definitions stress certain common elements.

1. The content is an experience of the poet, usually emotional, filtered through the poet's imagination.
2. The poet uses a special language that is concentrated, using words that suggest more than their exact meaning.
3. The poet creates rhythmic and sound patterns that contribute to the experience described. He or she frequently, but not necessarily, uses rhyme.

With these elements in mind, let us analyze the poem "Ozymandias" by Percy Bysshe Shelley.

WHAT REMAINS OF A ONCE POWERFUL KING

I met a traveler from an antique land
Who said: "Two vast and trunkless legs of stone
Stand in the desert... Near them, on the sand,
Half sunk, a shattered visage lies, whose frown
And wrinkled lip, and sneer of cold command,
Tell that its sculptor well those passions read
Which yet survive, stamped on these lifeless things,

The hand that mocked them, and the heart that fed;
And on the pedestal these words appear:
'My name is Ozymandias, king of kings:
Look on my works, ye Mighty, and despair!'
Nothing beside remains. Round the decay
Of that colossal wreck, boundless and bare
The lone and level sands stretch far away."

The poet meets someone who describes something seen in a desert. It is the colossal wreck of a statue of a powerful king that has decayed over time. The remains consist of several parts—two legs, a shattered face, and the pedestal on which the statue once stood. The poet wants to portray a scene of utter desolation. Only the shattered statue survives amidst the emptiness of the boundless, bare desert sands. The poem gains its power by means of irony—the opposite of what we expect for a powerful king, not a royal palace but a broken statue of a king, is described. The poet creates, in a few words, the character of the king—his frown, his wrinkled lip, his sneer of authority. All of these details lead to the lesson the poet wishes to teach the Mighty: life is brief; human desires are vain; power leads to despair. He does this in 14 lines and 111 words.

Technically the poem has faulty rhyme—stone and frown, appear and despair, and the word order in "Nothing beside remains" is unusual. Nevertheless, an emotional response from us results from the picture the poet creates and the message engraved on the pedestal: nothing lasts forever, not even the power of a mighty king.

DETERMINING TONE AND MOOD

Tone is the aspect of the author's style that reveals attitude toward the subject. *Mood* is the atmosphere, or emotional effect, created by the manner in which the author presents the material.

To determine the tone or mood of a passage, consider the feelings or attitudes that are expressed. Examine, for example, the following passages:

EXAMPLE

The room was dark—so dark that even after giving her eyes a while to accustom themselves to the blackness, she could still see nothing. Something soft—she hoped it was only a cobweb—brushed her lip.

And the throbbing sound, attuned to her own heavy heartbeat, became stronger and faster.

EXAMPLE

The room was dark—not dark as it is when your eyes are just not used to blackness, but really *dark* dark. Then some soft creepy thing brushed her lip, and she found herself hoping very hard that it was only a cobweb. And then there was that sound—baBoom, baBoom, baBoom—getting faster and louder all the time like her own heart going thump, thump, thump.

Consider the contrasting moods of the two passages above. The first passage presents a sustained mood of suspense and fear. The woman in the room can see nothing; something strange touches her; she hears a heavy and mysterious sound. We have the feeling that something is going to happen; the indication is that what will happen is dangerous, evil, or deadly.

The second paragraph relates essentially the same event. But we are distracted somewhat from what is happening by several devices. First, we are brought informally into the story—we know what a room is like when it's *really* dark. And the quality of darkness is also expressed informally—it is not pitch dark, or night dark, but "dark dark." "Then something creepy" is felt, and the sounds of the noise and the woman's heart are described—baBoom. The feeling conveyed by these devices is somehow made less frightening by the familiarity of the language, and the general impression is less one of total fear than of "scariness"—an easier emotion to deal with. Thus we have the impression from this second passage that whatever happens will probably not be all that bad or, if it is, it will somehow be easier to overcome,

INFERRING CHARACTER

Character is often implied by a person's words or actions, rather than by direct description. This has always been particularly true of drama, where the reader of a play is often called upon to interpret a character's personality without benefit of stage directions or other descriptive material. In the modern novel, too, the trend has been away from utilizing long descriptive passages and more toward allowing the characters' actions, speech, or thoughts (often called "inner dialogue") to reveal their personalities. The reader must rely, therefore, on the hints offered by the playwright or novelist to interpret character—and even then, a wide range of interpretation may be possible.

The following scene, from Oscar Wilde's comedy *The Importance of Being Earnest*, offers a good sketch of two minor characters. They are Miss Prism, a governess, and Canon (or Doctor) Chasuble, a clergyman.

EXAMPLE

MISS PRISM: You are too much alone, dear Dr. Chasuble. You should get married. A misanthrope, who hates everyone, I can understand—a womanthrope, never!

CANON CHASUBLE: Believe me, I do not deserve such a new-fangled phrase. The teaching as well as the practice of the early church was distinctly against marriage.

MISS PRISM: That is obviously the reason why the early church has not lasted up to the present day. And you do not seem to realize, dear Doctor, that by persistently remaining single, a man converts himself into a permanent public temptation. Men should be more careful; this very condition of remaining unmarried leads weaker persons astray.

CANON CHASUBLE: But is a man not equally attractive when married?

MISS PRISM: No married man is ever attractive except to his wife.

CANON CHASUBLE: And often, I've been told, not even to her.

MISS PR1SM: That depends on the intellectual sympathies of the woman. Maturity can always be depended on. Ripeness can be trusted. Young women are green. [Canon Chasuble shows surprise.] I spoke horticulturally. My metaphor was drawn from fruits.

What do we learn about Miss Prism? First, she is quick-witted. She quickly demolishes the Canon's argument about the teachings and practices of the Church. Then, we are given an example of her intellectual prowess. Her argument that bachelors become a permanent temptation to weaker women is a brilliant comment; also, when Chasuble questions it, she disposes of his observation that a married man may also be attractive. Finally, she marshals all the arguments on her own behalf since she is an intelligent and mature woman. She stresses "intellectual sympathies"; she mentions her doubts about the trustworthiness of young wives—only maturity and ripeness can really be trusted; young women do not make dependable wives. The conclusion: Miss Prism, who is no longer in the first flush of her youth, thinks she would make an ideal wife.

What has been revealed of Canon Chasuble? First, he is obviously something of a stuffed shirt; his first response to Miss Prism's unusual word—*womanthrope*—is to scold her for it. He then launches into a speech on the practices of the ancient Church regarding marriage of the clergy. Finally, Miss Prism manages to draw from him a more human response to the idea of marriage: the Canon sadly remarks that married men are not often attractive even to their wives. We can conclude from this remark that he is also somewhat shy, or frightened, by the idea of marriage, although not from personal experience; when a man like Dr. Chasuble says "I've been told," he means it. He is a man who speaks, and who must be spoken to, quite precisely; thus, when Miss Prism says "Young women are green," she feels obliged to explain that she is using the word *green* in a special sense.

Briefly, we may draw the following inferences from this passage: (1) the two characters are no longer youthful; (2) they have known each other for a long time; (3) Miss Prism is determined to marry Dr. Chasuble; (4) she understands his personality and has apparently made up her mind that she can adjust to it; and (5) the Canon is a stuffy, somewhat impractical man who is probably no match for a woman of Miss Prism's determination. If asked to draw any conclusions, we might well decide that Miss Prism will probably have her way, and that the two will probably make the necessary adjustments to a married life of limited happiness and total respectability.

Obviously, some ways of portraying character are easier to understand than others, and the personalities described may be more or less complex. The GED Examination questions, however, do not delve too deeply into the characters discussed; the answers can readily be found in the reading passages. You merely have to pick up the author's clues.

INFERRING SETTING

A number of factors are involved in the setting of a selection. These include not only *place* (physical location, type of locale—noisy, crowded, tranquil, etc.), but *time* (of day, of season, of historical period). See what clues to the setting you can find in the following passage.

EXAMPLE

He knew she would be late, but he could not keep himself from hurrying, pushing his way impatiently through the strolling, multilingual crowd. The Germans, their sunburned necks garlanded with camera straps, bargained gutturally with the indifferent women at their stalls, thinking to strike a sharp bargain on the price of a straw handbag or a painted box. The women let them struggle with the unfamiliar numbers, knowing exactly how much they would ultimately settle for. Three American girls, distinguishable by their short hair and madras skirts above sandalled feet and bare legs, dawdled along, giggling at the pleadings of two persistent *pappagalli* who seemed determined to improve international relations at all costs.

The sidestreet leading to the Signoria was hardly less busy, and he found it easier to dodge the small motorbikes bouncing noisily along the cobbled roadway than to struggle against the crowds pouring out of the great museum and onto the narrow sidewalks. He hated these annual floods of holiday-makers and culture-seekers who jammed the streets, the hotels, and the small restaurants so that the year-round residents found it necessary to retreat more than ever to the interiors of their cool, stone houses and their small, closed social circles. The more fortunate natives, of course, headed for Viareggio or the beaches of the South or the Riviera.

He finally found a table at the back of the cafe—a little too close to the bar but partially screened by a box hedge—and ordered a drink. The ancient *piazza* was mostly in shade now, except for the very tops of the towers which had been turned by the sun from the faded buff of the old stone to a rich gold against the blue sky.

What can we tell of the setting described?

Place: We can immediately pick up a number of clues. Obviously the setting is a city (crowds, sidewalks, a market, a museum). It is also not in the United States, since American girls are particularly distinguishable. By the mention of the Riviera as a nearby vacation spot, we know that we are somewhere in western Europe—but not Germany (the Germans are not familiar with the language). We can narrow the location down even further (although you are not expected to have all this extra information): two foreign words, *pappagalli* and *piazza*, might lead to the educated guess that the country is Italy.

Time: (1) Period—although the city itself is old (cobbled streets, narrow sidewalks, towers in an ancient piazza), the period is more recent. Motorbikes, barelegged girls, camera-carrying tourists all indicate the modern era. (2) Season—we can assume by the dress of the tourists, and by the fact that the natives usually head for the beach during this season, that it is summer. (3) Time of day—The piazza is in shade, except for the tops of the towers. It is unlikely, therefore, to be midday. Since the main character orders a drink in a cafe-bar, and since we have nowhere been given to understand that he has a drinking problem, we can assume it is late afternoon (cocktail time) and he has an appointment with someone for a predinner drink.

You should be made aware that the above passage was prepared solely to give you practice in inferring setting, and that you are not likely to find too many passages on the actual examination that concentrate on such description. However, you should learn to pick up small clues here and there that will give you an idea of the setting in a descriptive passage. Remember that, more often than not, the locale will be inferred rather than actually stated.

PRACTICE IN READING POPULAR AND CLASSICAL PROSE

WHAT IS ABOUT TO HAPPEN TO BORIS?

The light carriage swished through the layers of fallen leaves upon the terrace. In places, they lay so thick that they half covered the stone balusters and reached the knees of Diana's stag. But the trees were bare; only here and there a single golden leaf trembled high upon the black twigs. Following the curve of the road, Boris's carriage came straight upon the main terrace and the house, majestic as the Sphinx herself in the sunset. The light of the setting sun seemed to have soaked into the dull masses of stone. They reddened and glowed with it until the whole place became a mysterious, a glorified abode, in which the tall windows shone like a row of evening stars.

Boris got out of the britska in front of the mighty stone stairs and walked toward them, feeling for his letter. Nothing stirred in the house. It was like walking into a cathedral. "And," he thought, "by the time that I get into that carriage once more, what will everything be like to me?"

1. The title that expresses the main idea of this passage is
   (1) "The Lure of Autumn"
   (2) "Sphinx in the Sunset"
   (3) "A Mysterious Cathedral"
   (4) "A Terrifying Surprise"
   (5) "An Important Visit"

2. From the description of the house, we may most safely conclude that the house
   (1) is sometimes used as a place of worship
   (2) is owned by a wealthy family
   (3) was designed by Egyptian architects
   (4) is constructed of modern brick
   (5) is a dark, cold-looking structure

3. This story probably takes place in
   (1) the British Isles
   (2) the Far East
   (3) eastern Europe
   (4) southern United States
   (5) the Mediterranean

4. We may most safely conclude that Boris has come to the house in order to
   (1) secure a job
   (2) find out about his future
   (3) join his friends for the holidays
   (4) attend a hunting party
   (5) visit his old family home

5. In this passage, which atmosphere does the author attempt to create?
   (1) pleasant anticipation
   (2) quiet peace
   (3) carefree gaiety
   (4) unrelieved despair
   (5) vague uncertainty

6. From this passage, which inference can most safely be drawn?
   (1) The house was topped by a lofty tower.
   (2) Boris is tired from his journey.

(3) There is only one terrace before the house is reached.

(4) The most imposing feature of the house is the door.

(5) Boris intends to stay at the house for only a short time.

Answer Key

1. **5**   2. **2**   3. **3**   4. **2**   5. **5**   6. **5**

Summary of Prose Interpretation

You should·

1. *Read the selection carefully.*

2. *In **selecting a title** that expresses the main idea, go back to the selection constantly. Arrive at the correct answer by a process of elimination.* Eliminate the one or more possibilities that are clearly incorrect. Eliminate the possibilities that are based on minor details; there will be one or two of these. From the remaining choices, you must select the one that expresses the main rather than the subordinate idea.

3. *In **drawing inferences**, find the clues in the passage from which you can draw the proper conclusion.* The clue may be a name, a place, an adjective, an object, an unusual word. You may have to reread the selection a few times before you locate the clue or the two details that can be linked to make a clue.

4. *In **determining purpose**, ask yourself why the author wrote the passage; what he or she wanted you, the reader, to understand or feel.* After you have read the passage several times, try to define the *total impression* you get from your reading. The purposes of authors at various times may be to inform, to arouse anger, to poke fun at, to evoke pity, to amuse, and to urge to action, among others. Which of these predominates?

5. *In **determining mood**, try to find words that either create an atmosphere or evoke an emotion.* This is related to the author's purpose but may not necessarily be his or her main purpose. There are two main guides to determining atmosphere: selection of details and use of adjectives and adverbs.

Reading Poetry

Reading poetry requires a special set of skills because the poet uses both a special language and special writing techniques.

In poetry, words are not used in their normal, literal senses. Rather, they are used in such a way that you, the reader, must call on your imagination to fully understand them. Let's consider an example.

"I almost blew my top."

Here the words *blew* and *top* do not have their regular meanings, but are used figuratively to express the idea "I almost went crazy."

> *Skill One*. In poetry, words are often used in a figurative sense. Do not take these words literally. Use your imagination in order to understand them as the poet uses them.

In poetry, meaning is frequently compressed into a few words by the use of figures of speech such as metaphors.

"The road was a ribbon of moonlight."

In seven words, the poet Walter de la Mare tells us that the time is night, the moon was shining, and the road is a lighted area surrounded by darker ones.

"The moon was a ghostly galleon."

In six words, the poet tells us that the moon is like a ship, the sky is like an ocean, and the moon creates an eerie, supernatural feeling as it moves across the sky.

> *Skill Two*. In poetry, words often compress or condense extended meanings and pictures into a few words, usually by the use of figures of speech such as metaphors. Add to the words you read the implied meanings and pictures they create.

In poetry, meaning is closely related to rhythm. For this reason it helps to read poetry aloud.

> *Skill Three*. Read the poem aloud paying attention to the rhythm, because the rhythm of the poem will help you understand its meaning.

In poetry, in addition to rhythm, which is always present, you will frequently encounter rhyme. Rhyme, too, often helps to convey meaning. In Edgar Allan Poe's poem "The Raven," the rhyme is repeated in *door, more, Lenore, forevermore,* and *nevermore.*

"'Tis some visitor,' I muttered, 'tapping at my chamber door: Only this and nothing more.'"

The sound itself adds to the atmosphere of mystery.

> *Skill Four.* As you read the poem aloud, note the rhyme as well as the rhythm, since both add to the meaning and feelings expressed.

In poetry, the poet uses sounds in addition to rhyme to help convey meaning. The poet John Masefield describes the effect of the wind with a series of "w" and "wh" sounds. He wants to return

"To the gull's *w*ay and the *wh*ales's *w*ay *wh*ere the *w*ind's like a *wh*etted knife."

Another technique is the use of words whose sounds correspond to their meaning. Here is the way one poet describes the movement of the waters of a river:

"And rushing and flushing and brushing and gushing,
And flapping and rapping and clapping and slapping..."

> *Skill Five.* As you read the poem aloud, note the sounds of the words as well as their rhyme and their rhythm, since each adds to the meaning and feelings expressed by the poet.

In poetry, the poem itself has a certain shape or form. The poem can be in a very definite form, such as the sonnet, or in a very loose form. "The New Colossus," by Emma Lazarus, which follows below, is a sonnet with a definite rhythm and a definite rhyme scheme. The form of "The New Colossus" is appropriate because it lends itself to the main ideas expressed in each of the two stanzas of the poem.

Skill Six. As you read the poem, study its form and structure. If it is divided into stanzas or paragraph units, try to determine what each stanza adds to the meaning of the poem. The poem's form is another aid to your understanding its meaning.

Read the following poem carefully and answer the questions based on it. Compare your answers with the answer key: then study the analysis of the answers, particularly for questions that you have answered incorrectly.

Practice in Reading Poetry

WHAT DOES THE NEW STATUE REPRESENT?

The New Colossus

Not like the brazen giant of Greek fame,
With conquering limbs astride from land to land;
Here at our sea-washed, sunset gates shall stand
A mighty woman with a torch, whose flame
Is the imprisoned lightning, and her name
Mother of Exiles. From her beacon-hand
Glows world-wide welcome; her mild eyes command
The air-bridged harbor that twin cities frame.
"Keep, ancient lands, your storied pomp!" cries she
with silent lips. "Give me your tired, your poor,
Your huddled masses yearning to breathe free,
The wretched refuse of your teeming shore.
Send these, the homeless, tempest-tost, to me.
I lift my lamp beside the golden door!"

—Emma Lazarus

1. The main idea of the poem is that
    (1) the ancient lands of Europe should serve as a beacon to America
    (2) the Greek statue serves as a model for the American statue
    (3) the mighty are asked to come to these shores
    (4) America welcomes all persecuted freedom-lovers
    (5) the lamp guides those who come to the golden door

2. In the choices below, the incorrectly paired words are
   (1) brazen—of brass
   (2) sunset—east
   (3) beacon—guiding light
   (4) refuse—trash
   (5) pomp—splendor

3. The "mighty woman" and "Mother of Exiles" is the
   (1) United States of America
   (2) city of New York
   (3) Statue of Liberty
   (4) Plymouth Rock
   (5) Golden Gate

4. The title of this poem, "The New Colossus," implies
   (1) similarity to the old
   (2) replacement of the old
   (3) difference from the old
   (4) inferiority to the old
   (5) acceptance of the old

5. The *incorrectly* matched phrase from the poem with the figure of speech or poetic device it demonstrates is
   (1) "Her mild eyes"—epithet
   (2) "Keep, ancient lands, your storied pomp!" cries she—personification
   (3) "shall stand a mighty woman"—inversion
   (4) "world-wide welcome"—alliteration
   (5) "flame is the imprisoned lightning"—simile

6. The form of the poem is that of
   (1) a ballad
   (2) an octet
   (3) an ode
   (4) a sestet
   (5) a sonnet

Answer Key

1. **4**   2. **2**   3. **3**   4. **3**   5. **5**   6. **5**

Summary of Interpretation of Poetry

The skills needed in reading and interpreting poetry call for you to:

1. Try to get the extended meaning of words used figuratively by using your imagination to add to the usual meanings of the words.
2. Since poetry compresses meaning and description into a few words, fill in the suggested meanings and pictures they create by studying the figures of speech used, such as similes and metaphors.
3. Read the poem aloud, since the rhythm will help you determine its meaning.
4. Note the rhymes used, since they will also help you get meaning and feeling from the poem.
5. Note the sounds of the words, since they reinforce meaning.
6. Study the form of the poem, since its subdivisions (stanzas) can help you understand it better.

Note: First, read the poem through quickly to get an overall idea of its meaning and feeling. Then read it more slowly and carefully after you have read the questions based on it.

Reading Drama

Earlier, we indicated how character can be inferred from words or actions, since in drama, direct description, as in prose, is not possible. It is true that, of all the forms of literature, plays are among the most difficult to read. The playwright does not speak directly to the reader in modern drama, as do the novelist and short story writer. Sometimes the playwright sets the scene for those who produce or read the play, and sometimes he or she includes instructions to the actors about mood or action. For the most part, however, the playwright leaves it to the actor and the reader to figure out appearance, character, actions, and feelings. The only real help the playwright should and must give is through the dialogue, the conversation between the characters. From this dialogue alone, you must *imagine the setting, visualize the action,* including "hearing" the speech of the actors, and *draw conclusions about their character and motives.* In addition, you must understand the nature of the essence of drama, which is conflict between ideas or characters. This is made clear only through the dialogue. A final point: you may also be asked to predict what is likely to happen on the basis of what you have read.

Practice in Reading Drama

HOW ARE OLSON'S DREAMS DESTROYED?

OLSON: [*After a pause—worriedly*] I tank I should go after dem. Cocky iss very drunk, too, and Drisc—

FREDA: Aar! The big Irish is all right. Don't yer 'ear 'im say as 'ow they'd surely come back 'ere, an' fur you to wait fur 'em?

OLSON: Yes; but if dey don't come soon I tank I go see if dey are in boarding house all right.

FREDA: Where is the boardin' 'ouse?

OLSON: Yust little way back from street here.

FREDA: You stayin' there, too?

OLSON: Yes—until steamer sail for Stockholm—in two day.

FREDA: [*She is alternatingly looking at* JOE *and feverishly trying to keep* OLSON *talking so he will forget about going away after the others.*] Yer mother won't be 'arf glad to see yor agen, will she? [OLSON *smiles.*] Does she know yer comin'?

OLSON: No. I tought I would yust give her surprise. I write to her from Bonos Eres but I don't tell her I come home.

FREDA: Must be old, ain't she, yer ole lady?

OLSON: She iss eighty-two. [*He smiles reminiscently.*] You know, Miss Freda, I don't see my mother or my brother in—let me tank—[*He counts laboriously on his fingers.*] must be more than ten year. I write once in while and she write many time; and my brother he write me, too. My mother say in all letter I should come home right away. My brother he write same ting, too. He want me to help him on farm. I write back always I come soon; and I mean all time to go back home at end of voyage. But I come ashore, I take one drink, I take many drinks, I get drunk, I spend all money, I have to ship away for other voyage. So dis time I say to myself; Don't drink one drink, Ollie, or, sure, you don't get home. And I want go home dis time. I feel homesick for farm and to see my people again. [*He smiles.*] Yust like little boy, I feel homesick. Dat's why I don't drink noting tonight but dis— bellywash! [*He roars with childish laughter, then suddenly be-*

comes serious.] You know, Miss Freda, my mother get very old, and I want see her. She might die and I would never—

FREDA: [*Moved a lot in spite of herself*] Ow, don't talk like that! I jest 'ates to 'ear any one speakin' abaht dyin'. [*The door to the street is opened and* NICK *enters, followed by two rough-looking, shabbily dressed men, wearing mufflers, with caps pulled down over their eyes. They sit at the table nearest to the door.* JOE *brings them three beers, and there is a whispered consultation, with many glances in the direction of* OLSON.]

OLSON: [*Starting to get up—worriedly*] I tank I go around to boarding house. I tank something go wrong with Drisc and Cocky.

FREDA: Ow, down't go. They kin take care of theyselves. They ain't babies. Wait 'arf a mo'. You ain't 'ad yer drink yet.

JOE: [*Coming hastily over to the table, indicates the men in the rear with a jerk of his thumb*] One of them blokes wants yer to 'ave a wet wiv 'im.

FREDA: Righto! [*To* OLSON] Let's drink this. [*She raises her glass. He does the same.*] 'Ere's a toast fur yer: Success to yer bloomin' farm an' may yer live long an' 'appy on it. Skoal! [*She tosses down her brandy. He swallows half his glass of ginger beer and makes a wry face.*]

OLSON: Skoal! [*He puts down his glass.*]

FREDA: [*With feigned indignation*] Down't yer like my toast?

OLSON: [*Grinning*] Yes. It iss very kind, Miss Freda.

FREDA: Then drink it all like I done.

OLSON: Well—[*He gulps down the rest.*] Dere! [*He laughs.*]

FREDA: Done like a sport!

ONE OF THE ROUGHS: [*With a laugh*] Amindra, ahoy!

NICK: [*Warningly*] Sssshh!

OLSON: [*Turns around in his chair*] Amindra? Iss she in port? I sail on her once long time ago—three mast, full rig, skys'l yarder? Iss dat ship you mean?

THE ROUGH: [*Grinning*] Yus; right you are.

OLSON: [*Angrily*] I know dat damn ship—worst ship dat sail to sea. Rotten grub and dey make you work all time—and the Captain and Mate wus Bluenose devils. No sailor who know anything ever ship on her. Where iss she bound from here?

THE ROUGH: Round Cape 'Orn—sails at daybreak.

OLSON: Py yingo, I pity poor fallers make dat trip round Cape Stiff dis time year. I bet you some of dem never see port once again. [*He passes his hand over his eyes in a dazed way. His voice grows weaker.*] Py golly, I feel dizzy. All the room go round and round like I was drunk. [*He gets weakly to his feet.*] Good night, Miss Freda. I bane feeling sick. Tell Drisc—I go home. [*He takes a step forward and suddenly collapses over a chair, rolls to the floor, and lies there unconscious.*]

JOE: [*From behind the bar*] Quick, nawh! [NICK *darts forward with* JOE *following.* FREDA *is already beside the unconscious man and has taken the roll of money from his inside pocket. She strips off a note furtively and shoves it into her bosom, trying to conceal her action, but* JOE *sees her. She hands the roll to* JOE, *who pockets it.* NICK *goes through all the other pockets and lays a handful of change on the table.*]

JOE: [*Impatiently*] 'Urry, 'urry, can't yer? The other blokes'll be 'ere in 'arf a mo'. [*The two roughs come forward.*] 'Ere, you two, tike 'im in undor tho arms like 'e was drunk. [*They do so.*] Tike 'im to the Amindra—yer knows that, don't yer?—two docks above. Nick'll show yer. An' you, Nick, down't yer leave the bleedin' ship till the capt'n guvs yer this bloke's advance—full month's pay—five quid, d'yer 'ear?

NICK: I knows me bizness, ole bird. [*They support* OLSON *to the door.*]

THE ROUGH: [*As they are going out*] This silly bloke'll 'ave the s'prise of 'is life when 'e wakes up on board of 'er. [*They laugh. The door closes behind them.*]

—Eugene O'Neill

1. The playwright creates mood by his effective use of all of the following EXCEPT
    (1) stage directions
    (2) names of characters
    (3) dialogue
    (4) dialect
    (5) humor

2. The main purpose of the playwright is to describe
   (1) a sailor's life in port
   (2) the frustrated longings of a sailor
   (3) the weakness of character of a sailor
   (4) how a sailor is exploited
   (5) his admiration for sailors

3. Olson's mood is best described as one of
   (1) bitterness
   (2) nostalgia
   (3) happiness
   (4) resignation
   (5) despair

4. Sympathy for Olson is created by the playwright by all of the following EXCEPT his
   (1) devotion to his family
   (2) abandonment by his shipmates
   (3) resolution to stay sober
   (4) courtesy to Freda
   (5) description of the *Amindra*

5. The reader can correctly infer from the incident all of the following EXCEPT
   (1) Joe, Nick, Freda, and the two roughs plotted against Olson
   (2) Olson may never get to see his mother
   (3) Olson's life on board the *Amindra* will be difficult
   (4) Olson's drink was spiked
   (5) Freda regretted her role in the incident

6. Suspense is created by all the following EXCEPT
   (1) Drisc and Cocky's departure
   (2) Freda's encouraging Olson to stay
   (3) the entry of Nick and the roughs
   (4) Olson's reluctance to take a drink
   (5) Olson's talk about the *Amindra*

7. The playwright
   (1) feels sorry for Olson
   (2) criticizes the habitual drinking of the sailors

(3) despises Joe, Nick, Freda, and the roughs
(4) describes the action with no comment
(5) feels life is unfair

Answer Key

1. **5**   2. **2**   3. **2**   4. **2**   5. **5**   6. **1**   7. **4**

Summary of Interpretation of Drama Reading

The skills needed in reading and interpreting drama call for you to:

1. Try to imagine the setting. If no stage directions are given, deduce from the speech and dialogue of the characters where the action is taking place.
2. Visualize the action. As the characters speak, figure out *what they are doing* while they are speaking.
3. Determine their motives. Why are the characters speaking as they do? *Why are they doing what they do?*
4. Determine their character and personality. What sort of person talks and acts the way he does? Why?
5. Determine the conflict that is taking place. Since the essence of drama is conflict, who or what is in conflict with whom or what? Is the conflict physical? Is it emotional? Is it a conflict of ideas?
6. Try to predict on the basis of all of the above what is most likely to happen next.
7. Read the scene aloud, trying to project yourself into the character of each of the roles.

READING COMMENTARY ON THE ARTS

Selections that fall under the term commentary are limited to the aspects of contemporary writing that deal with the arts—music, art, theater, movies, television, literature, and dance. They are further limited to selections in which the author comments critically on the arts, discussing the value of the content and the style of these means of expression.

In reading commentaries, try to determine the point of view of the writer and whether his or her evaluation of the artist, the musician, the author, the playwright, the film, the television program, or the dancer is favorable or unfavorable. Also look for the insights of the critic into the meaning and emotion conveyed by the artist or the medium.

The writing style will be that of the author of a piece of popular literature, so sentence structure and vocabulary will be relatively simple. *Here is a helpful hint.* Since critics who comment on the arts are describing their reactions, they resort to many adjectives that express their judgment. Here are a couple of dozen of such adjectives: *adept, authentic, candid, credible, dynamic, eloquent, exquisite, graphic, inane, inept, laudable, lucid, naive, poignant, prosaic, spontaneous, superb, superlative, tedious, timeless, tiresome, trite, vivacious, witty.*

PRACTICE IN READING COMMENTARY ON THE ARTS

WHAT DID THE CREATOR OF THE MUPPETS CONTRIBUTE TO CHILDREN'S TELEVISION?

He built an empire on a discarded green coat and a Ping-Pong ball. Jim Henson, creator of Kermit the Frog and a menagerie of other furry creatures known as the Muppets, revolutionized puppetry and reinvented children's television.

The Muppets charmed audiences of all ages on *Sesame Street*, possibly the most influential children's show ever, and later on *The Muppet Show*, which became the mostly widely watched TV program in the world, attracting 135 million viewers in 100 countries.

Henson succeeded with craftsmanship and showmanship and salesmanship. But above all, he constantly challenged the status quo. Henson was one of the first producers to use television not merely as a medium but as a tool to enhance his performances.

While earlier puppet programs, such as *Kukla, Fran, and Ollie*, simply plluncked a camera in front of a traditional stage, Henson used a variety of camera lenses to create illusions which made his Muppets more agile and antic.

He also taught his puppeteers to work while using a TV monitor. For the first time, they could see not only their performances as they were unfolding, but also what the viewers could see.

That insight led Henson to create a new, softer-looking style of puppet that was extremely expressive in TV closeups.

Henson's unconventional approach to life came through in his

Muppets—a word he coined for the crossbreed of marionettes and puppets he developed in the mid-50s.

While companies like Disney were creating model characters that lived up to the era's model of perfection, such as Bambi, Henson's creatures, such as the proud Miss Piggy, the grumpy Oscar the Grouch, and the uncontrollable Animal, were wildly irreverent.

Henson also applied this irreverent approach to his work. He promoted productivity, not by demanding results, but by encouraging his associates to have fun. He promoted silliness, even chaos, on the set. In fact, he was most satisfied with a scene when it had grown so funny that no one could perform it without busting up, former associates say.

Despite his childlike enthusiasm, Henson was also a pragmatist who tackled situations by approaching them from new angles. He was a problem solver and had a knack for sidestepping complexity and finding a simpler, purer way of doing things.

1. The contributions of Jim Henson, according to the article,
    (1) retained earlier approaches
    (2) added little to current programming
    (3) climbed on the bandwagon of children's television
    (4) imitated Kukla, Fran, and Olllie
    (5) broke new ground in puppetry

2. The reinventing of children's TV was exemplified by the worldwide success of
    (1) *Sesame Street*
    (2) *The Muppet Show*
    (3) *Kukla, Fran, and Ollie*
    (4) Kermit the Frog
    (5) the status quo

3. The most important reason for the success of Jim Henson was
    (1) his craftsmanship
    (2) his showmanship
    (3) his salesmanship
    (4) his unconventional approach
    (5) his charm

4. Henson pioneered in using television
   (1) as a medium
   (2) to improve performance
   (3) as a traditional stage
   (4) to teach tried-and-true methods
   (5) to preserve the familiar puppets

5. Henson's Muppets
   (1) sought perfection
   (2) imitated Disney's creations
   (3) were disrespectful
   (4) were ideal role models
   (5) were static and serious

6. Jim Henson was all of the following EXCEPT
   (1) a man of childlike enthusiasm
   (2) a searcher for simple solutions
   (3) a pragmatist
   (4) an irreverent innovator
   (5) a conformist

Answer Key

1. **5**   2. **2**   3. **4**   4. **2**   5. **3**   6. **5**

7

MATHEMATICS

AN OVERVIEW

This chapter is designed to prepare you for the Mathematics Test of the High School Equivalency Exam. This 56-question test covers *arithmetic* and some of the main concepts and skills of *algebra* and *geometry*. About 50% of the questions in this 90-minute test will be in arithmetic, 20% in geometry, and 30% in algebra.

HOW TO READ AND SOLVE WORD PROBLEMS

It is helpful to use a systematic method for solving word problems. The following steps are suggested.

Plan for Solving Word Problems
1. Read the problem carefully.
2. Collect the information that is given in the problem.
3. Decide what must be found.
4. Develop a plan to solve the problem.
5. Use your plan as a guide to complete the solution of the problem.

The following example shows how this systematic method is used.

Algebra Problem

1. **Read the problem carefully.**
   A father is 15 years more than twice the age of his daughter. If the sum of the ages of the father and daughter is 48 years, what is the age of the daughter?
2. **Collect the information that is given in the problem.**
   Age of father = twice age of daughter + 15
   Age of father + age of daughter = 48

3. **Decide what must be found.**
   Find the age of the daughter.
4. **Develop a plan to solve the problem.**
   Set up an equation using the given facts. Then solve the equation.
5. **Use your plan as a guide to complete the solution of the problem.**
   Let n = age of daughter, and $2n + 15$ = age of father
   Age of daughter + age of father = 48

$$n \quad\quad + (2n + 15) = 48$$
$$3n + 15 = 48$$
$$3n = 33$$
$$n = \frac{33}{3}$$
$$= 11$$

The daughter's age is 11 years.

I. ARITHMETIC

I. A. BASIC OPERATIONS

On the GED Examination the word *number* always means *real number*, a number that can be represented by a point on the number line.

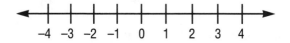

On the line above, we have indicated only the *integers* (positive, negative, and 0), but every number corresponds to a point on the line.

For example, $\frac{1}{2}$ is exactly midway between

0 and 1, and 2.01 is slightly to the right of 2. For now we will concern ourselves only with 0 and positive numbers.

In arithmetic we are basically concerned with the addition, subtraction, multiplication, and division of numbers. The correct terms for the results of these operations follow.

Operation	Symbol	Result
addition	**+**	*sum*

16 is the sum of 12 and 4.

16 = 12 + 4

subtraction	**–**	*difference*

8 is the difference of 12 and 4.

8 = 12 – 4

multiplication*	**×**	*product*

48 is the product of 12 and 4.

48 = 12 × 4

division	**÷**	*quotient*

3 is the quotient of 12 and 4.

3 = 12 ÷ 4

***Note:** Multiplication, especially in algebra, can also be indicated by a dot, parentheses, or the juxtaposition of symbols without any sign: $2^2 \cdot 2^4$, $3(4)$, $3(x + 2)$, $3a$, $4abc$.

EXAMPLE

What is the sum of the product and quotient of 10 and 5?

Product: $10 \times 5 = 50$ Quotient: $10 \div 5 = 2$ Sum: $50 + 2 = 52$

The sum, difference, and product of two integers is *always* an integer; the quotient of two integers may be, but is not necessarily, an integer. When 23 is divided by 10, the quotient

can be expressed as $\frac{23}{10}$ or $2\frac{3}{10}$ or 2.3.

If the quotient is to be an integer, we can also say that the quotient is 2 and there is a *remainder* of 3. It depends upon the items with which we are dealing. For example, if 23 dollars is to be divided among 10 people, each one will get $2.30 (2.3 dollars); but if 23 books are to be divided among 10 people, each one will get 2 books and 3 (the remainder) will be left over.

I. B. DIVISORS AND PRIME NUMBERS

Every whole number greater than 1 has at least two positive divisors, 1 and itself—and possibly many more. For example, 6 is divisible by 1 and 6, as well as by 2 and 3; whereas 7 is divisible only by 1 and 7. Whole numbers, such as 7, that have exactly two positive divisors are called *prime numbers* or *primes*.

Here are the first few primes:

    2, 3, 5, 7, 11, 13, 17, 19, 23

Memorize this list—it will come in handy. Note that 1 is *not* a prime.

The *even numbers* are all the multiples of 2:

    {..., –4, –2, 0, 2, 4, 6, ...}

The *odd numbers* are the integers that are not divisible by 2:

    {..., –5, –3, –1, 1, 3, 5, ...}

I. C. FRACTIONS

Working with Fractions

When a whole is *divided* into n equal parts, each part is called *one nth* of the whole, written as $\dfrac{1}{n}$. For example:

- If a pizza is cut (*divided*) into 8 equal slices, each slice is one eighth $\left(\dfrac{1}{8}\right)$ of the pizza.

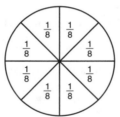

- A week is *divided* into 7 days, so a day is one seventh $\left(\dfrac{1}{7}\right)$ of a week.

$\frac{1}{7}$	$\frac{1}{7}$	$\frac{1}{7}$	$\frac{1}{7}$	$\frac{1}{7}$	$\frac{1}{7}$	$\frac{1}{7}$
Sun.	Mon.	Tues.	Wed.	Thurs.	Fri.	Sat.

- If Sam went to Paris for 5 days, he was there for five sevenths $\left(\dfrac{5}{7}\right)$ of a week.

$\frac{1}{7}$	$\frac{1}{7}$	$\frac{1}{7}$	$\frac{1}{7}$	$\frac{1}{7}$	$\frac{1}{7}$	$\frac{1}{7}$
Sun.	Mon.	Tues.	Wed.	Thurs.	Fri.	Sat.

$\dfrac{5}{7}$

- If Tom bought 10 slices of pizza, he bought ten eighths $\left(\dfrac{10}{8}\right)$ of a pie.

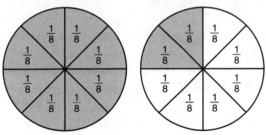

Numbers such as $\dfrac{5}{7}$ and $\dfrac{10}{8}$, in which

one integer is written over a second integer, are called *fractions*. The center line is called the *fraction bar*. The number above the bar is called the *numerator*, and the number below the bar is the *denominator*.

CAUTION: The denominator of a fraction can *never* be 0.

EXAMPLE

A baseball team won 37 games and lost 15 games. What fraction of the games played did the team win?

The required fraction is

$$\frac{\text{number of games won}}{\text{total number of games played}}$$

$$= \frac{37}{37+15} + \frac{37}{52}$$

Improper Fractions and Mixed Numbers

A fraction, such as $\dfrac{5}{24}$, whose numerator is less than its denominator, is called a *proper fraction*. Its value is less than 1.

A fraction, such as $\dfrac{30}{12}$, whose numerator is greater than its denominator, is called an *improper fraction*. Its value is greater than 1.

A fraction, such as $\frac{8}{8}$, whose numerator and denominator are the same, is also an *improper* fraction. Its value is 1.

A *mixed number* is a number, such as $5\frac{1}{2}$, that consists of a whole number followed by a fraction. It is an abbreviation for the *sum* of the integer and the fraction; thus, $5\frac{1}{2}$ is an abbreviation for $5 + \frac{1}{2}$.

Changing an Improper Fraction to a Mixed Number

To change an improper fraction to a mixed number, divide the numerator by the denominator; the quotient is the whole number and the remainder is placed over the denominator to form the fractional part.

EXAMPLE

Change $\frac{17}{5}$ to a mixed number. When 17

is divided by 5, the quotient is 3 and the remainder is 2, so

$$\frac{17}{5} = 3 + \frac{2}{5} = 3\frac{2}{5}$$

Changing a Mixed Number to an Improper Fraction

To change a mixed number to an improper fraction, multiply the whole number by the denominator and add the numerator; then write that sum over the denominator.

EXAMPLE

Change $2\frac{3}{7}$ to an improper fraction.

$2 \times 7 = 14$ and $14 + 3 = 17$, so

$$2\frac{3}{7} = \frac{17}{7}$$

Equivalent Fractions

If Bob and Joe shared a pizza, and Bob ate $\frac{1}{2}$ of the pizza and Joe ate $\frac{4}{8}$, they had exactly the same amount. We express this idea by saying that $\frac{1}{2}$ and $\frac{4}{8}$ are *equivalent fractions*; that is, they have the exact same value.

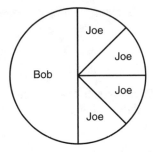

Two fractions are equivalent if multiplying or dividing both the numerator and the denominator of the first fraction *by the same number* gives the second fraction.

EXAMPLE

Are $\dfrac{3}{8}$ and $\dfrac{45}{120}$ equivalent?

Since $3 \times 15 = 45$ and $8 \times 15 = 120$, the fractions are equivalent.

Reducing a Fraction to Lowest Terms

A fraction is in *lowest terms* if no positive integer greater than 1 divides evenly into both the numerator and denominator.

For example, $\dfrac{9}{20}$ is in lowest terms, since no integer greater than 1 is a divisor of both 9 and 20; but $\dfrac{9}{24}$ is not in lowest terms, since 3 is a divisor of both 9 and 24.

EXAMPLE

Reduce $\dfrac{21}{28}$ to lowest terms.

The largest integer that is a divisor of both 21 and 28 is 7: $21 \div 7 = 3$ and $28 \div 7 = 4$.

Thus $\dfrac{21}{28} = \dfrac{3}{4}$, which is in lowest terms.

Multiplying Fractions

To multiply two or more fractions, multiply the numerators to obtain the numerator of the product. Then, multiply the denominators to obtain the denominator of the product.

EXAMPLE

Multiply $\frac{4}{7}$ by $\frac{3}{5}$.

$$\frac{4}{7} \times \frac{3}{5} = 4 \times \frac{3}{7} \times 5 = \frac{12}{35}$$

The process of multiplying fractions can be simplified by reducing each fraction to lowest terms before performing the multiplication.

EXAMPLE

Multiply $\frac{8}{15}$ by $\frac{5}{12}$.

$$\frac{8}{15} \times \frac{5}{12}$$

Since 8 and 12 are both divisible by 4, and 5 and 15 are both divisible by 5,

$$\frac{\overset{2}{\cancel{8}}}{\underset{3}{\cancel{15}}} \times \frac{\overset{1}{\cancel{5}}}{\underset{3}{\cancel{12}}} = 2 \times \frac{1}{3} \times 3 = \frac{2}{9}$$

If you are required to multiply a whole number by a fraction, write the whole number in fractional form, with 1 as the denominator, and proceed as before.

EXAMPLE

Multiply 12 by $\frac{5}{9}$.

$$12 \times \frac{5}{9} = \frac{12}{1} \times \frac{5}{9} = \frac{\overset{4}{\cancel{12}}}{1} \times \frac{5}{\underset{3}{\cancel{9}}} = \frac{4 \times 5}{1 \times 3} = \frac{20}{3}$$

If you are required to multiply two mixed numbers, convert them to improper fractions, and proceed as before. The product will be an improper fraction, which can be changed to a mixed number.

EXAMPLE

Multiply $3\frac{2}{3}$ by $1\frac{1}{5}$.

$$3\frac{2}{3} = 1\frac{1}{3} \text{ and } 1\frac{1}{5} = \frac{6}{5}$$

$$1\frac{1}{3} \times \frac{6}{5} = \frac{11}{\underset{1}{\cancel{3}}} \times \frac{\overset{2}{\cancel{6}}}{5} = \frac{11 \times 2}{1 \times 5} = \frac{22}{5} = 4\frac{2}{5}$$

Dividing Fractions

To divide one fraction by another fraction, invert the divisor and multiply the resulting fractions.

EXAMPLES

Divide $\frac{2}{3}$ by $\frac{5}{6}$.

$$\frac{2}{3} \div \frac{5}{6} = \frac{2}{3} \times \frac{6}{5} = \frac{2}{\cancel{3}_1} \times \frac{\cancel{6}^2}{5} = \frac{4}{5}$$

Divide 8 by $\frac{6}{7}$.

Write 8 in fractional form, as $\frac{8}{1}$, and proceed as before:

$$8 \div \frac{6}{7} = \frac{8}{1} \times \frac{7}{6} = \frac{\cancel{8}^4}{1} \times \frac{7}{\cancel{6}_3} = \frac{28}{3} = 9\frac{1}{3}$$

Divide $3\frac{3}{5}$ by $2\frac{1}{10}$.

$$3\frac{3}{5} = \frac{18}{5} \text{ and } 2\frac{1}{10} = \frac{21}{10}$$

$$\frac{18}{5} \div \frac{21}{10} = \frac{18}{5} \times \frac{10}{21} = \frac{\cancel{18}^6}{\cancel{5}_1} \times \frac{\cancel{10}^2}{\cancel{21}_7} = \frac{12}{7} = 1\frac{5}{7}$$

Adding and Subtracting Fractions

In the same way that $5 plus $2 is $7, and 5 boys plus 2 boys is 7 boys, five ninths plus two ninths is seven ninths. This example illustrates the following rule: To add or subtract fractions with the same denominator, add or subtract the numerators and keep the denominator:

$$\frac{5}{9} + \frac{2}{9} = \frac{7}{9} \text{ and } \frac{5}{9} - \frac{2}{9} = \frac{3}{9} = \frac{1}{3}$$

To add or subtract fractions with different denominators, first rewrite the fractions as equivalent fractions with the same denominators. For example,

$$\frac{1}{6} + \frac{3}{4} = \frac{2}{12} + \frac{9}{12} = \frac{11}{12}$$

Note that the *easiest* denominator to get is the product of the two denominators ($6 \times 4 = 24$, in this case), but the *best* denominator to use is the *least common denominator* (L.C.D.), which is the smallest integer (12 in this case) that is a multiple of each of the denominators. Using the least common denominator minimizes the amount of reducing necessary to express the answer in lowest terms.

EXAMPLE

Add $\frac{2}{3}$ and $\frac{5}{7}$.

The multiples of 7 are 7, 14, 21, 28, ... The smallest one that is also a multiple of 3 is 21, so that is the L.C.D. Now form equivalent fractions by multiplying the numerator and

denominator of $\frac{2}{3}$ by 7 and the numerator

and denominator of $\frac{5}{7}$ by 3:

$$\frac{2}{3} \times \frac{7}{7} = \frac{14}{21} \text{ and } \frac{5}{7} \times \frac{3}{3} = \frac{15}{21}$$

$$\frac{2}{3} + \frac{5}{7} = \frac{14}{21} + \frac{15}{21} = \frac{29}{21} = \frac{18}{21}$$

EXAMPLE

Subtract $\frac{1}{10}$ from $\frac{2}{15}$.

For a common denominator you *could* use $15 \times 10 = 150$, but using the L.C.D., which is 30, makes the problem easier.

$$\frac{2}{15} - \frac{1}{10} = \frac{4}{30} - \frac{3}{30} = \frac{1}{30}$$

To add mixed numbers, add the whole numbers and the fractions separately, and then combine the results.

EXAMPLE

Add $3\frac{5}{6}$ and $2\frac{3}{4}$.

The L.C.D. is 12.

$$3 + 2 = 5 \text{ and } \frac{5}{6} + \frac{3}{4} = \frac{10}{12} + \frac{9}{12} = \frac{19}{12} = 1\frac{7}{12}$$

$$5 + 1\frac{7}{12} = 6\frac{7}{12}$$

When mixed numbers are subtracted, it is sometimes necessary to borrow, as in the following example.

MATHEMATICS   **169**

EXAMPLE

Subtract $1\frac{5}{12}$ from $4\frac{1}{8}$.

The L.C.D. is 24.

$$4\frac{1}{8} = 4\frac{3}{24} \text{ and } 1\frac{5}{12} = 1\frac{10}{24}$$

Since $\frac{10}{24}$ cannot be subtracted from $\frac{3}{24}$, borrow 1, in the form

of $\frac{24}{24}$, from the 4. Then

$$4\frac{3}{24} = 3 + 1 + \frac{3}{24} = 3 + \frac{24}{24} + \frac{3}{24} = 3\frac{27}{24}$$

$$3\frac{27}{24}$$
$$-1\frac{10}{24}$$
$$\overline{2\frac{17}{24}}$$

Problems Involving Fractions

In general, there are two types of problems involving fractions.

1.   To find a number that is a fractional part of a number.

EXAMPLE

A dealer sold 70 television sets in September. If $\frac{2}{5}$ of the sets were color sets, how many color sets were sold?

The word *of* indicates that you need to multiply 70 by $\frac{2}{5}$.

$$\frac{70}{1} \times \frac{2}{5} = \frac{\overset{14}{\cancel{70}}}{1} \times \frac{2}{\underset{1}{\cancel{5}}} = 28$$

The dealer sold 28 color television sets.

2.   To find a number when a fractional part of the number is known.

EXAMPLE

In a package of stamps, 78 are French.

If $\frac{3}{5}$ of the stamps are French, how many stamps are in the package?

To visualize this problem, imagine that the stamps are divided into 5 equal piles, each

containing $\frac{1}{5}$ of the stamps.

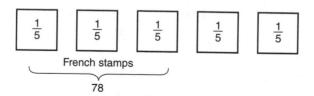

Assume that the first 3 piles contain the French stamps. Since the total number in those 3 piles is 78, each pile contains 78 ÷ 3 = 26 stamps. Finally, there are 5 piles, so there are

5 × 26 = 130 stamps in all.

Note that what you did was to divide 78 by 3 and then multiply by 5. This is exactly the same as multiplying 78 by $\frac{5}{3}$, which is equivalent to dividing by $\frac{3}{5}$:

$$78 \div \frac{3}{5} = 78 \times \frac{5}{3} = 130$$

Arranging Fractions in Order

To compare two fractions, cross-multiply as indicated below. Multiply each denominator by the opposite numerator (as indicated by the arrows), and write the products above the numerators (by the tips of the arrows).

If the two products are equal, the fractions are equivalent. If the products are unequal, the fraction with the larger product written next to it is greater. The symbol > means *is greater than*, and the symbol < means is *less than*.

$$\overset{6}{\underset{2}{1}} \times \overset{3}{\underset{6}{3}}$$

$$1 \times 6 = 2 \times 3$$

$$\frac{1}{2} = \frac{3}{6}$$

$$\overset{1}{\underset{4}{3}} \times \overset{8}{\underset{5}{2}}$$

$$3 \times 5 > 4 \times 2$$

$$\frac{3}{4} > \frac{2}{5}$$

$$\overset{18}{\underset{7}{3}} \times \overset{35}{\underset{6}{5}}$$

$$3 \times 6 < 7 \times 5$$

$$\frac{3}{7} < \frac{5}{6}$$

I. F. DECIMALS

A *decimal number* is equivalent to a fraction whose denominator is a power of 10 (10, 100, 1,000, etc.), but the number is not written in fractional form; rather, it is written with a decimal point. In writing a decimal number, be sure that there are the same number of digits to the right of the decimal point as there are zeros in the denominator. If necessary, insert zeros after the decimal point to have the correct number of digits. For example:

Written as Common Fractions	Written as Decimals
$\dfrac{3}{10}$	0.3
$\dfrac{5}{100}$	0.05
$\dfrac{7}{1,000}$	0.007
$\dfrac{163}{10,000}$	0.0163

To express a mixed number as a decimal number, write the whole number to the left of the decimal point, and the fractional part to the right. For example:

$$8\frac{3}{10} = 8.3$$

$$9\frac{7}{1,000} = 9.007$$

Note: The value of a decimal is *not* changed by annexing zeros after the last digit to the right of the decimal point. For example,

$$\frac{1}{2} = 0.5 = 0.50 = 0.500 = 0.5000$$

One reason to use decimals is that they are convenient to write and to work with. For example, it is more convenient to write that a shirt costs $8.25 than that it costs $8\frac{1}{4}$.

Addition of Decimals
In adding decimal numbers, always line up the decimal points. It is useful to add zeros at the ends of some numbers so that each number has the same number of digits.

EXAMPLE
Add 2.3, 0.789, 5, and 1.08.

$$\begin{array}{r} 2.300 \\ 0.789 \\ 5.000 \\ 1.080 \\ \hline 9.169 \end{array}$$

Subtraction of Decimals
Use the same procedure for subtraction as for addition: line up the decimal points and add zeros if necessary.

EXAMPLE
Subtract 9.7 from 15.58.

$$\begin{array}{r} 15.58 \\ -9.70 \\ \hline 5.88 \end{array}$$

Multiplication of Decimals
In multiplying decimals, the number of decimal places in the product is the sum of the number of decimal places in the numbers being multiplied.

EXAMPLES
Multiply 0.02 by 0.3.

$$\begin{array}{r} 0.02 \ \text{(2 decimal places)} \\ \times 0.3 \ \text{(1 decimal place)} \\ \hline 0.006 \ \text{(3 decimal places)} \end{array}$$

Multiply 1.02 by 0.004.

$$\begin{array}{r} 1.02 \ \text{(2 decimal places)} \\ \times 0.004 \ \text{(3 decimal places)} \\ \hline 0.00408 \ \text{(5 decimal places)} \end{array}$$

Division of Decimals

In dividing decimals, move the decimal point in the divisor all the way to the right, and then move the decimal point in the dividend the same number of places to the right. The decimal point in the quotient is always in the same place as in the new dividend.

EXAMPLES

$6.93 \div 0.3.$

$$\begin{array}{r} 23.1 \\ 0.3.\overline{)6.9.3} \end{array}$$

$35.75 \div 0.05.$

$$\begin{array}{r} 715. \\ 0.05.\overline{)35.75.} \end{array}$$

$0.08136 \div 0.006.$

$$\begin{array}{r} 13.56 \\ 0.006.\overline{)0.081.36} \end{array}$$

Sometimes, there is a remainder and you are told to find the answer to the nearest tenth, nearest hundredth, and so on. In such cases, carry out the division to one more place than is called for. *Regarding remainders:* If the digit just to the right of the desired decimal place is 5 or greater, add 1 to the desired decimal place number. Otherwise, drop the digit to the right of the desired decimal place.

EXAMPLES

Divide 3.734 by 0.9, and express the answer to the nearest tenth.

$$\begin{array}{r} 4.15 \\ 0.9.\overline{)3.7.38} \end{array} \quad \text{The answer is 4.2.}$$

Divide 2.4873 by 0.7, and express the answer to the nearest hundredth.

$$\begin{array}{r} 3.553 \\ 0.7.\overline{)2.4.873} \end{array} \quad \text{The answer is 3.55.}$$

Conversion of Fractions to Decimals

It is sometimes necessary to change a fraction to a decimal. To do this, divide the numerator by the denominator, annexing zeros after the decimal point in the numerator when they are needed.

EXAMPLES

Change $\frac{3}{8}$ to a decimal.

$$\begin{array}{r} 0.375 \\ 8\overline{)3.000} \end{array}$$

$$\frac{3}{8} = 0.375$$

Change $\frac{5}{12}$ to a decimal.

$$\begin{array}{r} 0.4166\frac{2}{3} \\ 12\overline{)5.0000} \end{array}$$

To the nearest tenth, $\frac{5}{12} = 0.4$.

To the nearest hundredth, $\frac{5}{12} = 0.42$.

To the nearest thousandth, $\frac{5}{12} = 0.417$.

I.G. PERCENT

You have seen that fractions may be expressed as decimals. A fraction may also be expressed as a percent. In this section, you will learn how to work with percents.

On a motor trip of 100 miles, 73 miles were on a parkway. To indicate this part of the trip, you may say that $\frac{73}{100}$ of the trip was on a parkway. Another way of stating the same fact is to say that 0.73 of the trip was on a parkway. A third way to express the same idea is to say that 73% of the trip was on a parkway. *Percent is just another way of writing a fraction in which the denominator is 100*. The % sign is used instead of writing the denominator 100. In short, 73% means $\frac{73}{100}$ or 0.73. It is a simple matter to change a percent to a fraction or to a decimal.

EXAMPLE

Change 45%: (a) to a decimal

$$45\% = 0.45$$

(b) to a fraction

$$45\% = \frac{45}{100} = \frac{9}{20}$$

EXAMPLES

Change 0.37 to a percent.

$$0.37 = \frac{37}{100} = 37\%$$

Change 0.025 to a percent.

$$0.025 = \frac{25}{1,000} = \frac{2.5}{100} = 2.5\% \text{ or } 2\frac{1}{2}\%$$

EXAMPLES

Change $\frac{3}{4}$ to a percent.

Change $\frac{3}{4}$ first to a decimal and then to a percent.

$$4\overline{)3.00}^{\,0.75}$$

$$\frac{3}{4} = 0.75 = 75\%$$

Change $\frac{5}{19}$ first to a decimal and then to a percent.

$$
\begin{array}{r}
0.26 \\
19\overline{)5.00} \\
3.8 \\
\hline
1\,20 \\
1\,14 \\
\hline
6
\end{array}
$$

$$\frac{5}{19} = 0.26\frac{6}{19} = 26\frac{6}{19}\%$$

Certain fractions and their equivalent percents are used frequently.

Helpful Equivalents to Memorize

$\frac{1}{2} = 50\%$	$\frac{3}{4} = 75\%$	$\frac{4}{5} = 80\%$	$\frac{3}{8} = 37\frac{1}{2}\%$
$\frac{1}{3} = 33\frac{1}{3}\%$	$\frac{1}{5} = 20\%$	$\frac{1}{6} = 16\frac{2}{3}\%$	$\frac{5}{8} = 62\frac{1}{2}\%$
$\frac{2}{3} = 66\frac{1}{3}\%$	$\frac{2}{5} = 40\%$	$\frac{5}{6} = 83\frac{1}{3}\%$	$\frac{7}{8} = 87\frac{1}{2}\%$
$\frac{1}{4} = 25\%$	$\frac{3}{5} = 60\%$	$\frac{1}{8} = 12\frac{1}{2}\%$	

Problems Involving Percents

Since percents are fractions in another form, problems involving percents are similar to problems involving fractions.

1. To find a percent of a given number.

EXAMPLE

In a factory, 4,775 machine parts were manufactured. When these were tested, 4% were found to be defective. How many machine parts were defective?

In this case, the word *of* indicates that you are to multiply 4,775 by 4%. Since 4% = 0.04:

$$\begin{array}{r} 4775 \quad \text{parts manufactured} \\ \times \quad 0.04 \quad \text{percent defective} \\ \hline 191.00 \quad \text{number of defective parts} \end{array}$$

191 machine parts were defective.

2. To find what percent one number is of another.

EXAMPLE

During the season, a professional basketball player tried 108 foul shots, and made 81 of them. What percent of the shots tried were made?

Form a fraction:

$$\frac{\text{number of shots made}}{\text{total number of shots tried}} = \frac{81}{108}$$

This fraction may be expressed as a percent by changing $\frac{81}{108}$ to a decimal and then to a percent:

$$\begin{array}{r} 0.75 \\ 108 \overline{)81.00} \\ \underline{75\,6} \\ 5\,40 \\ \underline{5\,40} \end{array}$$

$$\frac{81}{108} = 0.75 = 75\%$$

The player made 75% of his shots.

3. To find a number when a percent of it is given.

EXAMPLE

A businessman decided to spend 16% of his expense budget for advertising. If he spent $2,400, what was his total expense?

You know that 16%, or $\frac{16}{100}$, of his expenses amounted to $2,400.

To find the total expense, divide by $\frac{16}{100}$

$\left(\text{which means multiply by } \frac{16}{100}\right)$

$$\$2,400 \times \frac{100}{16} = \frac{\$240,000}{16} = \$15,000$$

Percent Increase and Decrease

The *percent increase* of a quantity is

$$\frac{\text{actual increase}}{\text{original amount}} \times 100\%$$

and the *percent decrease* of a quantity is

$$\frac{\text{actual decrease}}{\text{original amount}} \times 100\%.$$

If the price of a chair rises from $80 to $100, the actual increase is $20, and the percent increase is

$$\frac{20}{80} \times 100\% = \frac{1}{4} \times 100\% = 25\%$$

If a $100 chair is on sale for $80, the actual decrease in price is $20, and the percent decrease is

$$\frac{20}{100} \times 100\% = 20\%$$

Note that the percent increase in going from 80 to 100 is not the same as the percent decrease in going from 100 to 80. Sometimes you will need to work with percents greater than 100%.

EXAMPLE

Mr. Fowler bought some stock at $40 per share. Three years later he sold the stock at $90 per share. What percent of profit did he make?

$90 selling price of stock per share

$-\ 40$ cost of stock per share

$50 profit per share

$$\frac{50}{40} = \frac{\text{profit per share}}{\text{original cost per share}}$$

$$\begin{array}{r} 1.25 \\ 40\overline{)50.00} \\ \underline{40} \\ 100 \\ \underline{80} \\ 200 \\ \underline{200} \end{array}$$

Mr. Fowler made a profit of 125%.

Applications of Percents

Manufacturers will frequently suggest a price, called the *list price*, for which an article is to be sold. Dealers will sometimes reduce the list price, however, in order to meet competition. The amount by which the list price is reduced is called the *discount*, and the reduced price is called the *net price*, or *selling price*.

EXAMPLE

In a department store, a chair was marked as follows: "List price $44. For sale at $33." What was the rate of discount?

The rate of discount is just the percent decrease in the price. The actual discount was

$$\$44.00 - \$33.00 = \$11.00$$

and the percent discount was

$$\frac{\text{actual decrease in price}}{\text{original price}} \times 100\%$$

$$= \frac{11}{44} \times 100\% = \frac{1}{4} \times 100\% = 25\%$$

Sometimes one discount is followed by another; such discounts are called *successive* discounts. You must be careful not to add these discounts, but rather to take them one after another.

EXAMPLE

The list price of a VCR is $200. Appliance City, which normally sells all VCR's at 20% off the list price, is having a special sale in which all merchandise is reduced an additional 15%. How much does the VCR cost during this sale?

Adding 20% and 15% and taking 35% off the $200 list price would result in a sale price of $130. This is *not* correct. You must first take 20% off the $200 list price:

$$\$200 - 0.20 \times \$200 = \$200 - \$40 = \$160$$

You then take 15% off the $160 price:

$$\$160 - 0.15 \times \$160 = \$160 - \$24 = \$136$$

During the sale the VCR costs $136.

I. H. INVESTMENTS

In the most common type of investment, money is placed in a savings bank, where it draws interest. To compute interest, use the following formula:

Interest = Principal $\times$ Rate $\times$ Time
$$I = PRT$$

The principal is the amount invested, the rate is the percent of the principal given to the investor each year, and the time is stated in years.

EXAMPLE

What is the interest on $1,200 at 6% for 9 months?

$$I = PRT$$

In this case
$$\begin{cases} P = \$1,200 \\ R = \dfrac{6}{100} \\ T = \dfrac{9}{12} \text{ or } \dfrac{3}{4} \end{cases}$$

Therefore, $I = 1{,}200 \times \dfrac{6}{100} \times \dfrac{3}{4} = 54$

The interest is $54.00.

Add the interest to the principal to obtain the new *amount*.

In this case, the amount is $1,200 + $54.00 = $1,254.00.

I. I. SALES TAX

Many states in the United States have a *sales tax* on articles bought at retail. This may be 3%, 4%, 5% or a higher percent of the retail price of an article.

EXAMPLE

Mrs. Horn buys a small rug for $39.95. If she has to pay a sales tax of 3%, what is the total cost of the rug?

$$3\% \text{ of } \$39.95 = 0.03 \times \$39.95 = \$1.1985$$

In a case such as this, the amount of tax is rounded off to the nearest penny. Since the tax is $1.20, Mrs. Horn must pay $39.95 + $1.20, or $41.15.

I.J. PROPERTIES OF OPERATIONS

You know that

$$7 + 2 = 9$$
$$\text{and } 2 + 7 = 9.$$

In fact, the order in which two numbers are added does not matter as far as obtaining the correct sum is concerned. This mathematical principle is called the *commutative law of addition*, stated as follows:

> COMMUTATIVE LAW OF ADDITION
> If *a* and *b* are numbers, then
> $$a + b = b + a.$$

You also know that

$$4 \times 6 = 24$$
$$\text{and } 6 \times 4 = 24.$$

In fact, the order in which two numbers are multiplied does not matter as far as obtaining the correct product is concerned. This mathematical principle is called the *commutative law of multiplication*, stated as follows:

> COMMUTATIVE LAW OF MULTIPLICATION
> If *a* and *b* are numbers, then
> $$ab = ba.$$

To find the sum of 3, 6, and 5, you add 3 + 6 to obtain 9 and then add 5 to the result to obtain 14. This process is indicated by using parentheses to group 3 and 6 for addition before adding 5 to the result:

$$(3 + 6) + 5 = 9 + 5 = 14$$

Could the grouping be arranged differently? If 6 and 5 are grouped for addition before 3 is added to the result, you have

$$3 + (6 + 5) = 3 + 11 = 14$$

Thus,

$$(3 + 6) + 5 = 3 + (6 + 5)$$

This freedom in grouping is called the *associative law of addition*, stated as follows:

> **ASSOCIATIVE LAW OF ADDITION**
> If a, b, and c are numbers, then
> $$(a + b) + c = a + (b + c).$$

To multiply the numbers 4, 5, and 7, you multiply 4×5 to obtain 20 and then multiply the result by 7 to obtain $20 \times 7 = 140$. This process is indicated by using parentheses to group 4 and 5 for multiplication before multiplying the result by 7:

$$(4 \times 5) \times 7 = 20 \times 7 = 140$$

Could the grouping be arranged differently? If 5 and 7 are grouped for multiplication before multiplying by 4, you have

$$4 \times (5 \times 7) = 4 \times 35 = 140$$

Thus,

$$(4 \times 5) \times 7 = 4 \times (5 \times 7)$$

This freedom in grouping is called the *associative law of multiplication*, stated as follows:

> **ASSOCIATIVE LAW OF MULTIPLICATION**
> If a, b, and c are numbers, then
> $$(ab)c = a(bc).$$

EXAMPLE

A sales clerk earns $8.00 per hour. He works 7 hours on Friday and 4 hours on Saturday. How much does he earn on these 2 days?

You can compute his earnings as follows:

$8 \times 7 = \$56$ for Friday
$8 \times 4 = \underline{\$32}$ for Saturday
Total: $\$88$

You can compute the earnings more simply in this way:

$7 + 4 = 11$ (total hours worked)
$8 \times (7 + 4) = 8 \times 11 = \$88$ (total earnings)

Thus,

$$8 \times (7 + 4) = 8 \times 7 + 8 \times 4$$

The principle described above is called the *distributive law of multiplication* with respect to addition. It is usually called simply the *distributive law*, stated as follows:

DISTRIBUTIVE LAW
If *a*, *b*, and *c* are numbers, then
$$a(b + c) = ab + ac.$$

II. ALGEBRA

II. A. FUNDAMENTALS

So far we have dealt only with numbers. Now, we must review the use of letters as variables. If we let $J =$ Judy's age, and $A =$ Adam's age, we can express the statement "Judy is 8 years older than Adam" by the algebraic equation

$$J = A + 8$$

Then we can use this equation to answer each of the following questions:

If Adam is 21, how old is Judy?
Replace *A* by 21 and get:

$$J = 21 + 8 = 29$$

When Adam was 7, how old was Judy?
Replace *A* by 7 and get:

$$J = 7 + 8 = 15$$

When Adam is 55, how old will Judy be?

Replace *A* by 55 and get:

$$J = 55 + 8 = 63$$

In algebraic expressions, we express addition and subtraction by using the same signs as in arithmetic: + and − . To express division, we can use the division symbol, ÷, but more often we use the fraction bar; instead of writing $n \div 3$, we usually write $\dfrac{n}{3}$.

To express multiplication, we never use the multiplication sign, ×. The most common letter we use as a variable is *x*, and writing $3 \times x \times y$ to express "3 times *x* times *y*" would be very confusing. Instead, we have three other ways to express multiplication in algebraic expressions.

1. Write the numbers or letters with no symbol between them: $3xy$.
2. Use a raised dot between the numbers or letters: $3 \cdot x \cdot y$.
3. Write the numbers or letters in parentheses, with no symbol between the parentheses: $(3)(x)(y)$.

To use algebra effectively, we must learn how to translate from ordinary English into symbols and letters.

EXAMPLES

John is *x* years old. How old will he be 7 years from now?

ANSWER:

$$x + 7$$

One apple costs *a* cents. What is the cost of 6 apples?

ANSWER:

$$6a$$

Alice weighed *y* pounds a year ago. Since then she has lost 9 pounds. What is her present weight?

ANSWER:

$$y - 9$$

Take a number *z*. Increase it by 2. Multiply the result by 6.

ANSWER:

$6(z + 2)$. Note that this must be written with parentheses.

II. B. EXPONENTS AND EVALUATIONS

There are times when we wish to multiply a number by itself. Of course, if we wish to multiply 7 by itself, we can write 7×7. However, in modern science, where we may have occasion to multiply a number by itself many times, it becomes awkward to write such numbers as $7 \times 7 \times 7 \times 7 \times 7 \times 7 \times 7 \times 7 \times 7$. Instead, we use a shortcut and write the product of nine 7's as 7^9. In this case 9 is called the *exponent* and 7 is the *base*.

EXAMPLES

5^1 means 5.
6^3 means $6 \times 6 \times 6$
a^5 means $a \cdot a \cdot a \cdot a \cdot a$
$3b^4$ means $3 \cdot b \cdot b \cdot b \cdot b$
$(3b)^4$ means $(3b)(3b)(3b)(3b)$

We often wish to find the numerical value of an algebraic expression when we know the numerical value assigned to each letter of the expression.

When a calculation requires more than one operation, it is critical that the operations be carried out in the correct order. For decades students have memorized the sentence "Please Excuse My Dear Aunt Sally," or just the first letters, PEMDAS, to remember the proper order of operations. The letters stand for:

1. Parentheses: first do whatever appears in parentheses, following PEMDAS within the parentheses if necessary.
2. Exponents: next evaluate all terms with exponents.
3. Multiplication and Division: next do all multiplications and divisions *in order from left to right*—do not multiply first and then divide.
4. Addition and Subtraction: finally do all additions and subtractions *in order from left to right*—do not add first and then subtract.

EXAMPLES

Evaluate $3b^3$ and $(3b)^3$ when $b = 2$.
$$3b^3 = 3 \times 2^3 = 3 \times 8 = 24$$
$$(3b)3 = (3 \times 2)3 = (6)3 = 216$$

Notice that, in evaluating $(3b)^3$, we first evaluated what was in Parentheses ($3 \times 2 = 6$) and then took the Exponent ($6^3 = 216$). In evaluating $3b^3$, we first evaluated the Exponent ($2^3 = 8$) and then Multiplied by 3 ($3 \times 8 = 24$). The order matters!

Evaluate $5x + 3y \div 6z$ when $x = 6$, $y = 4$, and $z = 1$.
$$5x + 3y \div 6z = (5 \cdot 6) + (3 \cdot 4) \div (6 \cdot 1)$$
$$= 30 + 12 \div 6$$
$$= 30 + 2 = 32$$

Find the value of $4a^3 - 9c^2 \div 4b$ when $a = 5$, $b = 3$, and $c = 2$.
$$4a^3 - 9c^2 \div 4b = (4 \cdot 5^3) - (9 \cdot 2^2) \div (4 \cdot 3)$$
$$= (4 \cdot 125) - (9 \cdot 4) \div (4 \cdot 3)$$
$$= 500 - 36 \div 12$$
$$= 500 - 3 = 497$$

II. C. OPERATIONS WITH EXPONENTS AND SCIENTIFIC NOTATION

Multiplication and Division with Exponents

Since $2^3 = 2 \cdot 2 \cdot 2$ and $2^4 = 2 \cdot 2 \cdot 2 \cdot 2$,
$2^3 \cdot 2^4 = (2 \cdot 2 \cdot 2) \cdot (2 \cdot 2 \cdot 2 \cdot 2) = 2^7 = 2^{3+4}$.
This is a special case of the following law:

> For any numbers a, m, and n:
> $$a^m \cdot a^n = a^{m+n}$$

Expressing Large Numbers in Scientific Notation

Scientists such as astronomers and space engineers frequently deal with very large numbers in their work. In order for scientists to be able to write these numbers conveniently and to use them effectively, the *scientific notation* system was developed. The definition of scientific notation for writing a number is given below.

> **DEFINITION:** When a number is written in scientific notation it is written as the product of two numbers:
> **a.** a number greater than or equal to 1, but less than 10
> **b.** a power of 10

EXAMPLE

The distance between two planets is 460,000,000,000 miles. Write this number in scientific notation.

The number between 1 and 10 is 4.6. When you go from 4.6 to 460,000,000,000, you move the decimal point 11 places to the right. Each move of the decimal point to the right represents multiplication by 10. Thus, a move of the decimal point 11 places to the right is equivalent to multiplication by 10^{11}.

Therefore, $460,000,000,000 = 4.6 \times 10^{11}$.

EXAMPLE

Express 875,000,000 in scientific notation.

The number between 1 and 10 is 8.75. When you go from 8.75 to 875,000,000, you move the decimal point 8 places to the right.

Therefore, $875,000,000 = 8.75 \times 10^{8}$.

EXAMPLE

Express 3.35×10^{5} as an integer.

To multiply by 10^{5}, move the decimal point 5 places to the right, filling in 0's once the decimal point is all the way to the right.

Therefore, $3.35 \times 10^{5} = 335,000$.

Expressing Small Numbers in Scientific Notation

Atomic scientists and other physicists have occasion to work with very small numbers. The ability to express these small numbers in scientific notation is a great convenience. The definition of scientific notation previously given applies to very small, as well as to very large, numbers.

EXAMPLE

The length of a wave of violet light is 0.000016 inch. Express this number in scientific notation.

The number between 1 and 10 is 1.6. When you go from 1.6 to 0.000016, you move the decimal point 5 places to the left. Each move of the decimal point to the left represents division by 10, which we express as multiplication by 10^{-1}. Thus, a move of the decimal point 5 places to the left is equivalent to division by 10^5 or multiplication by 10^{-5}.

Therefore, $0.000016 = 1.6 \times 10^{-5}$.

EXAMPLE

Express 7.9×10^{-4} as an ordinary decimal number.

To multiply by 10^{-4}, move the decimal point 4 places to the left, filling in 0's once the decimal point is all the way to the left.
Therefore, $7.9 \times 10^{-4} = 0.00079$.

II. D. FORMULAS

Temperature readings given in weather reports use the *Fahrenheit* scale, on which the freezing point of water is 32° and the boiling point of water is 212°. However, in the science laboratory and in many European countries the Celsius scale is used. On the *Celsius* scale, the freezing point of water is 0° and the boiling point of water is 100°. The relationship between the Fahrenheit scale and the Celsius scale is given by the formula

$$F = \frac{9}{5} C + 32$$

where F represents the Fahrenheit temperature and C represents the Celsius temperature.

EXAMPLE

On a certain day the noon temperature in Paris is recorded as 20° Celsius. What is the corresponding Fahrenheit temperature?
Use the formula
$$F = \frac{9}{5} C + 32$$
In this case $C = 20$.
$$F = \frac{9}{\cancel{5}} \times \cancel{20}^4 + 32$$
$$= 9 \times 4 + 32 = 36 + 32 = 68°$$

II. E. SOLVING EQUATIONS

The ability to solve equations is important because it enables us to solve many different types of problems. In this section, you will learn how to solve some of the simpler kinds of equations. In a later section you will apply these skills in problem solving.

> An equation states that two quantities are equal.

For example, the equation

$$3x + 2 = 20$$

tells us that $3x + 2$ and 20 are different names for the same number. If this is so, then $3x$ must represent the number 18, since 18 is the only number that can be added to 2 to get 20. Then, since 3 times x equals 18, x must be equal to 6.

A number that yields a true statement when it replaces the variable in an equation is called a *solution* of that equation. To *solve* an equation means to find its solution. In the preceding paragraph, when we solved the equation $3x + 2 = 20$, we determined that the solution was $x = 6$.

On the GED Mathematics test, many of the equations that you will have to solve can be reasoned out in the same way. Try to use this method on the following eight practice problems.

You will now learn a systematic method of finding the solution of an equation. The basic principle is this: *do exactly the same thing to each side of the equation*. For example, you may always add the same number to each side, subtract the same number from each side, or multiply or divide each side by the same number (except 0).

Virtually every equation that you will have to solve on the GED Examination has only one variable and no exponents. The simple six-step method shown in the following example can be used on all of these equations.

EXAMPLE

If $\frac{1}{2}x + 3x - 3 = 2(x + 1) + 4$, what is the value of x?

Step	What to do	Example
1	Get rid of fractions by multiplying both sides by the LCD (Least Common Denominator).	Multiply each term by 2: $x + 6x - 6 = 4(x + 1) + 4$
2	Use the distributive law to get rid of all parentheses.	$x + 6x - 6 = 4x + 4 + 8$
3	Combine like terms on each side.	$7x - 6 = 4x + 12$
4	By adding or subtracting, get all the variables on one side.	Subtract $4x$ from each side: $3x - 6 = 12$
5	By adding or subtracting, get all the plain numbers on the other side.	Add 6 to each side: $3x = 18$
6	Divide both sides by the number in front of the variable.	Divide both sides by 3: $x = 6$

This example is actually harder than any equation on the GED Examination, because it requires all six steps. On the GED that never happens.

Think of the six steps as a list of questions that must be answered. Ask yourself whether each step is necessary. If it isn't, move on to the next one; if it is, do it.

Now let's look at some equations that require only a few steps to solve. We'll start with the equation we solved at the beginning of this section.

EXAMPLES

Solve the equation $3x + 2 = 20$.

There are no fractions or parentheses, there are no like terms, and the variable is on only one side of the equation, so skip steps 1 through 4.

Subtract 2 from each side: $3x = 18$
Divide each side by 3: $x = 6$

Solve the equation $\frac{x}{3} = 20$.

There is a fraction, so do step 1. Multiply both sides by the denominator, 3:

$$3\,\frac{x}{3} = 3(20)$$

$$x = 60$$

Solve the equation $\frac{3}{5}x - 1 = 8$.

There is a fraction, so do step 1. Multiply each side by the denominator, 5:

$$5\left(\frac{3}{5}x\right) - 5(1) = 5(8)$$

$$3x - 5 = 40$$

Skip to step 5. Add 5 to each side:

$$3x = 45$$

Do step 6. Divide each side by 3:

$$x = 15$$

II. F. SOLVING PROBLEMS

We may use equations to solve problems such as the following.

EXAMPLE

A plumber must cut a pipe 50 inches long into two pieces so that one piece will be 12 inches longer than the other piece. Find the length of each piece.

Let x = length of the shorter piece.

Then $x + 12$ = length of the longer piece.
Since the sum of the two pieces is 50 inches:

$$x + (x + 12) = 50$$

Combine like terms: $\quad 2x + 12 = 50$
Subtract 12 from each side: $2x = 38$
Divide each side by 2: $\quad x = 19$

The shorter piece is 19 in. long, and the longer piece is $19 + 12 = 31$ in. long.

EXAMPLE

Divide an estate of $46,000 among three sons so that the second son gets $6,000 more than the youngest, and the eldest son gets 3 times as much as the youngest.

Let x = amount the youngest son gets. Then x + 6,000 = amount the second son gets, and $3x$ = amount the eldest son gets.

$$x + (x + 6000) + 3x = 46,000$$
Combine like terms: $\quad 5x + 6000 = 46,000$
Subtract 6,000 from each side: $5x = 40,000$
Divide each side by 5: $\qquad x = 8,000$

The youngest son gets $8,000; the second son gets 8,000 + 6,000 = $14,000; and the eldest son gets 3(8,000) = $24,000.

Algebra problems are sometimes more easily understood and analyzed when approached through analogous problems in arithmetic.

EXAMPLE

Arithmetic Problem: If 1 pencil costs 10 cents, then 6 pencils cost _____cents.

Algebra Problem: If 1 pencil costs y cents, then 6 pencils cost _____ cents.

To solve the arithmetic problem, you need to multiply 6 times 10 cents, to arrive at 60 cents as the answer. In the algebra problem, you use the same procedure: multiply 6 times y cents to get the answer, $6y$.

Here is a more complicated example:

EXAMPLE

Arithmetic Problem: George has 50 dollars. He buys 5 articles for 8 dollars each. The number of dollars George has left is _____.

Algebra Problem: George has x dollars. He buys y articles for z dollars each. The number of dollars George has left is _____.

To solve the arithmetic problem, you need to multiply 5 times 8 and subtract the result from 50, to get $50 - (5)(8) = 50 - 40 = 10$ as the answer. In the algebra problem, you use the same procedure: multiply y times z, and subtract the result from x, to get $x - yz$ as the answer.

EXAMPLE

At a track meet the total score for each event was 20 points. First place counted twice as much as second place, and third place counted 4 points less than second place. How many points did first place count?

Let x = number of points for second place.

Then $2x$ = number of points for first place, and $x - 4$ = number of points for third place.

$$x + 2x + (x - 4) = 20$$

Combine like terms: $4x - 4 = 20$
Add 4 to each side: $4x = 24$
Divide each side by 4: $x = 6$

First place counted for $2(6) = 12$ points.

EXAMPLE

Two cars start at the same time from two cities that are 480 miles apart and travel toward each other. One car averages 35 miles per hour, and the other car averages 45 miles per hour. In how many hours will the two cars meet?

Let x = number of hours the two cars take to meet.

In problems involving motion, it is convenient to collect the information in a box, as shown below, with the formula

Rate $\times$ Time = Distance.

	Rate	$\times$ Time	= Distance
First car	35	x	$35x$
Second car	45	x	$45x$

Since the sum of the two distances covered is 480 miles:
$$35x + 45x = 480$$
Combine like terms: $80x = 480$
Divide each side by 80: $x = 6$

The cars will meet in 6 hr.

II. G. SOLVING INEQUALITIES

We recall that the symbol > means *is greater than* and that the symbol < means *is less than*. For example, 9 > 5 and 3 < 8.

An inequality is a statement in which two quantities are unequal. The inequality

$$3x + 2 > 20$$

tells us that $3x + 2$ names a number that is greater than 20. To solve such an inequality, we use the exact same six-step method that we use for solving equations.

$$3x + 2 > 20$$

Subtract 2 from each side: $3x > 18$

Divide each side by 3: $x > 6$

Since *any number* greater than 6 is a solution, the inequality $3x + 2 > 20$ has infinitely many solutions. Of course, 7, 8, 9, 10, . . . are all solutions, but solutions do not have to be integers—6.4, $117\frac{1}{2}$, and $\sqrt{55}$ are also solutions. For example,

$3(6.4) + 2 = 19.2 + 2 = 21.2$, which is greater than 20.

The symbol $\geq$ means *is greater than or equal to*, and the symbol $\leq$ means *is less than or equal to*. For example, $x \geq 5$ means that $x > 5$ or $x = 5$.

EXAMPLES

The positive integers that satisfy the inequality $x \geq 3$ are 3, 4, 5, ...

The positive integers that satisfy the inequality $x \leq 3$ are 1, 2, and 3. Of course, 0 and all of the negative integers also satisfy this inequality.

II. H. RATIO AND PROPORTION

A *ratio* is a fraction that compares two quantities that are measured in the same units. The first quantity is the numerator, and the second quantity is the denominator.

For example, if Mr. Carson earns $48 per day and Mr. Burns earns $16 per day, we may say that the ratio of Mr. Carson's earnings per day to Mr. Burns's earnings per day is $\frac{48}{16}$. We may reduce $\frac{48}{16}$ to $\frac{1}{3}$ or 3, which indicates that Mr. Carson earns 3 times as much per day as Mr. Burns.

The comparison of the two pay rates may be written as $\frac{48}{16}$ or as 48 : 16, which is read as "48 to 16." In general, the ratio of number a to number b is $\frac{a}{b}$, or $a : b$.

EXAMPLES

At a party there are 12 men and 8 women. What is the ratio of men to women?

The ratio is $\frac{12}{8}$, or 12 : 8. In simplest form, this is $\frac{3}{2}$, or 3 : 2.

At the same party, what is the ratio of women to men?

The ratio is $\frac{8}{12}$ or 8 : 12. In simplest form, this is $\frac{2}{3}$, or 2 : 3.

At the same party, what is the ratio of men to the number of people at the party?

Since there are 8 + 12 = 20 people at the party, the ratio is $\frac{12}{20}$, or 12 : 20. In simplest form this is $\frac{3}{5}$, or 3 : 5.

If two numbers are in the ratio of $a : b$, then, for some number x, the first number is ax and the second number is bx. Therefore, in any ratio problem, you should write the letter x after each number and use some given information to solve for x.

EXAMPLE

A B C

If $AB : BC = 2 : 3$, and if $AC = 30$ inches, what is the length of AB?

Let $AB = 2x$ and $BC = 3x$. Since

$$AB + BC = AC$$
$$\text{then } 2x + 3x = 30$$
$$5x = 30$$
$$x = 6$$

Therefore, $AB = 2x = 2(6) = 12$.

EXAMPLE

If the number of children at a picnic is between 40 and 50, and the ratio of boys to girls is 5 : 4, how many girls are at the picnic?

If $5x$ and $4x$ are the numbers of boys and girls, respectively, at the picnic, then the number of children present is $5x + 4x = 9x$. Therefore, the number of children must be a multiple of 9. The only multiple of 9 between 40 and 50 is 45, so $9x = 45$ and $x = 5$. Since the number of girls is $4x$, there are $4(5) = 20$ girls.

A **proportion** is an equation that states that two ratios are equivalent. Since ratios are just fractions, any equation such as $\frac{4}{6} = \frac{10}{15}$ in which each side is a single fraction is a proportion. The easiest way to solve a proportion is to cross-multiply:

$$\text{if } \frac{a}{b} - \frac{c}{d}, \text{ then } ad = bc$$

EXAMPLE

If $\frac{3}{7} = \frac{x}{84}$ what is the value of x?
Cross-multiply: $3(84) = 7x$, so $252 = 7x$ and $x = 36$.

EXAMPLE

If a tank contains 24 quarts of alcohol, how many quarts of water must be added to make an antifreeze mixture in which the ratio of alcohol to water is $3 : 4$?

Set up a proportion.

Let $x = $ number of quarts of water needed.

$$\frac{\text{alcohol}}{\text{water}} = \frac{3}{4} = \frac{24}{x}$$

Now, cross multiply.

$$\frac{3}{4} \diagdown \frac{24}{x}$$

$$3x = 4 \times 24$$
$$= 96$$
$$x = 32$$

A **rate** is a fraction that compares two quantities measured in different units. The word per often appears in rate problems: miles per hour, dollars per week, cents per ounce, children per classroom, and so on.

The following examples will indicate how ratios and proportions can be used to solve problems.

EXAMPLE

Sharon read 24 pages of her book in 15 minutes. At this rate, how many pages can she read in 40 minutes?

Handle this rate problem exactly as you do a ratio problem. Set up a proportion and cross-multiply:

$$\frac{\text{pages}}{\text{minute}} = \frac{24}{15} = \frac{x}{40}$$
$$15x = 40 \times 24 = 960 \text{ and}$$
$$x = 64$$

EXAMPLE

The scale on a map is 1 inch to 60 miles.

If the distance between two cities is $2\frac{3}{4}$ inches on the map, what is the actual distance between the two cities?

Let d = distance between the cities.

Set up a proportion and cross-multiply:

$$\frac{\text{inches}}{\text{miles}} = \frac{1}{60} = \frac{2.75}{d}$$
$$d = 60(2.75) = 165 \text{ mi.}$$

II. I. SIGNED NUMBERS

On the GED Examination the word *number* always means *real number*, a number that can be represented by a point on the number line.

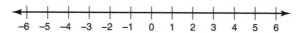

The numbers to the right of 0 on the number line are called ***positive***, and those to the left of 0 are called ***negative***. Negative numbers must be written with a *negative sign* (–2); positive numbers may be written with a *plus sign* (+2) but are usually written without a sign (2). All numbers can be called ***signed numbers***.

The ***absolute value*** of a number, *a*, denoted as |*a*|, is the distance between *a* and 0 on the number line. For example, since 3 is 3 units to the right of 0 on the number line and –3 is 3 units to the left of 0, both have an absolute value of 3:

|3| = 3 and |–3| = 3

Multiplying and dividing signed numbers is easy as long as you know when the result is positive and when it is negative. The product and quotient of two positive numbers or two negative numbers are positive; the product and quotient of a positive number and a negative number are negative. For example,

$6 \times 3 = 18$ $6 \div 3 = 2$

$(-6) \times (-3) = 18$ $(-6) \div (-3) = 2$

$6 \times (-3) = -18$ $6 \div (-3) = -2$

$(-6) \times 3 = -18$ $(-6) \div 3 = -2$

Adding and subtracting signed numbers requires a little more care. The sum of two positive numbers is positive, and the sum of two negative numbers is negative. To find the sum of a positive and a negative number, find the difference of their absolute values and use the sign of the number with the larger absolute value. For example:

$6 + 2 = 8$ $(-6) + (-2) = -8$

To calculate $6 + (-2)$ or $(-6) + 2$, take the *difference*, $6 - 2 = 4$, and use the sign of the number whose absolute value is 6.

$6 + (-2) = 4$ $(-6) + 2 = -4$

To subtract signed numbers, change the problem to an addition problem by changing the sign of the number that is being subtracted. For example:

$2 - 6 = 2 + (-6) = -4$

$2 - (-6) = 2 + (6) = 8$

$(-2) - (-6) = (-2) + (6) = 4$

$(-2) - 6 = (-2) + (-6) = -8$

In each case, the minus sign was changed to a plus sign, and either the 6 was changed to −6 or the −6 was changed to 6.

EXAMPLE

What is the product of the odd integers between −6 and 4?

The product of the odd integers between −6 and 4 is $(-5)(-3)(-1)(1)(3)$. To evaluate, just multiply from left to right: $(-5)(-3) = 15$, $15(-1) = -15$, $-15(1) = -15$, $-15(3) = -45$.

EXAMPLE

Solve for x and check: $-3x + 5 = -10$.

$$-3x = -10 - 5 = -15$$
$$x = (-15) \div (-3) = 5$$
$$\text{Check: } -3(5) + 5 = -15 + 5 = -10$$

II. J. PROBABILITY

The *probability* that an event will occur is a number between 0 and 1, usually written as a fraction, which indicates how likely it is that the event will happen. For example, if a person spins the spinner pictured below, there are 4 possible outcomes and it is equally likely that the spinner will stop in any of the 4 regions.

There is 1 chance in 4 that it will stop in the region marked 2, so we say that the probability of spinning a 2 is one-fourth and write $P(2) = \dfrac{1}{4}$. Since 2 is the only even number on the spinner, we can also say $P(\text{even}) = \dfrac{1}{4}$. There are 3 chances in 4 that the spinner will land in a region with an odd number in it, so $P(\text{odd}) = \dfrac{3}{4}$.

If E is any event, the probability that E will occur is given by

$$P(E) = \frac{\text{number of favorable outcomes}}{\text{total number of possible outcomes}}$$

assuming that all the possible outcomes are equally likely.

For the spinner shown above, each of the 4 regions is the same size, so it is equally likely that the spinner will land on the 2, 3, 5, or 7. Therefore,

$$P(\text{odd}) = \frac{\text{number of favorable outcomes}}{\text{total number of possible outcomes}} = \frac{3}{4}.$$

We note that the probability of *not* getting an odd number is 1 minus the probability of getting an odd number: $1 - \dfrac{3}{4} = \dfrac{1}{4}$.

Let's look at some other probabilities associated with spinning this spinner once.

$$P(\text{number} > 10) = \frac{\text{number of ways to get a number} > 10}{\text{number of possible outcomes}} = \frac{0}{4} = 0$$

$$P(\text{prime number}) = \frac{\text{number of ways to get prime}}{\text{total number of possible outcomes}} = \frac{4}{4} = 1$$

$$P(\text{number} < 4) = \frac{\text{number of ways to get a number} < 4}{\text{total number of possible outcomes}} = \frac{2}{4} = \frac{1}{2}$$

The following box contains six important facts about probabilities.

Facts about Probability

1. If event E is *impossible* (such as getting a number greater than 10), $P(E) = 0$.

2. If it is certain that event E will occur (such as getting a prime number), $P(E) = 1$.

3. In all cases $0 \leq P(E) \leq 1$.

4. The probability that event E will *not* occur is $1 - P(E)$.

5. If 2 or more events constitute all the outcomes, the sum of their probabilities is 1; for example:
$$P(\text{even}) + P(\text{odd}) = \frac{1}{4} + \frac{3}{4} = 1.$$

6. The more likely it is that an event will occur, the higher (the closer to 1) is its probability; the less likely it is that an event will occur, the lower (the closer to 0) its probability is.

EXAMPLE

John has a blue tie, a red tie, a brown tie, and a gray tie. If John selects a tie at random, what is the probability that he selects a blue tie?

In selecting a tie John may select any 1 of 4 colors. Therefore, the probability that John selects a blue tie is $\frac{1}{4}$.

EXAMPLE

A football squad consists of 29 linemen and 15 backfield men. If 1 man on the squad is chosen to be captain, what is the probability that the man chosen is a lineman?

In all, there are 29 + 15, or 44 men on the squad. Of the 44 men, 29 are linemen. Therefore, the probability that the choice is a lineman is $\frac{29}{44}$.

EXAMPLE

Joan had 3 dimes and 2 quarters in her purse. If she selected a coin at random from her purse, what is the probability that the coin chosen was a nickel?

Since Joan did not have a nickel in her purse, it was impossible for her to have withdrawn a nickel. Therefore, the probability is 0.

II. K. THE MEAN AND THE MEDIAN

The Mean (Average)

The **average**, A, of a set of n numbers is the sum of those numbers divided by n:

$$A = \frac{\text{sum of the } n \text{ numbers}}{n}$$

Although the technical name for this quantity is the *mean* or *arithmetic mean*, you will almost always hear it referred to as the average.

EXAMPLE

Mary's grades on a series of tests in history were 75, 90, 80, 65, and 70. What was the average, or mean, of Mary's grades?

To find the average, first add the scores:

$$75 + 90 + 80 + 65 + 70 = 380$$

Then divide this sum by the number of scores, namely, 5:

$$380 \div 5 = 76$$

The average of Mary's grades was 76.

Often on the GED Examination, you are *not* asked to find an average: rather, you are given the average of a set of numbers and asked for some other information. The key to solving such problems is to first find the sum of the numbers. Since $A = \frac{\text{sum}}{n}$, multiplying both sides by n yields

$$\text{sum} = nA$$

EXAMPLE

One day a truck driver picked up 20 packages whose average weight was 14.3 pounds. What was the total weight of all the packages?

Just multiply: $20 \times 14.3 = 286$ lb.

EXAMPLE

In its first 5 games the Cardinal Basketball Team scored 58, 49, 62, 53, and 41 points. How many points must the team score in its sixth game to achieve an average score of 56 points per game?

To average 56 points per game, the team needs a total of $6 \times 56 = 336$ points. In its first 5 games it earned

$$58 + 49 + 62 + 53 + 41 = 263 \text{ points.}$$

Therefore, in the sixth game the team needs to score $336 - 263 = 73$ points.

EXAMPLE

In an office there are four clerks, each of whom receives a salary of $300 per week, and an office manager who receives a salary of $950 per week. What is the mean salary earned by this office staff?

To find the mean of the salaries, find the sum and divide it by 5.

$$(300 + 300 + 300 + 300 + 950) \div 5 = 2,150$$
$$\div 5 = 430$$

Thus, the mean salary of the staff is $430.

In the above example, the mean salary does not fairly represent the situation. Only one person receives a salary above the mean of $430, whereas four people receive salaries well below the mean. To avoid having one or two extreme scores creating a misleading impression about a set of data, we often use another measure, called the *median*.

The Median

When we arrange a set of numbers in increasing or decreasing order, the number in the middle is the *median*.

EXAMPLE

The weights, in pounds, of the starting team of the Madison football team are 186, 195, 207, 173, 192, 201, 236, 228, 198, 215, and 179. What is the median weight of the members of this team?

Arrange the weights in decreasing order, starting with the heaviest.

236, 228, 215, 207, 201, 198, 195, 192, 186, 179, 173

↓

median

Listing the weights in increasing order, starting with the lightest, will yield the same result.

Note: In all cases where there is an even number of scores, there will be two middle scores. To find the median, take the average of the two middle scores.

EXAMPLE

Find the median of the following set of numbers:

47, 56, 79, 83, 45, 64, 72, 53

First, arrange the numbers in order:

83, 79, 72, 64, 56, 53, 47, 45

In this case, there are two middle numbers (64 and 56). To find the median, take the average of these numbers:

$(64 + 56) \div 2 = 120 \div 2 = 60.$

The median is 60.

III. GEOMETRY

III. A. POINTS, LINES, AND SPACE

By a *point* in geometry we mean a definite location in space. A point has no length, width, or thickness. We usually name a point with a capital letter.

When we use the word *line* in geometry, we always mean a straight line. Moreover, a line extends infinitely, in either direction. For this reason, arrows are frequently shown on a line, as follows:

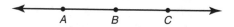

We can think of a line as a special set of points. A line is usually named by indicating two points on the line and adding an overhead double-arrowed symbol. For example, the line above could be named $\overleftrightarrow{AB}$, or $\overleftrightarrow{BA}$ or $\overleftrightarrow{AC}$, and so on.

A *segment*, or *line segment*, consists of two points on a line, together with points between those two points. The two points are called the *endpoints* of the segment. We usually name a segment by indicating the endpoints and placing a bar above. For example, the segment below could be called $\overline{CD}$ or $\overline{DC}$

C   D

In geometry, a *ray* consists of a point, *A*, on a line, together with all of the points on that line that are on the same side of *A*. Point A is called the *endpoint* of the ray. We name a ray by indicating its endpoint and another point on the ray with an overhead arrow symbol. For example, the ray shown below is called $\overrightarrow{AE}$ or $\overrightarrow{AF}$.

A   E   F

We can think of a *plane* in geometry as a set of points making up a perfectly flat surface. A plane is suggested by the floor of a room or the cover of a book.

By *space* in geometry we mean the set of all points in three dimensions.

III. B. GEOMETRIC FIGURES

Geometric figures may be classified in two groups, plane figures and solid figures. *If all the points of a figure lie in the same plane, it is called a plane figure. If the points of a figure lie in more than one plane, the figure is called a solid figure.* Below are diagrams of some important plane and solid figures.

PLANE FIGURES

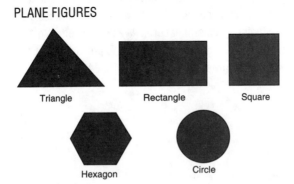

Triangle   Rectangle   Square

Hexagon   Circle

SOLID FIGURES

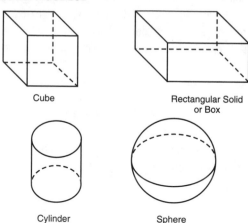

Cube

Rectangular Solid
or Box

Cylinder

Sphere

III. C. GEOMETRIC CONCEPTS
AND RELATIONSHIPS

Angles

An *angle* is a set of points consisting of two rays having the same endpoint. For example, rays $\overrightarrow{AB}$ and $\overrightarrow{AC}$ having the same endpoint, *A*, form the angle shown below. We name an angle by indicating a point on one ray, then the common endpoint, and finally a point on the other ray. The symbol for angle is $\angle$. The angle shown may be called $\angle BAC$ or $\angle CAB$. When there is no ambiguity in meaning, an angle may be named by indicating only its *vertex*, the endpoint of the two rays that form its sides. Thus, $\angle BAC$ may be called $\angle A$.

On the GED Mathematics test, angles are always measured in degrees. As shown in the box headed "Basics on Angles," angles are classified according to their degree of measures. We use the letter "m" to represent the measure of an angle; for example, to express the fact that the measure of $\angle BAC$ is 45 degrees, we write $m\angle BAC = 45°$.

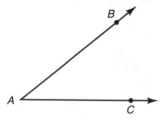

Basics on Angles

An *acute angle* is an angle whose measure is less than 90°. ∠*RST* is an acute angle: m∠*RST* < 90°.

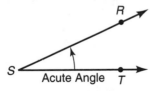

Acute Angle

A *right angle* is an angle whose measure is 90°. ∠*VWX* is a right angle: m∠*VWX* = 90°. A small square drawn in an angle *always* means that the angle is a right angle.

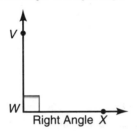

Right Angle

An *obtuse angle* is an angle whose measure is greater than 90° and less than 180°. ∠*OFG* is an obtuse angle:

90° < m∠*OFG* < 180°

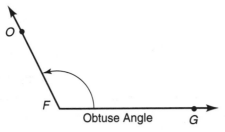

Obtuse Angle

A *straight angle* is an angle whose measure is 180°. ∠*LOC* is a straight angle:

m∠*LOC* = 180°

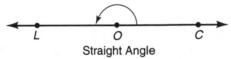

Straight Angle

When two lines meet to form right angles, we say that the lines are *perpendicular* to each other. The symbol ⊥ is used to indicate perpendicular lines. In the diagram, $\overleftrightarrow{DE}$ is perpendicular to $\overleftrightarrow{BC}$; this may be expressed as $\overleftrightarrow{DE} \perp \overleftrightarrow{BC}$. The four right angles formed are ∠*DAB*, ∠*DAC*, ∠*EAB*, and ∠*EAC*.

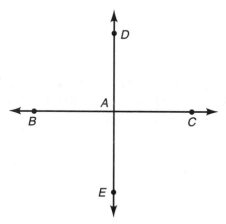

When two lines intersect, four angles are formed. The two angles in each pair of opposite angles are called *vertical angles*. In the diagram, ∠1 and ∠3 are vertical angles, and ∠2 and ∠4 are vertical angles. Vertical angles have equal measures; m∠1 = m∠3 and m∠2 = m∠4.

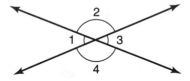

When two lines in the same plane do not meet, no matter how far they are extended in either direction, the lines are said to be *parallel* to each other. The symbol ∥ is used to indicate parallel lines.

In the diagram below, $\overleftrightarrow{RS} \parallel \overleftrightarrow{PQ}$.

Since parallel lines don't intersect, they form no angles. However, if a third line, called a *transversal*, intersects a pair of parallel lines, eight angles are formed, and the relationships between these angles are very important.

If the transversal is not perpendicular to the parallel lines, as in the diagram below, four of the angles are acute and four are obtuse; and the following important relationships hold:

1. All four acute angles are equal: m∠2 = m∠4 = m∠6 = m∠8
2. All four obtuse angles are equal: m∠1 = m∠3 = m∠5 = m∠7
3. The sum of the measures of any acute angle and any obtuse angle is 180°: for example, m∠6 + m∠5 = 180° and m∠3 + m∠8 = 180°.

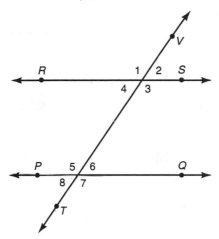

Circles

Here are some important terms and facts that you need to know about circles.

A *radius* of a circle is a line segment joining the center of the circle and any point on the circle. In the following diagram, each of $\overline{OA}$, $\overline{OC}$, and $\overline{OD}$ is a radius.

A *diameter* of a circle is a line segment that passes through the center of the circle and has its two endpoints on the circle. $\overline{CD}$ is a diameter. The length of the diameter is twice the length of the radius: $d = 2r$.

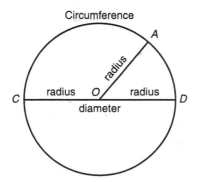

The *circumference* of a circle is the distance around the circle. In all circles, the ratio of the length of the circumference to the length of the diameter is the same. The Greek letter π (pi) is used to represent this ratio: $\pi = \dfrac{C}{d}$. Multiplying both sides of this equation by d gives $C = \pi d$ or, since $d = 2r$, $C = \pi (2r) = 2\pi r$.

The approximate value of π is 3.14; a slightly less accurate approximation is $\dfrac{22}{7}$.

Basics on Circles

Let r, d, and C represent the radius, diameter and circumference of a circle. Then

$$d = 2r$$
$$\pi = \frac{C}{d}$$
$$C = \pi d = 2\pi r$$

EXAMPLE

If the diameter of a circle is 12 inches, what is its circumference, in inches?

Use the formula $C = \pi d$:

$$C = \pi(12) = 12\pi \text{ in.}$$

This is approximately $12(3.14) = 37.68$ in.

Triangles

More geometry questions on the GED Mathematics test concern triangles than any other figure. The following box contains several important facts about triangles.

Basics on Triangles

The sum of the measures of the three angles in any triangle is 180°.

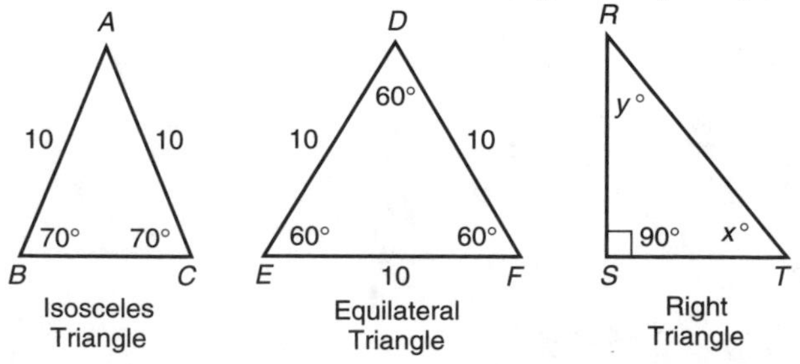

Isosceles Triangle

Equilateral Triangle

Right Triangle

A triangle that has two sides of equal length is called an *isosceles triangle*. The two angles opposite the equal sides are called *base angles*; their measures are equal. The third angle is called a *vertex angle*. △*ABC* is isosceles.

A triangle in which all three sides have the same length is called an *equilateral triangle*. Each of the three angles measures 60°. △*DEF* is equilateral.

A *right triangle* is a triangle that has one right angle. △*RST* is a right triangle; ∠*RST* is the right angle. The other two angles are acute, and the sum of their measures is 90°: $x + y = 90$. The longest side (*RT*), which is opposite the 90° angle, is called the *hypotenuse*; the other two sides (*RS* and *ST*) are *legs*.

EXAMPLE

If each base angle of an isosceles triangle measures x°, what is an expression for the measure of the third angle?

Let x = measure of each base angle,
and y = measure of the third angle.
Then $180° = x + x + y = 2x + y$
and $y = (180 - 2x)°$.

III. D. INDIRECT MEASUREMENT

If we wish to measure a length, we ordinarily use a ruler. However, this is not practicable if we wish to find the height of a mountain or the distance across a river. Such measurements are made indirectly. In this section, we will discuss one very important method of indirect measurement.

EXAMPLE

A nature group hikes 8 miles east and then 6 miles north. How many miles is the group from its starting point?

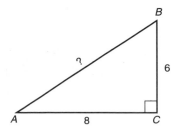

If you look at the diagram, you see that the triangle formed by the hikers is a right triangle. To solve the problem, you may make use of a well-known property of right triangles that is stated in the *Pythagorean theorem*.

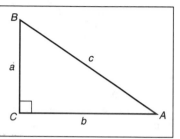

Pythagorean Theorem

Let a, b, and c be the sides of $\triangle ABC$, with $a \leq b \leq c$. If $\triangle ABC$ is a right triangle, then $a^2 + b^2 = c^2$; conversely if $a^2 + b^2 = c^2$, then $\triangle ABC$ is a right triangle.

To solve the problem about the hikers, let c = the length of the side opposite $\angle c$, and use the Pythagorean theorem:

$$c^2 = 6^2 + 8^2 = 36 + 64 = 100$$

The equation $c^2 = 100$ asks the question, "What number multiplied by itself is equal to 100?" The number that makes this statement true is $c = 10$. Thus, the nature group is 10 mi. from its starting point.

EXAMPLE

Next, suppose that the nature group had hiked 7 miles east and then 5 miles north. How many miles would the group be from the starting point?

Draw a diagram, and use the Pythagorean theorem.

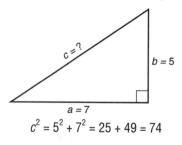

$$c^2 = 5^2 + 7^2 = 25 + 49 = 74$$

No whole number multiplied by itself equals 74. But the Pythagorean theorem assures us that such a number exists. This number is called the "square root of 74" (symbolized as $\sqrt{74}$). Since $8^2 = 64$ and $9^2 = 81$, $\sqrt{74}$ is a number between 8 and 9.

A whole number multiplied by itself is called a *perfect square.* Thus the square roots of perfect squares are whole numbers. It is useful to memorize perfect squares up to 15. These are summarized in the following table:

$1^2 = 1$	$\sqrt{1} = 1$	$9^2 = 81$	$\sqrt{81} = 9$
$2^2 = 4$	$\sqrt{4} = 2$	$10^2 = 100$	$\sqrt{100} = 10$
$3^2 = 9$	$\sqrt{9} = 3$	$11^2 = 121$	$\sqrt{121} = 11$
$4^2 = 16$	$\sqrt{16} = 4$	$12^2 = 144$	$\sqrt{144} = 12$
$5^2 = 25$	$\sqrt{25} = 5$	$13^2 = 169$	$\sqrt{169} = 13$
$6^2 = 36$	$\sqrt{36} = 6$	$14^2 = 196$	$\sqrt{196} = 14$
$7^2 = 49$	$\sqrt{49} = 7$	$15^2 = 225$	$\sqrt{225} = 15$
$8^2 = 64$	$\sqrt{64} = 8$		

There are special right triangles, called *Pythagorean triples,* in which the lengths of all three sides are whole numbers. Two of these triangles appear frequently in problems and, therefore, should be memorized:

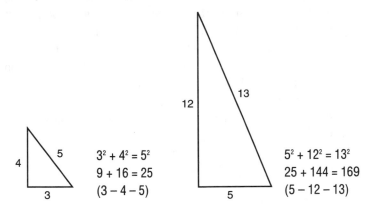

$$3^2 + 4^2 = 5^2$$
$$9 + 16 = 25$$
$$(3 - 4 - 5)$$

$$5^2 + 12^2 = 13^2$$
$$25 + 144 = 169$$
$$(5 - 12 - 13)$$

Multiples of these are also Pythagorean triples. For example, a triangle with side lengths 6, 8, and 10, or 10, 24, and 26, is also a right triangle.

EXAMPLE
A ladder 13 feet long leans against a building and reaches the ledge of a window. If the foot of the ladder is 5 feet from the foot of the building, how high, in feet, is the window ledge?

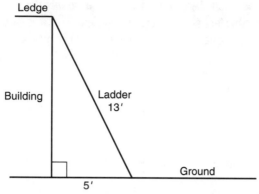

You can see that the ladder, the side of the building, and the ground form a right triangle. Two sides of the right triangle are known: 5 and 13. Therefore the third side—the height of the ledge—is 12.

III. E. CONGRUENCE AND SIMILARITY

Two geometric figures are said to be *congruent* if they have exactly the same size and the same shape. The symbol for congruence is ≅. The two triangles shown in the diagram below are congruent; that is, $\triangle ABC \cong \triangle DEF$. Since congruent triangles can be made to fit if one is placed on top of the other, corresponding sides have the same length. Also, corresponding angles of congruent triangles have the same measure. For example, in the diagram $AB = DE$, $AC = DF$, $BC = EF$, $m\angle A = m\angle D$, $m\angle B = m\angle E$, and $m\angle C = m\angle F$. Congruent triangles can be used to make measurements indirectly.

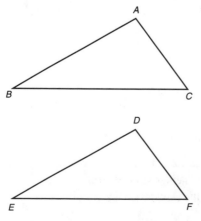

EXAMPLE

Find the distance (*DE*) across the river shown in the diagram.

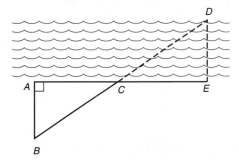

At point *E*, sight a point, *D*, on the other bank of the river. Measure *EA* at right angles to *ED*. At *C*, the midpoint of *EA*, set a stake. Then mark off distance *AB* so that ∠*A* is a right angle and point *B* lines up with points *C* and *D*. It can be shown that △*BAC* ≅ △*DEC* and that *AB* and *DE* are corresponding sides. Thus, distance *AB*, which can be measured, is equal to *DE*, the distance across the river.

Two geometric figures are said to be *similar* if they have the same shape. Because similar figures have the same shape, their corresponding angles have equal measures and the lengths of their corresponding sides are in proportion. The symbol for similarity is ~. The two triangles shown in the following diagram are similar; that is, △*ABC* ~ △*DEF*. Since the lengths of corresponding sides of similar triangles are in proportion:

$$\frac{AB}{DC} = \frac{AC}{DF} = \frac{BC}{EF}$$

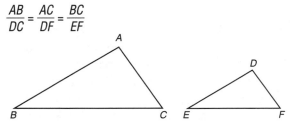

If all three angles in one triangle are equal to the measures to all three angles of a second triangle, then the triangles are similar. Similar triangles can be used to make measurements indirectly.

EXAMPLE

At a certain hour, a tree casts a shadow 24 feet long. At the same time, a post 5 feet high casts a shadow 2 feet long. What is the height of the tree?

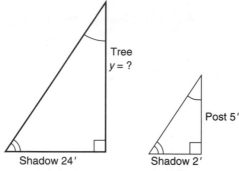

Since the measures of the angles of the two triangles are equal, the triangles are similar, and so their sides are in proportion.

$$\frac{y}{5} = \frac{24}{2}$$

$$2y = 120$$

$$y = \frac{120}{2} = 60$$

The tree is 60 ft. high.

III. F. COORDINATE GEOMETRY

There are times when we find it convenient to use pairs of numbers to locate points. For example, suppose you make an appointment to meet a friend. We might say, "Meet me at the corner of 5th Avenue and 3rd Street." We write this number pair as (5,3), where it is understood that the first number (5) indicates the avenue and the second number (3) locates the street of the meeting. On the other hand, if we wrote (3,5), we would mean that the meeting place is the corner of 3rd Avenue and 5th Street. The order in which the numbers are written is important. For this reason, such pairs of numbers are called *ordered number pairs*.

Recall that we can locate points on the number line. For example:

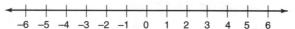

However, we may wish to locate points in the plane that are *not* on the number line. To do this, we use two number lines that are perpendicular to each other as shown below:

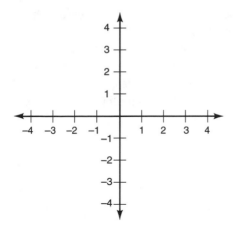

In this case, the horizontal number line is called the *x*-axis, and the vertical number line is the *y*-axis. For convenience in locating points, we draw lines parallel to the axes to form a graph chart as shown:

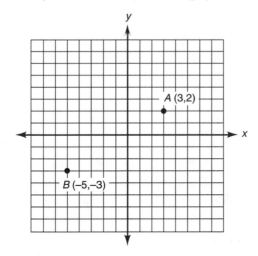

Consider point *A*. We locate point *A* in the plane by using the number pair (3,2). This indicates that point *A* is 3 units to the right of the *y*-axis and 2 units above the *x*-axis.

Consider point *B*. Point *B* is 5 units to the left of the *y*-axis and 3 units below the *x*-axis. Its number pair is (−5,−3).

To avoid confusion, we agree that the first number of the ordered pair will indicate the number of units to the right or left of the *y*-axis and the second number will indicate the number of units above or below the x-axis. The first number of the ordered pair is called the *abscissa* of the point, and the second number is the *ordinate* of the point.

Note that the two axes divide the plane into four regions. Each of these regions is called a *quadrant*. The quadrants are numbered I, II, III, and IV. The point where the coordinate axes meet is called the *origin*. The coordinates, or number pair, of the origin are (0,0).

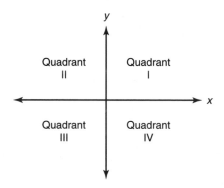

We may use the Pythagorean theorem to find the distance between two points whose coordinates are given.

EXAMPLES

Find the distance between points A (2,1) and B (6,4).

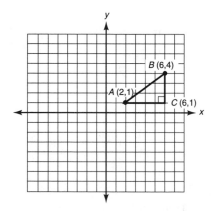

Draw $\overline{AC}$ parallel to the x-axis and $\overline{BC}$ parallel to the y-axis to form right triangle ACB with hypotenuse $\overline{AB}$.

In right triangle ACB,

$$(AB)^2 = (AC)^2 + (BC)^2$$

The coordinates of C are (6,1). To find the length of horizontal line segment $\overline{AC}$, count the number of boxes from A to C to discover that $AC = 4$. To find the length of vertical line segment $\overline{BC}$, count the number of boxes from B to C to discover that $BC = 3$.

$$(AB)^2 = (3)^2 + (4)^2 = 9 + 16 = 25$$
$$AB = \sqrt{25} = 5$$

We may use the Pythagorean theorem to derive a formula for finding the distance between two points $A\,(x_1,y_1)$ and $B\,(x_2,y_2)$.

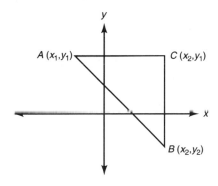

We draw $\overline{AC}$ and $\overline{BC}$ to complete a right triangle. The coordinates of point C are $(x_1 - y_2)$.

$$BC = x_2 - x_1$$
$$AC = y_2 - y_1$$

Since $(AB)^2 = (BC)^2 + (AC)^2$, $(AB)^2 = (x_2 - x_1)^2 + (y_2 - y_1)^2$

If we let $AB = d$, we have

$$d^2 = (x_2 - x_1)^2 + (y_2 - y_1)^2$$
$$d = \sqrt{(x_2 - x_1)^2 + (y_2 - y_1)^2}$$

The Distance Formula

The distance, d, between two points $A\,(x_1, y_1)$ and $B\,(x_2, y_2)$ is given by $\boldsymbol{d = \sqrt{(x_2 - x_1)^2 + (y_2 - y_1)^2}}$

EXAMPLE

Find the distance between $P(10,9)$ and $Q(2,3)$.

Use the formula $d = \sqrt{(x_2 - x_1)^2 + (y_2 - y_1)^2}$.

In this case, $x_2 = 10$, $x_1 = 2$, $y_2 = 9$, and $y_1 = 3$.

$$d = \sqrt{(10 - 2)^2 + (9 - 3)^2}$$
$$= \sqrt{8^2 + 6^2} = \sqrt{64 + 36}$$
$$= \sqrt{100} = 10$$

The Slope of a Line

In designing a road, engineers are concerned with the steepness, or slope, of the road. In this section, we will discuss the meaning and the measurement of the slope of a line.

The *slope of a line* between two points on the line is defined as the distance that the line rises between the points divided by the horizontal distance between the two points. For example, in the following diagram

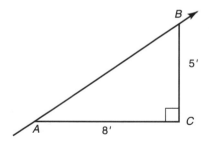

if BC represents the distance the line rises between points A and B, and AC represents the horizontal distance between points A and B, then the slope of $\overline{AB}$ is $\dfrac{5}{8}$.

In general, we can define the slope of a line as the change in the y-coordinates divided by the change in the x-coordinates of the two points.

The Slope Formula

The slope, m, of the line passing through two points $A(x_1, y_1)$ and $B(x_2, y_2)$ is given by

$$m = \frac{y_2 - y_1}{x_2 - x_1}$$

EXAMPLE

Find the slope of the line joining points A (2,1) and B (5,8).

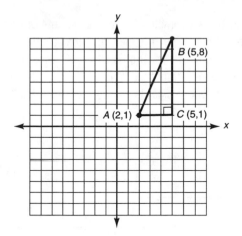

Of course, you should just use the slope formula:

$$m = \frac{8-1}{5-2} = \frac{7}{3}.$$

If you forget the formula, however, you can proceed as follows:

Draw $\overline{AC}$ parallel to the x-axis and $\overline{BC}$ parallel to the y-axis.

Slope of $\overline{AB} = \dfrac{\text{change in } y\text{-coordinates}}{\text{change in } x\text{-coordinates}} = \dfrac{CB}{AC}$

By counting, you find that $CB = 7$ and that $AC = 3$.

The slope of $\overline{AB} = \dfrac{CB}{AC} = \dfrac{7}{3}.$

III. G. PERIMETERS

Mr. Wells had a garden 60 feet long and 40 feet wide. He wished to fence in the garden. How many feet of fencing did he need?

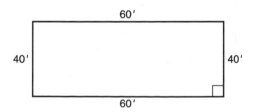

We can see that Mr. Wells needed two lengths of 60 feet each and two widths of 40 feet each. Thus, he needed $(2 \times 60) + (2 \times 40)$, or $120 + 80 = 200$ feet.

The *perimeter* of any plane geometric figure is a measure of its outside boundary. For a circle, the perimeter is the circumference; for a polygon, the perimeter is the sum of the lengths of all of the sides. For example, the perimeter of a 3–4–5 right triangle is $3 + 4 + 5 = 12$, and the perimeter of a square each of whose sides is 5 is $5 + 5 + 5 + 5 = 4(5) = 20$.

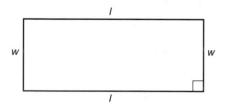

Perimeter of a Rectangle

   If the length and width of a rectangle are denoted by *l* and *w*, and its perimeter by *P*, then

$$P = l + w + l + w = 2l + 2w = 2(l + w)$$

III. H. AREAS

If we wish to find the amount of carpeting needed to cover a floor, we have the problem of finding the surface area of the floor. In finding a length, we use units such as 1 foot, 1 yard, or 1 mile. To find the area of a floor, our unit of measure is 1 square foot or 1 square yard. Below are diagrams of 1 square foot and 1 square yard.

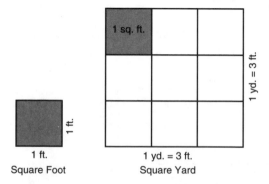

1 ft.
Square Foot

1 yd. = 3 ft.
Square Yard

If we wish to find the number of square feet in a floor, we must find the number of square feet units that will cover the floor. Similarly, if we wish to find the number of square yards in the floor, we must find the number of square yard units that will cover the floor. Let us see how this works in the following example.

EXAMPLE

The wooden board shown below measures 6 feet by 9 feet. What is the area of the board (a) in square feet, (b) in square yards?

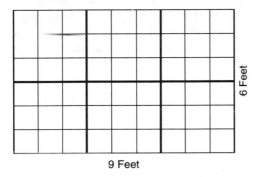

9 Feet

(a) Since there are 9-ft. units along the length and 6-ft. units along the width, the area of the board is 54 sq. ft.

(b) Since there are 3-yd. units along the length and 2-yd. units along the width, the area of the board is 6 sq. yd. As the diagram indicates, there are 9 sq. ft. in 1 sq. yd.

The following box contains all of the area formulas that you need to know for the GED Mathematics test.

AREA FORMULAS
Rectangle
The area of a rectangle is the product of its length (*l*) and width (*w*): $A = lw$.

w (width)

l (length)

Square

Since a square is a rectangle, its area is also given by $A = lw$. In a square, however, the length and width are equal and each is usually called a side (s), so $A = s^2$.

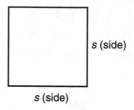

s (side)

s (side)

Parallelogram

The area of a parallelogram is the product of its base (b) and height (h). Note in the diagram below that the base is a side of the parallelogram, but the height is not—the height is perpendicular to the base:

$A = bh.$

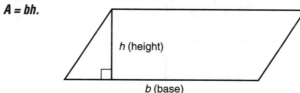

h (height)

b (base)

Triangle

Since a triangle is half a parallelogram, its area is given by the formula:

$A = \dfrac{1}{2}bh.$

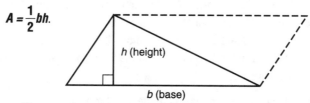

h (height)

b (base)

Trapezoid

The two parallel sides of a trapezoid are called bases (b_1 and b_2). The area of a trapezoid is the product of the height and the average of the two bases:

$$A = h\left(\dfrac{b_1 + b_2}{2}\right) \ \text{ or } \ A = \dfrac{1}{2}h(b_1 + b_2).$$

b_2 (upper base)

h (height)

b_1 (lower base)

Circle
The area of a circle is given by the formula $A = \pi r^2$.

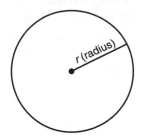

EXAMPLE
Find the area of a rectangle whose length is twice its width and whose perimeter is 60 inches.

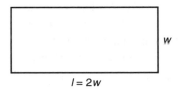

$l = 2w$

In the formula $P = 2(l + w)$, replace l by $2w$:

$60 = 2(2w + w) = 2(3w) = 6w$

Then $w = 10$ in. and $l = 20$ in., so

$A = 20(10) = 200$ sq. in.

EXAMPLE
Find the area of a circle whose diameter is 20 centimeters.

Since the radius is one-half of the diameter, $r = 10$ cm, and $A = \pi(10)^2 = 100\pi$ sq. cm.

You can get a more useful answer, however, by approximating π by 3.14:

$A \approx 100(3.14) = 314$ sq. cm

III. I. VOLUMES

If we want to know the amount of space that a box occupies, we must determine its *volume*. Just as length is measured in units such as inches, feet, and meters, and area is measured in square inches, square feet, and square meters, volume is measured in cubic inches, cubic feet, and cubic meters. One cubic inch is the amount of space that is taken up by a cube each of whose edges is 1 inch long.

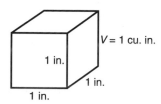

Thus, if we want to find the volume of a box that is 4 inches long, 3 inches wide, and 2 inches high, we have to determine how many 1-inch cubes can fit in the box. From the following figure, we can see that we can fit 4 cubes along the length and 3 cubes along the width. We can therefore fit 12 cubes in one layer. Since we can place 2 layers in the box, the volume of the box is $2 \times 12 = 24$ cubic inches. In general, the volume of a box (called a *rectangular solid*) is obtained by multiplying the number of units in the length by the number of units in the width by the number of units in the height. In this case, $V = 4 \times 3 \times 2 = 24$ cubic inches.

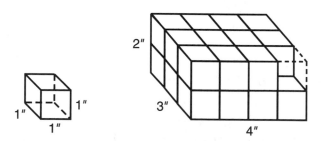

The formula for the *volume of a rectangular solid* is

$$V = lwh$$

If we wish to find the volume of a cube, we note that, in a cube, the length, width, and height are equal. If we represent each dimension of a cube by *s*, then:

The formula for the *volume* of a cube is

$$V = s^3$$

EXAMPLE

A coal bin is in the form of a rectangular solid. The bin is 14 feet long, 10 feet wide, and 6 feet high. If 1 ton of coal occupies 35 cubic feet of space, and the bin is two-thirds full, how many tons of coal are in the bin?

Volume of bin = *lwh* = $14 \times 10 \times 6$ = 840 cu. ft.

Since the bin is two-thirds full, the number of cubic feet of coal in the bin is $\frac{2}{3} \times 840 = 560$. To find the number of tons in the bin, divide: $560 \div 35 = 16$.

An important solid figure that we encounter frequently is the cylinder. In a cylinder, the upper and lower bases are circles that lie in parallel planes. The volume of a cylinder is obtained by multiplying the area of one base by the height.

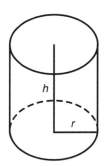

The formula for the *volume of a cylinder* is

$$V = \pi r^2 h$$

EXAMPLE

A storage oil tank in the form of a cylinder is three-fourths full. The radius of the base of the tank is 10 feet, and the height of the tank is 20 feet. Find the number of gallons of oil in the tank if each cubic foot of space holds 8 gallons of oil. [Approximate π by 3.14.]

$$\text{Volume of cylinder} = \pi r^2 h$$
$$= 3.14(10)(10)(20)$$
$$= 6,280 \text{ cu. ft.}$$

Since the tank is $\frac{3}{4}$ full, it contains

$\frac{3}{4} \times 6,280 = 4,710$ cu. ft. of oil.

Since each cubic foot of oil is 8 gal., the number of gallons of oil is $8(4,710) = 37,680$.

III. J. AREAS OF SURFACES OF SOLIDS

We are sometimes interested in the area of the surface of a solid figure. For example, a room is in the form of a rectangular solid. If we wish to paint the room, we will be interested in the area of the walls and ceiling.

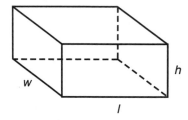

We can see that the area of the surface of the rectangular solid in the diagram is obtained by adding *lw* (bottom) + *lw* (top) + *wh* (side) + *wh* (side) + *lh* (front) + *lh* (back).

A formula for the area of the *surface of a rectangular solid* is

$$A = 2lw + 2wh + 2lh$$

As another example, the label on a cylindrical can (or cylinder) covers only the area on the side of the can.

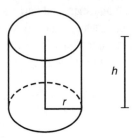

The formula for the *side area of a cylinder*, called the *lateral area*, is

$$A = 2\pi rh$$

EXAMPLE

Find the number of square feet of cardboard used to make a carton 4 feet long, 3 feet wide, and 2 feet high.

Use the formula

$A = 2lw + 2wh + 2lh$

In this case, $l = 4$, $w = 3$, and $h = 2$:

$A = 2 \times 4 \times 3 + 2 \times 3 \times 2 + 2 \times 4 \times 2$

$A = 24 + 12 + 16 = 52$

EXAMPLE

A can has a radius of $3\frac{1}{2}$ inches and is 5 inches high. What is the area of the label used on the can? [Use $\pi = \frac{22}{7}$.]

Lateral area of cylinder = $2\pi rh$

$$= 2 \times \frac{22}{7} \times \frac{7}{2} \times 5$$
$$= 110$$

The area of the label is 110 sq. in.

IV. GRAPHS

Pictures or graphs are often used in reports, magazines, and newspapers to present a set of numerical facts. These visual devices enable the viewer to make comparisons and to draw quick conclusions. In this section, we will learn how to interpret *pictographs, bar graphs, line graphs, circle graphs,* and *formula graphs.*

IV. A. PICTOGRAPHS

A *pictograph* is a graph in which objects are used to represent numbers.

EXAMPLE

**POPULATIONS OF VARIOUS CITIES
IN A CERTAIN STATE**

Each House Symbol Represents 10,000 People

1.   Which city has the largest population?
     ANSWER: City E

2.   What is the ratio of the population of city B to city C?
     ANSWER: City B has 45,000 people.
              City C has 60,000 people.
              Ratio is 45,000 : 60,000, which reduces to 3 : 4.

IV. B. BAR GRAPHS

A *bar graph* is used to show relationships among a set of quantities. Here, bars are used as opposed to the pictures in a pictograph.

EXAMPLE
In a recent year, a large industrial concern used each dollar of its sales income as shown in the following graph.

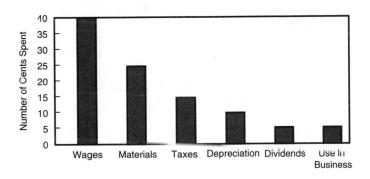

1. How many cents of each dollar of sales income did the company use to pay wages?
   ANSWER: 40

2. How many more cents of each sales dollar were spent on wages than on materials?
   answer.   40 − 25 = 15

IV. C. LINE GRAPHS

A *line graph* is especially helpful in showing changes over a period of time.

EXAMPLE
The graph below shows the growth in motor vehicle registration in a certain state.

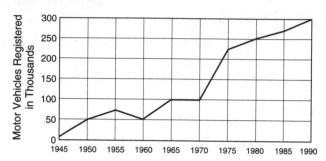

1. Approximately how many times as many motor vehicles were registered in 1980 as in 1950?

   ANSWER: Registered in 1980—250,000
   Registered in 1950—50,000

   There were 5 times as many motor vehicles registered in 1980 as in 1950.

2. What percent increase in registration took place between 1960 and 1990?

   ANSWER: Registered in 1960—50,000
   Registered in 1990—300,000
   Increase in registration—250,000
   Percent increase =

   $\dfrac{\text{original}}{\text{increase}} = \dfrac{50,000}{250,000}$ or 500%

IV. D. CIRCLE GRAPHS

A *circle graph* is used when a quantity is divided into parts, and we wish to make a comparison of the parts. Recall that a circle can be divided into 360°. Thus, if we wish to mark off one-quarter of the circle, the angle at the center must be $\dfrac{1}{4} \times 360°$, or 90°. For the same reason, a part of the circle with an angle at the center of 60° will be $\dfrac{60}{360}$, or $\dfrac{1}{6}$ of the circle.

EXAMPLE

The circle graph below shows how the wage earners in a certain city earned their livings in a certain year.

WHAT WAGE EARNERS DID

1. What fractional part of the labor force worked in personal services?

    ANSWER: $\dfrac{45}{360} = \dfrac{1}{8}$

2. If there were 180,000 workers in the city, how many were engaged in manufacturing?

    ANSWER: The fractional part of the workers engaged in manufacturing

    was $\dfrac{120}{360} = \dfrac{1}{3}$.

    $\dfrac{1}{3}$ of 180,000 = 60,000

V. MEASUREMENT

V. A. LENGTH

The most *common measures of length* are

12 inches = 1 foot
3 feet = 1 yard
5,280 feet = 1 mile

We often use the following abbreviations: *in.* for inches, *ft.* for feet, and *yd.* for yards.

EXAMPLE

A plumber has a pipe $\frac{3}{4}$ yard in length. If he cuts off a piece 23 inches long, how much pipe does he have left?

1 yd. = 3 ft. = 3(12 in.) = 36 in.

$\frac{3}{4}$ yd. = $\frac{3}{4}$ (36 in.) = 27 in.

There are 27 − 23 = 4 in. of pipe left.

V. B. TIME

The most *common measures of time* are

$$60 \text{ seconds} = 1 \text{ minute}$$
$$60 \text{ minutes} = 1 \text{ hour}$$
$$24 \text{ hours} = 1 \text{ day}$$
$$7 \text{ days} = 1 \text{ week}$$
$$12 \text{ months} = 1 \text{ year}$$
$$365 \text{ days} = 1 \text{ year}$$

EXAMPLE

A man works from 9:45 a.m. until 1:30 p.m. How many hours does he work?

From 9:45 a.m. to 10:00 a.m. is 15 min.

15 min. = $\frac{15}{60}$ hr. = $\frac{1}{4}$ hr.

From 10:00 a.m. to 1:00 p.m. is 3 hrs.

From 1:00 p.m. to 1:30 p.m. is 30 min.

30 min. = $\frac{30}{60}$ hr. = $\frac{1}{2}$ hr.

The man works $\frac{1}{4}$ + 3 + $\frac{1}{2}$ = $3\frac{3}{4}$ hr.

V. C. WEIGHT

The most *commonly used measures of weight* are

$$16 \text{ ounces} = 1 \text{ pound}$$
$$2,000 \text{ pounds} = 1 \text{ ton}$$

We often use the following abbreviations: *lb.* for pound and *oz.* for ounce.

EXAMPLE

How many 2-ounce portions of candy can be obtained from a 10-pound box?

Since there are 16 oz. in 1 lb., each lb. of candy will yield $\frac{16}{2}$, or 8 portions. Therefore,

10 lbs. of candy will yield 8×10, or 80, portions.

V. D. LIQUID MEASURE

The most *commonly used liquid measures* are

8 ounces = 1 cup
2 cups = 1 pint

2 pints = 1 quart
4 quarts = 1 gallon

We often use the following abbreviations: *pt.* for pint, *qt.* for quart, and *gal.* for gallon.

CAUTION: The word *ounce* is used as both a unit of weight and a unit of liquid measure, but the two are unrelated. For example, 1 ounce of water does *not* weigh 1 ounce.

EXAMPLE

A snack bar sells milk in half-pint containers for 15 cents. If 3 gallons of milk are sold one morning, how much money is taken in?

Since a half-pint container sells for 15 cents, a full pint sells for 30 cents. Thus, 1 qt. sells for 60 cents, 1 gal. sells for $2.40, and 3 gal. sell for $3 \times \$2.40 = \$7.20$.

V. E. THE METRIC SYSTEM

The *metric system* of measures is used in most scientific work and for all purposes in most foreign countries. The metric system is also used to some degree in the United States for nonscientific measurements, and it may be used more extensively in the future. It is especially useful because its units are related by powers of 10. In this section we will consider the most frequently used metric measures and will cover the aspects of the metric system that may appear on the GED Examination.

In the metric system, the basic unit of length is the *meter,* the basic unit of weight is the *gram*, and the basic unit of liquid measure is the *liter*. To name units that are larger or smaller than these, we use prefixes. The most common prefixes are:

- *kilo-*, which means 1,000
- *centi-*, which means $\dfrac{1}{100}$
- *milli-*, which means $\dfrac{1}{1,000}$

Metric Units of Length

One *meter* (m) is slightly more than 1 yard (approximately 39 inches) and is useful for measuring distances between a few feet and a mile.

Large distances, such as the distance between cities or the distance from the Earth to the Sun, are measured in *kilometers* (km).

One kilometer is approximately $\dfrac{5}{8}$ mile.

1 kilometer = 1,000 meters

1 meter = $\dfrac{1}{1,000}$ kilometer

For measuring short distances, such as the dimensions of a piece of paper or the length of a pencil, the *centimeter* (cm) is used.

One centimeter is slightly less than $\dfrac{1}{2}$ inch.

1 centimeter = $\dfrac{1}{100}$ meter

1 meter = 100 centimeters

For even smaller lengths, such as the width of a human hair or the thickness of a piece of paper, the *millimeter* (mm) is used.

1 millimeter = $\dfrac{1}{1,000}$ meter

1 meter = 1,000 millimeters

EXAMPLES

How many meters are there in 5 kilometers?

Since 1 km = 1,000 m, 5 km = 5 × 1,000 = 5,000 m.

How many centimeters are there in 8,000 millimeters?

$$8,000 \text{ mm} = 8,000 \left(\frac{1}{1,000}\right) \text{ m} = 8 \text{ m}$$
$$8 \text{ m} = 8 (100 \text{ cm}) = 800 \text{ cm}$$

Metric Units of Weight

A *gram* (g) is a light weight. There are approximately 28 grams in 1 ounce, or 454 grams in 1 pound. For example, a pat of butter weighs about 3 grams, and an apple may weigh 150 or 200 grams. Heavier weights, such as the weight of a person, a truck, or even the Earth, are measured in *kilograms* (kg). A *kilogram* is approximately 2.2 pounds.

1 kilogram = 1,000 grams

$$1 \text{ gram} = \frac{1}{1,000} \text{ kilogram}$$

For measuring very light objects, like the small quantities of drugs that a pharmacist uses, the *milligram* (mg) is used.

$$1 \text{ milligram} = \frac{1}{1,000} \text{ gram}$$

1 gram = 1,000 milligrams

EXAMPLE

A cake weighs 250 grams. How many kilograms does the cake weigh?

$$250g = 250 \left(\frac{1}{1,000}\text{kg}\right) = \frac{1}{4} \text{ kg} = 0.25 \text{ kg}$$

Metric Units of Liquid Measure

In the metric system, the basic unit of liquid measure is the *liter*. One liter contains a little more than 1 quart. In countries where the metric system is used, it is convenient to sell milk and gasoline in liter units.

For measuring large liquid quantities, the *kiloliter* may be used.

1 kiloliter = 1,000 liters

$$1 \text{ liter} = \frac{1}{1,000} \text{ kiloliter}$$

Small quantities of liquid, in a pharmacy or a laboratory, for example, are measured in *milliliters*.

1 milliliter = $\dfrac{1}{1,000}$ liter

1 liter = 1,000 milliliters

EXAMPLE

A glass contains 0.5 liter of milk. How many milliliters is this?

0.5 liter = 0.5(1,000) = 500 milliliters

8

A PRACTICE EXAMINATION

The direction sheets, mathematics formulas,* and question formats of this examination are constructed like the actual test you will take. The examination consists of five parts.

Tests	Questions	Time Allowance
Test 1: The Writing Skills Test, Part I	55	1 hour, 15 minutes
The Writing Skills Test, Part II	Essay	45 minutes
Test 2: The Social Studies Test	64	1 hour, 25 minutes
Test 3: The Science Test	66	1 hour, 35 minutes
Test 4: The Interpreting Literature and the Arts Test	45	1 hour, 5 minutes
Test 5: The Mathematics Test	56	1 hour, 30 minutes
	Total:	7 hours, 35 minutes

For this examination, we have included an answer sheet and a self-appraisal chart. Mark yourself on each test, checking your answers against the answer key. Read the answer explanations to be sure you understand the correct answer choices. After you have calculated the scores for all five tests, refer to the self-appraisal materials to determine your subject area strengths and weaknesses as well as your total GED score.

The main purpose of the test is to help you discover your strengths and your weaknesses. IMPORTANT: You should spend more time studying those chapters that deal with the tests in which you are weakest. In that way, you will improve your score when you take the two practice examinations at the end of this book.

SIMULATE TEST CONDITIONS

To make conditions similar to those on the actual examination, do not take more time than that allowed for each test.

*Directions and mathematics formulas are reprinted by permission of the GED Testing Service of the American Council on Education.

ANSWER SHEET—PRACTICE EXAMINATION

Test 1: The Writing Skills Test

1. ① ② ③ ④ ⑤
2. ① ② ③ ④ ⑤
3. ① ② ③ ④ ⑤
4. ① ② ③ ④ ⑤
5. ① ② ③ ④ ⑤
6. ① ② ③ ④ ⑤
7. ① ② ③ ④ ⑤
8. ① ② ③ ④ ⑤
9. ① ② ③ ④ ⑤
10. ① ② ③ ④ ⑤
11. ① ② ③ ④ ⑤
12. ① ② ③ ④ ⑤
13. ① ② ③ ④ ⑤
14. ① ② ③ ④ ⑤
15. ① ② ③ ④ ⑤
16. ① ② ③ ④ ⑤
17. ① ② ③ ④ ⑤
18. ① ② ③ ④ ⑤
19. ① ② ③ ④ ⑤

20. ① ② ③ ④ ⑤
21. ① ② ③ ④ ⑤
22. ① ② ③ ④ ⑤
23. ① ② ③ ④ ⑤
24. ① ② ③ ④ ⑤
25. ① ② ③ ④ ⑤
26. ① ② ③ ④ ⑤
27. ① ② ③ ④ ⑤
28. ① ② ③ ④ ⑤
29. ① ② ③ ④ ⑤
30. ① ② ③ ④ ⑤
31. ① ② ③ ④ ⑤
32. ① ② ③ ④ ⑤
33. ① ② ③ ④ ⑤
34. ① ② ③ ④ ⑤
35. ① ② ③ ④ ⑤
36. ① ② ③ ④ ⑤
37. ① ② ③ ④ ⑤
38. ① ② ③ ④ ⑤

39. ① ② ③ ④ ⑤
40. ① ② ③ ④ ⑤
41. ① ② ③ ④ ⑤
42. ① ② ③ ④ ⑤
43. ① ② ③ ④ ⑤
44. ① ② ③ ④ ⑤
45. ① ② ③ ④ ⑤
46. ① ② ③ ④ ⑤
47. ① ② ③ ④ ⑤
48. ① ② ③ ④ ⑤
49. ① ② ③ ④ ⑤
50. ① ② ③ ④ ⑤
51. ① ② ③ ④ ⑤
52. ① ② ③ ④ ⑤
53. ① ② ③ ④ ⑥
54. ① ② ③ ④ ⑤
55. ① ② ③ ④ ⑤

Test 2: The Social Studies Test

1. ① ② ③ ④ ⑤
2. ① ② ③ ④ ⑤
3. ① ② ③ ④ ⑤
4. ① ② ③ ④ ⑤
5. ① ② ③ ④ ⑤
6. ① ② ③ ④ ⑤
7. ① ② ③ ④ ⑤
8. ① ② ③ ④ ⑤
9. ① ② ③ ④ ⑤
10. ① ② ③ ④ ⑤
11. ① ② ③ ④ ⑤
12. ① ② ③ ④ ⑤

13. ① ② ③ ④ ⑤
14. ① ② ③ ④ ⑤
15. ① ② ③ ④ ⑤
16. ① ② ③ ④ ⑤
17. ① ② ③ ④ ⑤
18. ① ② ③ ④ ⑤
19. ① ② ③ ④ ⑤
20. ① ② ③ ④ ⑤
21. ① ② ③ ④ ⑤
22. ① ② ③ ④ ⑤
23. ① ② ③ ④ ⑤
24. ① ② ③ ④ ⑤

25. ① ② ③ ④ ⑤
26. ① ② ③ ④ ⑤
27. ① ② ③ ④ ⑤
28. ① ② ③ ④ ⑤
29. ① ② ③ ④ ⑤
30. ① ② ③ ④ ⑤
31. ① ② ③ ④ ⑤
32. ① ② ③ ④ ⑤
33. ① ② ③ ④ ⑤
34. ① ② ③ ④ ⑤
35. ① ② ③ ④ ⑤
36. ① ② ③ ④ ⑤

37. ① ② ③ ④ ⑤   47. ① ② ③ ④ ⑤   56. ① ② ③ ④ ⑤
38. ① ② ③ ④ ⑤   48. ① ② ③ ④ ⑤   57. ① ② ③ ④ ⑤
39. ① ② ③ ④ ⑤   49. ① ② ③ ④ ⑤   58. ① ② ③ ④ ⑤
40. ① ② ③ ④ ⑤   50. ① ② ③ ④ ⑤   59. ① ② ③ ④ ⑤
41. ① ② ③ ④ ⑤   51. ① ② ③ ④ ⑤   60. ① ② ③ ④ ⑤
42. ① ② ③ ④ ⑤   52. ① ② ③ ④ ⑤   61. ① ② ③ ④ ⑤
43. ① ② ③ ④ ⑤   53. ① ② ③ ④ ⑤   62. ① ② ③ ④ ⑤
44. ① ② ③ ④ ⑤   54. ① ② ③ ④ ⑤   63. ① ② ③ ④ ⑤
45. ① ② ③ ④ ⑤   55. ① ② ③ ④ ⑤   64. ① ② ③ ④ ⑤
46. ① ② ③ ④ ⑤   55. ① ② ③ ④ ⑤

Test 3: The Science Test

1. ① ② ③ ④ ⑤   24. ① ② ③ ④ ⑤   47. ① ② ③ ④ ⑤
2. ① ② ③ ④ ⑤   25. ① ② ③ ④ ⑤   48. ① ② ③ ④ ⑤
3. ① ② ③ ④ ⑤   26. ① ② ③ ④ ⑤   49. ① ② ③ ④ ⑤
4. ① ② ③ ④ ⑤   27. ① ② ③ ④ ⑤   50. ① ② ③ ④ ⑤
5. ① ② ③ ④ ⑤   28. ① ② ③ ④ ⑤   51. ① ② ③ ④ ⑤
6. ① ② ③ ④ ⑤   29. ① ② ③ ④ ⑤   52. ① ② ③ ④ ⑤
7. ① ② ③ ④ ⑤   30. ① ② ③ ④ ⑤   53. ① ② ③ ④ ⑤
8. ① ② ③ ④ ⑤   31. ① ② ③ ④ ⑤   54. ① ② ③ ④ ⑤
9. ① ② ③ ④ ⑤   32. ① ② ③ ④ ⑤   55. ① ② ③ ④ ⑤
10. ① ② ③ ④ ⑤   33. ① ② ③ ④ ⑤   56. ① ② ③ ④ ⑤
11. ① ② ③ ④ ⑤   34. ① ② ③ ④ ⑤   57. ① ② ③ ④ ⑤
12. ① ② ③ ④ ⑤   35. ① ② ③ ④ ⑤   58. ① ② ③ ④ ⑤
13. ① ② ③ ④ ⑤   36. ① ② ③ ④ ⑤   59. ① ② ③ ④ ⑤
14. ① ② ③ ④ ⑤   37. ① ② ③ ④ ⑤   60. ① ② ③ ④ ⑤
15. ① ② ③ ④ ⑤   38. ① ② ③ ④ ⑤   61. ① ② ③ ④ ⑤
16. ① ② ③ ④ ⑤   39. ① ② ③ ④ ⑤   62. ① ② ③ ④ ⑤
17. ① ② ③ ④ ⑤   40. ① ② ③ ④ ⑤   63. ① ② ③ ④ ⑤
18. ① ② ③ ④ ⑤   41. ① ② ③ ④ ⑤   64. ① ② ③ ④ ⑤
19. ① ② ③ ④ ⑤   42. ① ② ③ ④ ⑤   65. ① ② ③ ④ ⑤
20. ① ② ③ ④ ⑤   43. ① ② ③ ④ ⑤   66. ① ② ③ ④ ⑤
21. ① ② ③ ④ ⑤   44. ① ② ③ ④ ⑤
22. ① ② ③ ④ ⑤   45. ① ② ③ ④ ⑤
23. ① ② ③ ④ ⑤   46. ① ② ③ ④ ⑤

Test 4: The Interpreting Literature and Arts Test

1. ① ② ③ ④ ⑤
2. ① ② ③ ④ ⑤
3. ① ② ③ ④ ⑤
4. ① ② ③ ④ ⑤
5. ① ② ③ ④ ⑤
6. ① ② ③ ④ ⑤
7. ① ② ③ ④ ⑤
8. ① ② ③ ④ ⑤
9. ① ② ③ ④ ⑤
10. ① ② ③ ④ ⑤
11. ① ② ③ ④ ⑤
12. ① ② ③ ④ ⑤
13. ① ② ③ ④ ⑤
14. ① ② ③ ④ ⑤
15. ① ② ③ ④ ⑤

16. ① ② ③ ④ ⑤
17. ① ② ③ ④ ⑤
18. ① ② ③ ④ ⑤
19. ① ② ③ ④ ⑤
20. ① ② ③ ④ ⑤
21. ① ② ③ ④ ⑤
22. ① ② ③ ④ ⑤
23. ① ② ③ ④ ⑤
24. ① ② ③ ④ ⑤
25. ① ② ③ ④ ⑤
26. ① ② ③ ④ ⑤
27. ① ② ③ ④ ⑤
28. ① ② ③ ④ ⑤
29. ① ② ③ ④ ⑤
30. ① ② ③ ④ ⑤

31. ① ② ③ ④ ⑤
32. ① ② ③ ④ ⑤
33. ① ② ③ ④ ⑤
34. ① ② ③ ④ ⑤
35. ① ② ③ ④ ⑤
36. ① ② ③ ④ ⑤
37. ① ② ③ ④ ⑤
38. ① ② ③ ④ ⑤
39. ① ② ③ ④ ⑤
40. ① ② ③ ④ ⑤
41. ① ② ③ ④ ⑤
42. ① ② ③ ④ ⑤
43. ① ② ③ ④ ⑤
44. ① ② ③ ④ ⑤
45. ① ② ③ ④ ⑤

Test 5: The Mathematics Test

1. ① ② ③ ④ ⑤
2. ① ② ③ ④ ⑤
3. ① ② ③ ④ ⑤
4. ① ② ③ ④ ⑤
5. ① ② ③ ④ ⑤
6. ① ② ③ ④ ⑤
7. ① ② ③ ④ ⑤
8. ① ② ③ ④ ⑤
9. ① ② ③ ④ ⑤
10. ① ② ③ ④ ⑤
11. ① ② ③ ④ ⑤
12. ① ② ③ ④ ⑤
13. ① ② ③ ④ ⑤
14. ① ② ③ ④ ⑤
15. ① ② ③ ④ ⑤
16. ① ② ③ ④ ⑤
17. ① ② ③ ④ ⑤
18. ① ② ③ ④ ⑤
19. ① ② ③ ④ ⑤

20. ① ② ③ ④ ⑤
21. ① ② ③ ④ ⑤
22. ① ② ③ ④ ⑤
23. ① ② ③ ④ ⑤
24. ① ② ③ ④ ⑤
25. ① ② ③ ④ ⑤
26. ① ② ③ ④ ⑤
27. ① ② ③ ④ ⑤
28. ① ② ③ ④ ⑤
29. ① ② ③ ④ ⑤
30. ① ② ③ ④ ⑤
31. ① ② ③ ④ ⑤
32. ① ② ③ ④ ⑤
33. ① ② ③ ④ ⑤
34. ① ② ③ ④ ⑤
35. ① ② ③ ④ ⑤
36. ① ② ③ ④ ⑤
37. ① ② ③ ④ ⑤
38. ① ② ③ ④ ⑤

39. ① ② ③ ④ ⑤
40. ① ② ③ ④ ⑤
41. ① ② ③ ④ ⑤
42. ① ② ③ ④ ⑤
43. ① ② ③ ④ ⑤
44. ① ② ③ ④ ⑤
45. ① ② ③ ④ ⑤
46. ① ② ③ ④ ⑤
47. ① ② ③ ④ ⑤
48. ① ② ③ ④ ⑤
49. ① ② ③ ④ ⑤
50. ① ② ③ ④ ⑤
51. ① ② ③ ④ ⑤
52. ① ② ③ ④ ⑤
53. ① ② ③ ④ ⑤
54. ① ② ③ ④ ⑤
55. ① ② ③ ④ ⑤
56. ① ② ③ ④ ⑤

PRACTICE EXAMINATION

TEST 1: WRITING SKILLS, PART I

Directions

Alloted Time: 75 minutes

The Writing Skills test is intended to measure your ability to use clear and effective English. It is a test of English as it should be written, not as it might be spoken. This test includes both multiple-choice questions and an essay. These directions apply only to the multiple-choice section; a separate set of directions is given for the essay.

The multiple-choice section consists of paragraphs with numbered sentences. Some of the sentences contain errors in sentence structure, usage, or mechanics (spelling, punctuation, and capitalization). After reading the numbered sentences, answer the multiple-choice questions that follow. Some questions refer to sentences that are correct as written. The best answer for these questions is the one that leaves the sentence as originally written. The best answer for some questions is the one that produces a sentence that is consistent with the verb tense and point of view used throughout the paragraph.

You should spend no more than 75 minutes on the multiple-choice questions and 45 minutes on your essay. Work carefully, but do not spend too much time on any one question. You may begin working on the essay part of this test as soon as you complete the multiple-choice section.

To record your answers, mark the numbered space on the answer sheet beside the number that corresponds to the question in the test.

FOR EXAMPLE:

Sentence 1: **We were all honored to meet governor Phillips.**

What correction should be made to this sentence?

(1) insert a comma after <u>honored</u>
(2) change the spelling of <u>honored</u> to <u>honered</u>
(3) change <u>governor</u> to <u>Governor</u>
(4) replace <u>were</u> with <u>was</u>
(5) no correction is necessary

In this example, the word "governor" should be capitalized; therefore, answer space 3 would be marked on the answer sheet.

Questions 1 to 9 refer to the following paragraph.

(1) A combination of attributes make vegetable gardening a national hobby with both young and old. (2) For an ever-increasing number of individuals seed catalogs and the thoughts of spring gardening provide a happy escape from the winter doldrums. (3) Vegetable gardeners unanimously agree that many home-grown vegetables picked at their peak of maturity have quality. seldom found in vegetables purchased from commercial markets. (4) From Spring to late Fall, a well-planned and maintained garden can provide a supply of fresh vegetables, thus increasing the nutritional value of the family diet. (5) Freezers make it possible to preserve some of the surplus vegetables to be enjoyed at a later date other vegetables can be stored for a few months in a cool area. (6) Not to be overlooked is the finger-tip convenience of having vegetables in the backyard; this in itself justifies home gardening for many individuals. (7) In addition, vegetable gardening provides excercise and recreation for both urban and suburban families. (8) Although your initial dollar investment for gardening may be nominal, one cannot escape the fact that gardening requires manual labor and time. (9) Neglecting jobs that should be performed on a regular basis may result in failure and a negative feeling toward gardening.

1. Sentence 1: **A combination of attributes make vegetable gardening a national hobby with both young and old.**

   What correction should be made to this sentence?
   (1) insert a comma after <u>attributes</u>
   (2) change <u>make</u> to <u>makes</u>
   (3) capitalize vegetable gardening
   (4) reverse <u>with</u> and <u>both</u>
   (5) no correction is necessary

2. Sentence 2: **For an ever-increasing number of individuals seed catalogs and the thoughts of spring gardening provide a happy escape from the winter doldrums.**

   What correction should be made to this sentence?
   (1) remove the hyphen from <u>ever-increasing</u>
   (2) change <u>number</u> to <u>amount</u>
   (3) insert a comma after <u>individuals</u>
   (4) insert a comma after <u>catalogs</u>
   (5) no correction is necessary

3. Sentence 3: **Vegetable gardeners unanimously agree that many home-grown vegetables picked at their peak of maturity have <u>quality, seldom</u> found in vegetables purchased from commercial markets.**

   Which of the following is the best way to write the underlined portion of this sentence? If you think the original is the best way, choose option (1).
   (1) quality. seldom
   (2) quality. Seldom
   (3) quality seldom
   (4) quality; seldom
   (5) quality, seldom

4. Sentence 4: **From Spring to late Fall, a well-planned and maintained garden can provide a supply of fresh vegetables, thus increasing the nutritional value of the family diet.**

   What correction should be made to this sentence?
   (1) remove capitals from <u>Spring</u> and <u>Fall</u>
   (2) remove the hyphen from <u>well-planned</u>
   (3) remove the comma after <u>vegetables</u>
   (4) change <u>thus</u> to <u>however</u>
   (5) no correction is necessary

5. Sentence 5: **Freezers make it possible to preserve some of the surplus vegetables to be enjoyed at a later <u>date other</u> vegetables can be stored for a few months in a cool area.**

   Which of the following is the best way to write the underlined portion of this sentence? If you think the original is the best way, choose option (1).
   (1) date other
   (2) date, other
   (3) date. Other
   (4) date, while other
   (5) date; while other

6. Sentence 6: **Not to be overlooked is the finger-tip convenience of having vegetables in the backyard; this in itself justifies home gardening for many individuals.**

   What correction should be made to this sentence?
   (1) insert a comma after <u>overlooked</u>
   (2) change the spelling of <u>vegetables</u> to <u>vegtables</u>
   (3) replace the semicolon after <u>backyard</u> with a comma
   (4) change the spelling of gardening to <u>gardning</u>
   (5) no correction is necessary

7. Sentence 7: **In addition, vegetable gardening provides excercise and recreation for both urban and suburban families.**

   What correction should be made to this sentence?
   (1) remove the comma after <u>addition</u>
   (2) change the spelling of <u>excercise</u> to <u>exercise</u>
   (3) insert a comma after <u>recreation</u>
   (4) change <u>for both</u> to <u>both for</u>
   (5) no correction is necessary

8. Sentence 8: **Although your initial dollar investment for gardening may be nominal, one cannot escape the fact that gardening requires manual labor and time.**

   What correction should be made to this sentence?
   (1) change <u>Although</u> to <u>Because</u>
   (2) remove the comma after <u>nominal</u>
   (3) change <u>one</u> to <u>you</u>
   (4) change <u>requires</u> to <u>require</u>
   (5) no correction is necessary

9. Sentence 9: **Neglecting jobs that should be performed on a regular basis may result in failure and a negative feeling toward gardening.**

   What correction should be made to this sentence?
   (1) insert a comma after <u>jobs</u>
   (2) insert a comma after <u>basis</u>
   (3) change <u>may result</u> to <u>results</u>
   (4) change <u>and</u> to <u>despite</u>
   (5) no correction is necessary

<u>Questions 10 to 19</u> refer to the following paragraph.

(1) In coming years, families will need to learn to turn to their computers for assistence. (2) With the increasing amounts of information a family is required to process, the home computer will become a necessity for both decision making and family record storage and retrieval. (3) A home communications revolution is predicted with the arrival of the home computer. It will serve as a source and processor of information. (4) A virtually infinite amount of information from many sources will be at the instantaneous disposal of the family for more efficient decision making. (5) The computer will plan meals, turn lights on at appropriate times, keep track

of family members' schedules, calculate budget information, and oversee credit, spending, and bank accounts. (6) Just as home equiptment frees the homemaker from the labor of housekeeping, the computer releases family members from some repetitious managerial duties. (7) The home terminal may serve as a home education center for children's homework and part of the lifelong learning program of parents and elderly family members. (8) The change that will have the most immediate effect on family decision making will be increased discretionary time. (9) For economic reasons, many families will decide to use they're "free" time to hold a second job. (10) With the increasing interest in personal development, a segment of the time might be allotted by some to develop alternative interests through lifelong educational programs that will facilitate career changes, to increase skills for effective citizenship, and learning new skills to enhance their family living.

10. Sentence 1: **In coming years, families will need to learn to turn to their computers for assistence.**

   What correction should be made to this sentence?
   (1) remove the comma after years
   (2) change will need to need
   (3) change the spelling of their to they're
   (4) change the spelling of assistence to assistance
   (5) no correction is necessary

11. Sentence 2: **With the increasing amounts of information a family is required to process, the home computer will become a necessity for both decision making and family record storage and retrieval.**

   What correction should be made to this sentence?
   (1) change With the to Despite
   (2) change is to are
   (3) remove the comma after process
   (4) change the spelling of necessity to neccesity
   (5) no correction is necessary

12. Sentence 3: **A home communications revolution is predicted with the arrival of the home computer. It will serve as a source and processor of information.**

   Which of the following is the best way to write the underlined portion of the sentence? If you think the original is the best way, choose option (1).
   (1) computer. It
   (2) computer, It

(3) computer, it
(4) computer it
(5) computer; It

13. Sentence 4: **A virtually infinite amount of information from many sources will be at the instantaneous disposal of the family for more efficient decision making.**

What correction should be made to this sentence?
(1) insert a comma after <u>information</u>
(2) insert a comma after <u>sources</u>
(3) insert a comma after <u>family</u>
(4) change the spelling of <u>efficient</u> to <u>eficient</u>
(5) no correction is necessary

14. Sentence 5: **The computer will plan meals, turn lights on at appropriate times keep track of family members' schedules, calculate budget information, and oversee credit, spending, and bank accounts.**

What correction should be made to this sentence?
(1) remove comma after <u>meals</u>
(2) insert comma after <u>times</u>
(3) change <u>members'</u> to <u>member's</u>
(4) change the spelling of <u>schedules</u> to <u>skedules</u>
(5) no correction is necessary

15. Sentence 6: **Just as home equiptment frees the homemaker from the labor of housekeeping, the computer releases family members from some repetitious managerial duties.**

What correction should be made to this sentence?
(1) change <u>Just</u> as to <u>Although</u>
(2) change the spelling of <u>equiptment</u> to <u>equipment</u>
(3) remove the comma after <u>housekeeping</u>
(4) change <u>releases</u> to <u>will have released</u>
(5) no correction is necessary

16. Sentence 7: **The home terminal may serve as a home education center for children's homework and part of the lifelong learning program of parents and elderly family members.**

If you rewrote sentence 7 beginning with
<u>Children's homework and part of the lifelong learning program of parents and elderly family members</u>
the next words should be

(1) are served
(2) may serve
(3) may be served
(4) serve
(5) will serve

17. Sentence 8: **The change that will have the most immediate effect on family decision making will be increased discretionary time.**

What correction should be made to this sentence?
(1) change <u>will have</u> to <u>having</u>
(2) change the spelling of <u>effect</u> to <u>affect</u>
(3) change <u>family</u> to <u>family's</u>
(4) change <u>will be</u> to <u>is</u>
(5) no correction is necessary

18. Sentence 9: **For economic reasons, many families will decide to use they're "free" time to hold a second job.**

What correction should be made to this sentence?
(1) remove the comma after <u>reasons</u>
(2) ohango tho opolling of <u>familioc</u> to <u>familyc</u>
(3) change the spelling of <u>they're</u> to <u>their</u>
(4) change <u>to</u> to <u>and</u>
(5) no correction is necessary

19. Sentence 10: **With the increasing interest in personal development, a segment of the time might be allotted by some to develop alternative interests through lifelong educational programs that will facilitate career changes, to increase skills for effective citizenship, and learning new skills to enhance their family living.**

What correction should be made to this sentence?
(1) change the spelling of <u>development</u> to <u>developement</u>
(2) change the spelling of <u>through</u> to <u>thorough</u>
(3) remove the comma after <u>changes</u>
(4) change learning to <u>to learn</u>
(5) no correction is necessary

Questions 20 to 28 refer to the following paragraphs.

(1) To lessen the threat of faulty car repair work or repair frauds, they're a number of constructive steps you can take. (2) While these measures can't offer full protection they are wise insurance against dented pocketbooks and expanded time schedules.

(3) First, never wait until a small problem becomes a big and costly one. (4) Always take your car in for a check at the first sign of trouble.

(5) But before you take the car in, make a list of all problems and "symptoms" so you are prepared to describe the trouble as accurately and specifically as possible.

(6) Don't just ask to have the car put in "working order," (7) that kind of general statement can lead directly to unnecessary work.

(8) On your initial visit, make certain you get a copy of the work authorization that you sign or a general estimate of the total cost of the repairs. (9) Don't leave until you do.

(10) Ask the repair garage to telephone you when the exact work to be done has been determinned. (11) When you recieve the call, say you now want to return to the station to obtain another work order itemizing the cost of each repair to be made.

20. Sentence 1: **To lessen the threat of faulty car repair work or repair frauds, they're a number of constructive steps you can take.**

    What correction should be made to this sentence?
    (1) change <u>lessen</u> to <u>lesson</u>
    (2) remove the comma after <u>frauds</u>
    (3) change the spelling of <u>they're</u> to <u>there are</u>
    (4) change <u>can</u> to <u>might</u>
    (5) no correction is necessary

21. Sentence 2: **While these measures can't offer full protection they are wise insurance against dented pocketbooks and expanded time schedules.**

    What correction should be made to this sentence?
    (1) change <u>while</u> to <u>nevertheless</u>
    (2) insert a comma after <u>protection</u>
    (3) change <u>insurance</u> to <u>insurence</u>
    (4) insert a hyphen in <u>pocketbooks</u>
    (5) no correction is necessary

22. Sentence 3: **First, never wait until a small problem becomes a big and costly one.**

    What correction should be made to this sentence?
    (1) change <u>first</u> to <u>firstly</u>
    (2) remove the comma after <u>first</u>

(3) change the spelling of <u>until</u> to <u>untill</u>
(4) change <u>becomes</u> to <u>will become</u>
(5) no correction is necessary

23. Sentence 4: **Always take your car in for a check at the first sign of trouble.**

    What correction should be made to this sentence?
    (1) change <u>always</u> to <u>allways</u>
    (2) change <u>take</u> to <u>you should take</u>
    (3) change <u>your</u> to <u>your'e</u>
    (4) insert a comma after <u>check</u>
    (5) no correction is necessary

24. Sentence 5: **But before you take the car in, make a list of all problems and "symptoms" so you are prepared to describe the trouble as accurately and specifically as possible.**

    What correction should be made to this sentence?
    (1) change <u>take</u> to <u>will take</u>
    (2) remove the comma after <u>in</u>
    (3) change <u>are</u> to <u>will be</u>
    (4) change the spelling of <u>specifically</u> to <u>specificaly</u>
    (5) no correction is necessary

25. Sentences 6 and 7: **Don't just ask to have the car put in "working <u>order," that</u> kind of general statement can lead directly to unnecessary work.**

    Which of the following is the best way to write the underlined portion of these sentences? If you think the original is the best way, choose option (1).
    (1) order," that
    (2) order" that
    (3) order": that
    (4) order". that
    (5) order." That

26. Sentence 8: **On your initial visit, make certain you get a copy of the work authorization that you sign or a general estimate of the total cost of the repairs.**

    What correction should be made to this sentence?
    (1) change the spelling of <u>initial</u> to <u>initail</u>
    (2) remove the comma after <u>visit</u>

(3) insert a comma after <u>sign</u>
(4) change the spelling of <u>estimate</u> to <u>estemate</u>
(5) no correction is necessary

27. Sentence 10: **Ask the repair garage to telephone you when the exact work to be done has been determinned.**

What correction should be made to this sentence?
(1) insert a comma after <u>you</u>
(2) change <u>when</u> to <u>while</u>
(3) change <u>has been</u> to <u>will have been</u>
(4) change the spelling of <u>determinned</u> to <u>determined</u>
(5) no correction is necessary

28. Sentence 11: **When you recieve the call, say you now want to return to the station to obtain another work order itemizing the cost of each repair to be made.**

What correction should be made to this sentence?
(1) change the spelling of <u>recieve</u> to <u>receive</u>
(2) remove the comma after <u>call</u>
(3) insert a comma after <u>order</u>
(4) change <u>to be made</u> to <u>that will have been made</u>
(5) no correction is necessary

<u>Questions 29 to 37</u> refer to the following paragraphs.

(1) Total dollars available, family tastes storage and preparation facilities, end use, and item cost all affect a buying decision. (2) Unit pricing can help by taking the guesswork out of the price factor and simplifying cost comparisons.

(3) Unit price is just what its name implies—the price per unit. (4) To be more specific, unit pricing gives you the cost per ounce or per pound or per 100 or per square foot. (5) This price per unit enables you to readily find the best buy dollarwise among several items in different size packages with different total prices.

(6) Thousands of retail food chain stores now have unit pricing programs. (7) Such programs are required by local laws in several areas, but generally the programs are voluntary.

(8) Stores that offer unit pricing generally use a shelf tag system—a label on the shelf edge below the item gives the name of the item, the size, the total price, and the unit price.

(9) When unit pricing was first introduced there were some problems with the shelf tag system since just keeping the tags on the shelves in the right location can be difficult. (10) But as unit pricing has gained acceptance, some of these mechanical problems have been overcome, and the label information has become more usable from the shoppers standpoint.

29. Sentence 1: **Total dollars available, family tastes storage and preparation facilities, end use, and item cost all affect a buying decision.**

    What correction should be made to this sentence?
    (1) insert a comma after <u>tastes</u>
    (2) change <u>all</u> to <u>each</u>
    (3) change <u>affect</u> to <u>effect</u>
    (4) change the spelling of <u>buying</u> to <u>bying</u>
    (5) no correction is necessary

30. Sentence 1: **Total dollars available, family tastes storage and preparation facilities, end use, and item cost all affect a buying decision.**

    If you rewrote sentence 1 beginning with
    <u>A buying decision</u> is affected
    the next words should be
    (1) because of
    (2) by
    (3) depending on
    (4) however
    (5) therefore

31. Sentence 2: **Unit pricing can help by taking the guesswork out of the price factor and simplifying cost comparisons.**

    What correction should be made to this sentence?
    (1) change <u>can</u> to <u>could</u>
    (2) change <u>by taking</u> to <u>to take</u>
    (3) insert a hyphen in <u>guesswork</u>
    (4) insert a comma after <u>factor</u>
    (5) no correction is necessary

32. Sentences 3 and 4: **Unit price is just what its name implies—the price per unit. To be more specific, unit pricing gives you the cost per ounce or per pound or per 100 or per square foot.**

Which of the following is the best way to write the underlined portion of these sentences? If you think the original is the best way, choose option (1).

(1) . To be more specific
(2) , To be more specific
(3) ; To be more specific
(4) : To be more specific
(5) —To be more specific

33. Sentence 5: **This price per unit enables you to readily find the best buy dollarwise among several items in different size packages with different total prices.**

    What correction should be made to this sentence?
    (1) change <u>you</u> to <u>one</u>
    (2) insert comma before and after <u>dollarwise</u>
    (3) change among to <u>between</u>
    (4) change <u>size</u> to <u>sized</u>
    (5) no correction is necessary

34. Sentences 6 and 7: **Thousands of retail food chain stores now have unit pricing programs. Such programs are required by local laws in several areas, but generally the programs are voluntary.**

    The most effective combination of sentences 6 and 7 would include which of the following groups of words?
    (1) and such programs
    (2) although such programs
    (3) whereas such programs
    (4) programs that are
    (5) programs some being

35. Sentence 8: **Stores that offer unit pricing generally use a shelf tag <u>system—a label</u> on the shelf edge below the item gives the name of the item, the size, the total price, and the unit price.**

    Which of the following is the best way to write the underlined portion of this sentence? If you think the original is the best way, choose option (1).
    (1) system—a label
    (2) system. a label
    (3) system; a label

(4) system: a label
(5) system, a label

36. Sentence 9: **When unit pricing was first introduced there were some problems with the shelf tag system since just keeping the tags on the shelves in the right location can be difficult.**

    What correction should be made to this sentence?
    (1) change was to had been
    (2) insert a comma after introduced
    (3) change there to their
    (4) insert commas before and after in the right location
    (5) no correction is necessary

37. Sentence 10: **But as unit pricing has gained acceptance, some of these mechanical problems have been overcome, and the label information has become more usable from the shoppers standpoint.**

    What correction should be made to this sentence?
    (1) change the spelling of acceptance to acceptence
    (2) remove the comma after acceptance
    (3) change the spelling of usable to useable
    (4) add an apostrophe after shoppers
    (5) no correction is necessary

Questions 38 to 47 refer to the following paragraphs.

(1) You are going to move. (2) That statement will ring true for most Americans. (3) You will be the exception if you maintain your present residence for the rest of your life. (4) About one in five persons moves each year, put another way, the average person moves once every five years.

(5) Again dealing in averages most moves of household goods are completed without difficulty, although some are not. (6) The moving experience can be uneventful, but it should be recognized that many of the factors involved can lead to frustrations uncertainties, and expected courses of action that suddenly must be changed.

(7) Most moves involve fulfilment of a positive development. (8) A promotion has come through, (9) or perhaps an opportunity to move to a better climate. (10) Maybe there's a long-sought chance to be closer to the home folks or the grandchildren.

(11) On the other side of the coin, a familar neighborhood is being left behind. (12) The personal effort that must be put into a move can leave family members exhausted just at the time when they need to be at their sharpest.

38. Sentences 1 and 2: **You are going to move. That statement will ring true for most Americans.**

The most effective combination of sentences 1 and 2 would include which of the following groups of words.
(1) would be a statement that will ring
(2) is a statement that will ring
(3) might be a statement that will ring
(4) being a statement that will ring
(5) will be a statement that will ring

39. Sentence 3: **You will be the exception if you maintain your present residence for the rest of your life.**

What correction should be made to this sentence?
(1) change <u>will be</u> to <u>are</u>
(2) change the spelling of <u>exception</u> to <u>exeption</u>
(3) insert a comma after <u>exception</u>
(4) change <u>your</u> to <u>you're</u>
(5) no correction is necessary

40. Sentence 4: **About one in five persons moves each <u>year, put</u> another way, the average person moves once every five years.**

Which of the following is the best way to write the underlined portion of this sentence? If you think the original is the best way, choose option (1).
(1) year, put
(2) year, although put
(3) year, and put
(4) year, because put
(5) year, or put

41. Sentence 5: **Again dealing in averages most moves of household goods are completed without difficulty, although some are not.**

What correction should be made to this sentence?
(1) insert a comma after <u>averages</u>
(2) insert a hyphen in <u>household</u>

(3) change the spelling of <u>difficulty</u> to <u>dificulty</u>
(4) remove the comma after <u>difficulty</u>
(5) no correction is necessary

42. Sentence 6: **The moving experience can be uneventful, but it should be recognized that many of the factors involved can lead to frustrations uncertainties, and expected courses of action that suddenly must be changed.**

What correction should be made to this sentence?
(1) change the spelling of <u>experience</u> to <u>experiance</u>
(2) remove the comma after <u>uneventful</u>
(3) change <u>but</u> to <u>and</u>
(4) insert a comma after <u>frustrations</u>
(5) no correction is necessary

43. Sentence 7: **Most moves involve fulfilment of a positive development.**

What correction should be made to this sentence?
(1) change <u>most moves</u> to <u>most every move</u>
(2) change <u>involve</u> to <u>could involve</u>
(3) change the spelling of <u>fulfilment</u> to <u>fulfillment</u>
(4) change the spelling of <u>development</u> to <u>developement</u>
(5) no correction is necessary

44. Sentences 8 and 9: **A promotion has come <u>through, or</u> perhaps an opportunity to move to a better climate.**

Which of the following is the best way to write the underlined portion of these sentences? If you think the original is the best way, choose option (1).
(1) through, or
(2) through. or
(3) through : or
(4) through ; or
(5) through—or

45. Sentence 10: **Maybe there's a long-sought chance to be closer to the home folks or the grandchildren.**

What correction should be made to this sentence?
(1) change <u>there's</u> to <u>they're is</u>
(2) remove the hyphen from <u>long-sought</u>

(3) add an apostrophe to <u>folks</u>
(4) change the spelling of <u>grandchildren</u> to <u>grandchildern</u>
(5) no correction is necessary

46. Sentence 11: **On the other side of the coin, a familar neighborhood is being left behind.**

    What correction should be made to this sentence?
    (1) remove the comma after <u>coin</u>
    (2) change the spelling of <u>familar</u> to <u>familiar</u>
    (3) change the spelling of <u>neighborhood</u> to <u>nieghborhood</u>
    (4) change <u>is being</u> to <u>has been</u>
    (5) no correction is necessary

47. Sentence 12: **The personal effort that must be put into a move can leave family members exhausted just at the time when they need to be at their sharpest.**

    What correction should be made to this sentence?
    (1) insert commas around that <u>must be put into a move</u>
    (2) change <u>can</u> to <u>could</u>
    (3) change the spelling of <u>exhausted</u> to <u>exausted</u>
    (4) insert a comma after <u>time</u>
    (5) no correction is necessary

<u>Questions 48 to 55</u> refer to the following paragraphs.

(1) In fishing, the first step for the angler is to upgrade his equipment so that the availible range of lures, line weights, distances, etc., is substantially increased. (2) Usually a spinning reel and rod are selected as the next phase in advancement.

(3) The spinning reel consists of a stationery spool carrying a length of monofilament line, a bail or pickup device to direct the line onto the reel and a crank that rotates the pickup device restoring the line to the spool.

(4) In operation, the lure, attached to the monofilament line and dangling several inches beyond the rod tip is cast by swinging the rod from a position slightly behind the shoulder through a forward arc to a position in front at approximately eye level.

(5) Proper timing of the finger pressure on the line as it leaves the reel, combined with the rod acceleration, control the distance the lure will travel.

(6) Lures as light as a sixteenth of an ounce with two-pound test

monofilament line will provide enjoyable sport with any of the panfish, heavier lures and lines will more than adequately subdue far larger fish.

(7) Lures are available in a near infinite range of weights, sizes, shapes, and colors and include such items as spoons, spinners, jogs, plugs, and bugs as well as natural baits.

(8) With adequate spinning gear, anyone is prepared to pursue the fascinating and challenging game fish. (9) This category includes the world-famous and aristocratic salmon, the trout, the chars, the grayling, the basses, and the pike family.

48. Sentence 1: **In fishing, the first step for the angler is to upgrade his equipment so that the availible range of lures, line weights, distances, etc., is substantially increased.**

What correction should be made to this sentence?

(1) change the spelling of availible to available
(2) remove the comma after lures
(3) remove the period after etc.
(4) change the spelling of substantially to substantialy
(5) no correction is necessary

49. Sentence 2: **Usually a spinning reel and rod are selected as the next phase in advancement.**

If you rewrote sentence 2 beginning with
The next phase in advancement
the next words would be
(1) are selected a spinning
(2) are selecting a spinning
(3) selects a spinning
(4) is the selection of a spinning
(5) will be selecting a

50. Sentence 3: **The spinning reel consists of a stationery spool carrying a length of monofilament line, a bail or pickup device to direct the line onto the reel, and a crank that rotates the pick-up device restoring the line to the spool.**

What correction should be made to this sentence?

(1) change the spelling of stationery to stationary
(2) change the spelling of length to lenth
(3) remove the comma after line

(4) insert a comma after <u>device</u>

(5) no correction is necessary

51. Sentence 4: **In operation, the lure, attached to the monofilament line and dangling several inches beyond the rod tip is cast by swinging the rod from a position slightly behind the shoulder through a forward arc to a position in front at approximately eye level.**

What correction should be made to this sentence?

(1) change the spelling of <u>attached</u> to <u>attatched</u>

(2) insert a comma after <u>tip</u>

(3) insert a comma after <u>shoulder</u>

(4) change the spelling of <u>approximately</u> to <u>approximatly</u>

(5) no correction is necessary

52. Sentence 5: **Proper timing of the finger pressure on the line as it leaves the reel, combined with the rod acceleration, control the distance the lure will travel.**

What correction should be made to this sentence?

(1) insert a comma after <u>pressure</u>

(2) insert a comma after <u>line</u>

(3) insert commas before and after <u>reel</u>

(4) change <u>control</u> to <u>controls</u>

(5) no correction is necessary

53. Sentence 6: **Lures as light as a sixteenth of an ounce with two-pound test monofilament line will provide enjoyable sport with any of the <u>panfish, heavier</u> lures and lines will more than adequately subdue far larger fish.**

Which of the following is the best way to write the underlined portion of this sentence? If you think the original is the best way, choose option (1).

(1) panfish, heavier

(2) panfish: heavier

(3) panfish; heavier

(4) panfish. heavier

(5) panfish. Heavier

54. Sentence 7: **Lures are available in a near infinite range of weights, sizes, shapes, and colors and include such items as spoons, spinners, jogs, plugs, and bugs as well as natural baits.**

What correction should be made to this sentence?

(1) change <u>near</u> to <u>nearly</u>
(2) change the spelling of <u>infinite</u> to <u>infinate</u>
(3) remove the comma after <u>shapes</u>
(4) remove the comma after <u>plugs</u>
(5) no correction is necessary

55. Sentences 8 and 9: **With adequate spinning gear, anyone is prepared to pursue the fascinating and challenging game fish. This category includes the world-famous and aristocratic salmon, the trout, the chars, the grayling, the basses, and the pike family.**

The most effective combination of sentences 8 and 9 would include which of the following groups of words?

(1) and this category includes
(2) since this category includes
(3) which category includes
(4) which include
(5) and including

TEST 1: WRITING SKILLS, PART II

Directions

Alloted Time: 45 minutes

This part of the Writing Skills test is intended to determine how well you write. You are asked to write an essay that explains something or presents an opinion on an issue. In preparing your essay, you should take the following steps:

1. Read carefully the directions and the essay topic given below.
2. Plan your essay carefully before you write.
3. Use scratch paper to make any notes.
4. Write your essay on the lined pages of a separate answer sheet.
5. Read carefully what you have written and make any changes that will improve your essay.
6. Check your paragraphs, sentence structure, spelling, punctuation, capitalization, and usage, and make any necessary corrections.

You will have 45 minutes to write on the topic below.

Many Americans feel that the current state of world affairs requires continued involvement of the United States as a world superpower.

Others feel that America should concentrate on domestic problems and limit alliances and political relations with foreign nations.

Write a composition of about 200 words in which you indicate your views on this issue. Give appropriate reasons to support your position.

END OF EXAMINATION

TEST 2: SOCIAL STUDIES

Directions

Alloted Time: 85 minutes

The Social Studies test consists of multiple-choice questions intended to measure general social studies concepts. The questions are based on short readings that often include a graph, chart, or figure. Study the information given and then answer the question(s) following it. Refer to the information as often as necessary in answering the questions.

You should spend no more than 85 minutes answering the questions. Work carefully, but do not spend too much time on any one question. Be sure you answer every question. You will not be penalized for incorrect answers.

To record your answers, mark the numbered space on the answer sheet beside the number that corresponds to the question in the test.

FOR EXAMPLE:

Early colonists of North America looked for settlement sites that had adequate water supplies and were accessible by ship. For this reason, many early towns were built near

(1) mountains   ① ② ● ④ ⑤

(2) prairies

(3) rivers

(4) glaciers

(5) plateaus

The correct answer is "rivers"; therefore, answer space 3 would be marked on the answer sheet.

Questions 1 to 3 are based on the following passage.

The governor is empowered to veto single items of the budget bill, appending to each a message, and to return the same to the legislature if it is still in session. Such items can be enacted over his veto. This authority, not possessed by the president of the United States, lays a heavy responsibility on the governor for the integrity of the budget in all its parts.

All bills passed within the last ten days of a legislative session fall under what is called the "30-day" rule. None can become a law unless within 30 days (Sundays included) it has been signed by the governor.

The veto power is not used sparingly. More than one out of four bills falls to the deadly stroke of the executive pen.

1. The passage indicates that the governor
   (1) vetoes about one-fourth of the bills
   (2) vetoes about three-fourths of the bills
   (3) vetoes all bills during the legislative session
   (4) vetoes no bills during the legislative session
   (5) uses the veto power very sparingly

2. The "30-day" rule applies to
   (1) the time limit for exercising the veto
   (2) the pocket veto
   (3) the amount of time in which to appeal the governor's action
   (4) bills passed within the last ten days of a legislative session
   (5) the limitation on passing a law over the governor's veto

3. The governor's veto power is greater than that of the president in that the governor has the ability to
   (1) take as much time as he wishes before signing a bill
   (2) veto a bill in less than 10 days
   (3) ignore all bills during the last month of the legislature
   (4) veto single items of the budget bill
   (5) override the two-thirds vote of the legislature

Questions 4 to 6 are based on the following passage.

The consumer's first line of defense is information. Before you buy any product—especially before you make a major purchase of any kind—get all the information you can about the manufacturer's guarantee or warranty provisions.

Remember, a guarantee is a statement by the manufacturer or vendor that he stands behind his product or service. Guarantees and warranties usually have limitations or conditions, so get all promises in writing.

Before you buy any product or service covered by a guarantee or warranty, make sure you resolve these questions:

—What, exactly, is covered?

—Whom should you call when you need repairs under the warranty?

—Must repairs be made at the factory or by an "authorized service representative" to keep the warranty in effect?

—Who pays for parts, for labor, for shipping charges?

—How long does the warranty last?

—If pro rata reimbursement is provided, what is the basis for it?

—If the warranty provides for reimbursement, is it in cash or credit toward a replacement?

Keep the warranty and sales receipt for future reference.

4. The advice given to the consumer in this passage deals chiefly with
   (1) business ethics
   (2) unconditional guarantees
   (3) product safety
   (4) unwarranted promises
   (5) pre-purchase information

5. Guarantees and warranties, the passage implies, should be
   (1) conditional
   (2) in writing
   (3) made by the salesman
   (4) cancelable
   (5) dependent on the use of the product

6. Warranties usually include all of the following EXCEPT
   (1) what is covered
   (2) who does the repairs
   (3) where the repairs are made
   (4) who pays for expenses incurred in doing the repairs
   (5) return of monies paid

<u>**Questions 7 and 8**</u> are based on the following chart.

MEDIAN AGE IN THE UNITED STATES

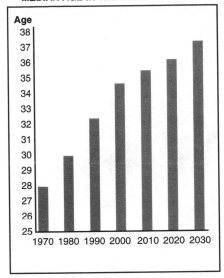

7. Which situation will be most likely to occur after the period shown
    in the graph?
    (1) Advertisers will increase their emphasis on youth.
    (2) The size of the average family will increase.
    (3) School districts will build more elementary schools.
    (4) The cost of the Social Security program will rise.
    (5) Population will begin to decline.

8. Which factor would most likely reverse the direction of the trend indi-
    cated by the graph?
    (1) development of a cure for cancer
    (2) a large increase in the birth rate
    (3) a prolonged period of economic depression
    (4) an increase in infant mortality
    (5) pollution control

9. Government policies designed to foster economic growth by encouraging
    greater consumption would probably meet with the greatest opposition
    from which group?
    (1) labor leaders
    (2) business executives

(3) military leaders
(4) environmentalists
(5) individual entrepreneurs

Questions 10 and 11 are based on the following cartoon.

10. What is the main idea of the cartoon?
(1) The world lacks sufficient energy resources to survive much longer.
(2) Concerns of environmentalists have had little impact on the actions of industrialists.
(3) The struggle between energy and the environment cannot be resolved.
(4) The need to produce energy comes into conflict with the need to preserve the environment.
(5) A stalemate has been arrived at between industrialists and environmentalists.

11. In dealing with the situation referred to in the cartoon during the late 1970s, the United States federal government generally followed a policy that
(1) gave priority to energy demands over environmental concerns
(2) sided with environmentalists against corporations
(3) sought new energy sources outside the United States
(4) attempted to divert national attention to other issues
(5) dealt evenhandedly with industrialists and environmentalists

12. The presidents of the United States from the time of World War II to the present have been most influential in the area of
(1) civil rights

(2) urban affairs
(3) foreign affairs
(4) states' rights
(5) human rights

Questions 13 and 14 are based on the following passage.

American industry in general, and America's highest paid industries in particular, export more goods to other markets than any other nation; and command our own market here in the United States.

Given this strength, accompanied by increasing productivity and wages in the rest of the world, there is less need to be concerned over the level of wages in the low-wage countries. These levels, moreover, are already on the rise, and we would hope, will continue to narrow the current wage gap, encouraged by appropriate consultations on an international basis.

This philosophy of the free market—the wider economic choice for men and nations—is as old as freedom itself. It is not a partisan philosophy. For many years our trade legislation has enjoyed bipartisan backing from those members of both parties who recognized how essential trade is to our basic security abroad and our economic health at home. This is even more true today.

—John F. Kennedy

13. In this passage, President Kennedy is emphasizing the need for
  (1) the free market
  (2) increasing our imports
  (3) reducing our tariffs
  (4) increasing our exports
  (5) American industrial efficiency

14. The immediate purpose of President Kennedy's message was to
  (1) try to restrict foreign competition
  (2) increase benefits for the American worker
  (3) close the wage gap between the United States and other countries
  (4) gain congressional support for trade legislation
  (5) decrease American imports

Questions 15 and 16 are based on the following passage.

Fourscore and seven years ago our fathers brought forth on this continent a new nation, conceived in liberty, and dedicated to the proposition that all men are created equal.

Now we are engaged in a great civil war, testing whether that nation, or any nation so conceived and so dedicated, can long endure. We are met on a great battlefield of that war. We have come to dedicate a portion of that field as a final resting-place for those who here gave their lives that that nation might live. It is altogether fitting and proper that we should do this.

But, in a larger sense, we cannot dedicate—we cannot consecrate—we cannot hallow—this ground. The brave men, living and dead, who struggled here, have consecrated it far above our poor power to add or detract.

—Abraham Lincoln

15. In the first paragraph, the speaker refers to
(1) the Declaration of Independence
(2) the Articles of Confederation
(3) the United States Constitution
(4) the Northwest Ordinance
(5) the Monroe Doctrine

16. The purpose of the speech was to
(1) commemorate a battle
(2) remember the founding of our nation
(3) dedicate a cemetery
(4) deplore civil war
(5) seek political support in an election

Questions 17 to 19 are based on the following chart, which lists some characteristics of Nations *A* and *B*.

Factors of Production	Nation A	Nation B
Land (natural resources)	Relative scarcity	Relative abundance
Labor	Relative abundance	Relative abundance
Capital	Relative abundance	Relative scarcity
Business management	Relative abundance	Relative scarcity

17. Which economic decision would most probably be in the best interests of Nation *A*?
(1) permitting an unfavorable balance of payments
(2) seeking foreign markets

(3) attracting investments from foreign nations
(4) encouraging immigration
(5) increasing imports

18. During the early 19th century, which nation most nearly resembled Nation *A*?
(1) the United States
(2) Great Britain
(3) Russia
(4) Turkey
(5) China

19. If Nation *B* wishes to industrialize, how can it best encourage its own citizens to invest their capital in domestic industries?
(1) by permitting an unfavorable balance of payments and seeking colonies
(2) by permitting an unfavorable balance of payments and encouraging immigration
(3) by attracting investments from foreign nations and encouraging immigration
(4) by instituting high protective tariffs and giving tax concessions to business
(5) by lowering taxes on imports

---

20. "Our policy in regard to Europe . . . is not to interfere in the internal concerns of any of its powers"—President Monroe, 1823

"It must be the policy of the United States to support free peoples who are resisting attempted subjugation by armed minorities or by outside pressures."—President Truman, 1947

The most valid conclusion to be drawn from these statements is that
(1) President Truman followed President Monroe's theory of foreign relations
(2) during the 19th and 20th centuries, the United States was not interested in international affairs
(3) during the 19th century, events in Europe did not affect the United States
(4) President Truman changed the policy of President Monroe
(5) conditions were different in 1947 from those in 1823

Questions 21 and 22 are based on the following graphs.

Of all women with children
under 6 and living with
their husbands, how
many work?

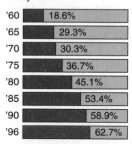

'60	18.6%
'65	29.3%
'70	30.3%
'75	36.7%
'80	45.1%
'85	53.4%
'90	58.9%
'96	62.7%

Of all woman who work, how
many have children under
6 years old?

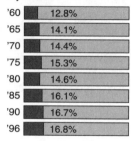

'60	12.8%
'65	14.1%
'70	14.4%
'75	15.3%
'80	14.6%
'85	16.1%
'90	16.7%
'96	16.8%

Of all working women with
children under 6 and living
with their husbands, how
many work...

	FULL TIME	PART TIME
'60	69.6%	30.4%
'65	68.8%	31.2%
'70	64.9%	35.1%
'75	64.9%	35.1%
'80	64.9%	35.1%
'85	65.7%	34.3%
'90	64.2%	35.8%
'96	62.8%	37.2%

Source: Bureau of Labor Statistics

21. The period with the greatest increase in the percentage of working
    women having children under 6 and living with their husbands was
    (1) '60–'65
    (2) '70–'75
    (3) '80–'85
    (4) '85–'90
    (5) '90–'96

22. The percentage of women working part time remained steadiest between
    (1) '60 and '70
    (2) '70 and '80
    (3) '75 and '85
    (4) '80 and '90
    (5) '90 and '96

23. Ethnocentrism is a belief that one's own ethnic group, nation, or culture
    is inherently superior to all others. An example of ethnocentrism is

(1) the use of the word *barbarian* to describe people of differing backgrounds
(2) the singing of a country's national anthem at sports events
(3) Japanese acceptance and imitation of Western culture
(4) the spread of Chinese culture to Southeast Asia
(5) a liberal immigration policy

Question 24 is based on the following diagram.

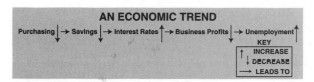

24. Which is occurring in the economy illustrated above?
    (1) increase in real income
    (2) devaluation of currency
    (3) growth
    (4) recession
    (5) recovery

25. "All forms of life developed from earlier forms. In every case the fittest survived and the weak died out. It is the same for people and nations."

    This passage expresses a view most often found in
    (1) fundamentalism
    (2) social Darwinism
    (3) liberalism
    (4) utopian socialism
    (5) egalitarianism

Questions 26 to 28 are based on the following passage.

The problems we face in conserving natural resources are laborious and complex. The preservation of even small bits of marshlands or woods representing the last strands of irreplaceable biotic communities is interwoven with the red tape of law, conflicting local interests, the overlapping jurisdiction of governmental and private conservation bodies, and an intricate tangle of economic and social considerations. During the time spent in resolving these factors, it often happens that the area to be preserved is swallowed up. Even more formidable is the broad-scale conservation problem raised by the spread of urban belts in such places as the northeastern part of the United States. The pressures of human growth are so acute in such instances that they raise issues that would tax the wisdom of Solomon.

26. The author of this passage is primarily concerned with
    (1) biotic communities
    (2) legal red tape
    (3) obstacles to conservation
    (4) private conservation organizations
    (5) encroaching suburbs

27. The most perplexing problem of conservationists is the one involving
    (1) population growth
    (2) public indifference
    (3) favorable legislation
    (4) division of authority
    (5) increased taxes

28. The author's attitude toward the situation he describes is
    (1) optimistic
    (2) realistic
    (3) apathetic
    (4) illogical
    (5) combative

Questions 29 to 31 are based on the following passage.

We must pursue a course designed not merely to reduce the number of delinquents. We must increase the chances for young people to lead productive lives.

For these delinquent and potentially delinquent youth, we must offer a New Start. We must insure that the special resources and skills essential for their treatment and rehabilitation are available. Because many of these young men and women live in broken families, burdened with financial and psychological problems, a successful rehabilitation program must include family counseling, vocational guidance, education and health services. It must strengthen the family and the schools. It must offer courts an alternative to placing young delinquents in penal institutions.

I recommend the Juvenile Delinquency Prevention Act of 1967.

—Lyndon B. Johnson

29. The emphasis in this speech is on
  (1) diagnosis and research
  (2) prevention and rehabilitation
  (3) rehabilitation and research
  (4) treatment and diagnosis
  (5) research and diagnosis

30. The main purpose of this speech is to
  (1) provide federal financial aid
  (2) give advice to broken families
  (3) support research and experimentation
  (4) praise "halfway houses"
  (5) advocate legislation to combat juvenile delinquency

31. The passage implies that
  (1) delinquents cannot lead productive lives
  (2) detention of delinquents is unnecessary
  (3) delinquency is caused by family problems
  (4) the federal government must assume responsibility for preventing juvenile delinquency
  (5) courts must place young delinquents in the proper penal institutions

Questions 32 and 33 are based on the following cartoon.

THE GREASED PIG

PRICES

ECONOMIC CONTROLS

Buffalo Evening News

32. Which statement best summarizes the main idea of the cartoon?
  (1) Prices should be regulated by a committee of private business people.
  (2) Competition among major industries has led to economic chaos.
  (3) Strict price-and-wage controls would assure a stable economy.
  (4) Government has been unable to deal effectively with a major economic problem.
  (5) Deregulation leads to lower prices.

33. A likely response to the problem referred to in the cartoon would be an increase in the
  (1) interest rates on bank loans
  (2) amount of government spending
  (3) amount of money in circulation
  (4) number of loans approved by banks
  (5) number of housing starts

---

34. Humanism as an intellectual and cultural movement stressed human values and welfare rather than religious interests.

The statement most in agreement with the humanist view is
  (1) Life on earth is only a preparation for another life.
  (2) Individuals are important and should be treated with dignity.
  (3) Degree of faith is an accurate measure of a person's worth.
  (4) The best education comes from a thorough understanding of religious doctrines and values.
  (5) Man does not have the free will to determine his own destiny.

Questions 35 to 37 are based on the following quotation.

"...American social development has been continually beginning over again on the frontier. This perennial rebirth, this fluidity of American life, this expansion westward with its new opportunities, its continuous touch with the simplicity of primitive society, furnish the forces dominating American character. The true point of view in the history of this nation is not the Atlantic coast, it is the Great West. The frontier is the line of most rapid and effective Americanization. The wilderness masters the colonists."

—Frederick Jackson Turner,
"The Significance of the Frontier in
American History"—1893

35. According to Frederick Jackson Turner, the culture of the United States was primarily the result of the

(1) dependence of each generation upon its predecessors
(2) Western settlers' experience in adjusting to new surroundings
(3) pioneers' ability to maintain contact with the settled areas back East
(4) influence of the frontier in making settlers more like Easterners
(5) original thirteen colonies

36. In this quotation Turner describes the frontier not only as an area but also as a
(1) process of developing culture
(2) preserver of traditions
(3) solution to European problems
(4) developer of economic systems
(5) refuge for colonists

37. Which characteristic of the West as described by Turner is most applicable to contemporary society in the United States?
(1) simplicity of life
(2) westward expansion
(3) new opportunities
(4) frontier environment
(5) urban redevelopment

---

38. A primary source is an eyewitness account of an event or events in a specific time period. Which would be an example of a primary source of information about life in the 18th-century American colonies?
(1) a diary of a colonial shopkeeper
(2) a painting of the colonial period by a 20th century artist
(3) a novel about the American Revolutionary War
(4) a reproduction of furniture used during the colonial period
(5) a social history of the period

Questions 39 and 40 are based on the following graph.

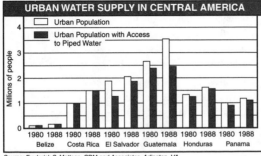

Source: Frederick S. Mattson, CDM and Associates, Arlington, VA

39. Which statement is best supported by the data in the graph?
   (1) The urban areas of Honduras and Panama require the largest supply of water in Central America.
   (2) Belize and Costa Rica are meeting the water needs of their urban population.
   (3) Urban water supplies are declining in many Central American countries.
   (4) Most Central American countries experienced a decrease in urban population between 1980 and 1988.
   (5) The supply of water increased in Central America between 1980 and 1988.

40. In 1988 the country with the largest urban population without access to piped water was
   (1) Costa Rica
   (2) El Salvador
   (3) Honduras
   (4) Panama
   (5) Guatemala

Questions 41 to 43 are based on the statements made by Speakers *A*, *B*, *C*, *D*, and *E*.

Speaker *A:*   Government could not function very well without them. The flow of information they provide to Congress and the federal agencies is vital to the functioning of our democratic system.

Speaker *B:*   Yes, but the secrecy under which they generally operate makes me suspicious that they are influencing lawmakers in improper ways.

Speaker *C:*   Don't forget that they not only try to influence Washington opinion but also attempt to shape public opinion across the nation in order to create a favorable climate for their views.

Speaker *D:*   That's true. Any politician who ignores 40,000 letters does so at great risk. We have to pay attention to them whether we accept their views or not.

Speaker *E:*   I agree with Speaker C. Public opinion is essential to the functioning of our American way of life.

41. Which group are the speakers most likely discussing?
   (1) lawyers
   (2) reporters
   (3) government workers
   (4) media analysts
   (5) lobbyists

42. Which speaker is most concerned about the impact of the methods used by this group upon democratic government?
   (1) A
   (2) B
   (3) C
   (4) D
   (5) E

43. Which speaker implies that lawmakers frequently must deal with a great many issues about which they know very little?
   (1) A
   (2) B
   (3) C
   (4) D
   (5) E

Question 44 is based on the following cartoon.

44. Which statement best summarizes the main point of the above cartoon?
   (1) The citizen's vote is a powerful means of influencing legislators seeking reelection.
   (2) Citizens are dependent upon the legislative branch of government for protection.
   (3) Federal and state legislators usually agree on major campaign issues.
   (4) The public generally does not favor consumer protection legislation.
   (5) Voters are easily fooled by politicians seeking votes.

Questions 45 to 47 are based on the following passage.

The people and groups that provide the stimulation and contact necessary for social development—the socializing agents—usually fall into two classes: (1) those people with authority over the individual, such as parents and teachers, and (2) those in positions of equality with him or her—age peers, such as playmates or a circle of friends. Since the family is the socializing agent during the critical first years of life, it naturally has had great influence. But because of the increased specialization of the functions of the family, the rapidity of social change that tends to divide the generations, and the high degree of mobility and social fluidity, the peer group is of growing importance in modern urban life.

45. Parents, teachers, and age peers share the role of
   (1) people with authority over the individual
   (2) peer group members
   (3) the friendly circle
   (4) the family circle
   (5) socializing agents

46. All of these reasons are given for the increased role of peers in an individual's social development EXCEPT
   (1) social mobility
   (2) social fluidity
   (3) generation gap
   (4) growing number of peers
   (5) specialization of family functions

47. The family, in modern urban life, is
 (1) exerting influence
 (2) growing in importance
 (3) being replaced by the peer group
 (4) filling a broadening role
 (5) influential only in the early years of life

Questions 48 and 49 refer to the following statements made by Speakers _A_, _B_, and _C_.

Speaker _A:_ Increased contact among nations and peoples is characteristic of our times. A single decision by OPEC or a multinational corporation can send ripples of change throughout our global society.

Speaker _B:_ If we are to survive, all passengers on our Spaceship Earth must participate in efforts to solve the issues that threaten humankind—poverty, resource depletion, pollution, violence, and war.

Speaker _C:_ We must understand that no single culture's view of the world is universally shared. Other people have different value systems and ways of thinking and acting. They will not see the world as we do.

48. Which concept is discussed by both Speakers _A_ and _B_?
 (1) self-determination
 (2) nationalism
 (3) conservation
 (4) interdependence
 (5) protectionism

49. Speaker _C_ indicates a desire to reduce
 (1) ethnocentrism
 (2) globalism
 (3) social mobility
 (4) religious tolerance
 (5) interdependence

Questions 50 and 51 are based on the following cartoon.

"Witnesses for the Prosecution"

50. The cartoon is concerned primarily with determining responsibility for which situation?
(1) use of poison gas during World War I
(2) slave labor camps in the Soviet Union during the Stalin era
(3) the Holocaust in Europe during the 1930s and 1940s
(4) apartheid practices in South Africa
(5) the blitzkrieg of World War II

51. The trial symbolized in the cartoon is significant because it was the first time that
(1) the United Nations International Court of Justice worked effectively
(2) individuals were prosecuted for crimes against humanity
(3) war guilt was applied to a whole nation
(4) international law was enforced
(5) the United States cooperated with the United Nations

Questions 52 to 54 are based on the following passage.

Organized economic studies date only from the 17th century. Since then, there have been a number of major schools of economic thought. They can be briefly identified as follows:

(1) mercantilism—advocates, in foreign trade, a surplus of exports over imports to accumulate gold and supports development of local industries protected by tariffs from foreign trade competition

(2) laissez-faire—opposes state intervention in economic affairs to allow free trade and competition

(3) Marxism—teaches that value created by labor and profit is surplus value skimmed off by the capitalist who owns the means of production, which should be eventually controlled by the proletariat or the industrial workers

(4) Keynes theory—focuses on the need to create demand by government spending and the curbing of excess demand by tight budget policies

(5) supply-side economics—supports stimulating production rather than demand by drastic tax reductions to increase business investment and advocates a cutback in government spending to eliminate deficits

Each of the following describes an action or proposal relating to the economic policies described above. Indicate which school of economic thought would approve the action.

52. The president recommends drastic cuts in defense and nondefense spending.
(1) mercantilism
(2) laissez-faire
(3) Marxism
(4) Keynes theory
(5) supply-side economics

53. Congress is considering a tariff on Japanese imports to protect the United States electronics industry.
(1) mercantilism
(2) laissez-faire
(3) Marxism
(4) Keynes theory
(5) supply-side economics

54. A company is bought out by its employees.
(1) mercantilism
(2) laissez-faire
(3) Marxism
(4) Keynes theory
(5) supply-side economics

55. Cultural diffusion is the spread of one culture to other areas of the world. An example is
   (1) an immigrant learning a new language
   (2) a child learning to walk
   (3) conflict between old and new cultures
   (4) the superiority of the United States' culture over all others
   (5) a Russian playing basketball

56. "Under a government which imprisons anyone unjustly, the true place for a just man is also a prison."

—Henry David Thoreau

   Which does this quotation most strongly support?
   (1) social control
   (2) conformity
   (3) suspension of civil liberties
   (4) dictatorship
   (5) civil disobedience

Questions 57 and 58 are based on the following cartoon.

57. Which best states the main idea of the cartoon?
   (1) The United States establishes immigration policies that meet its specific needs.
   (2) There is a surplus of highly trained people in foreign countries.
   (3) Highly trained people will be able to pass literacy tests required to enter the United States.

(4) The United States lags behind other nations in technological development.

(5) Untrained people are not welcome in the United States.

58. One similarity between immigration policy suggested in the cartoon and United States immigration policy in the 1920s is that both show a

(1) reluctance to admit non-English speaking people

(2) preference for certain groups

(3) desire to encourage increased immigration

(4) desire to adopt the values of international human rights organizations

(5) desire to increase ethnic diversity

Question 59 is based on the following headline.

NIXON MUST SURRENDER TAPES,
SUPREME COURT RULES, 8 TO 0;
HE PLEDGES FULL COMPLIANCE
House Committee Begins Debate on Impeachment

---

59. Which feature of the United States constitutional system is best illustrated by the above headline?

(1) checks and balances

(2) executive privilege

(3) power to grant pardons

(4) federalism

(5) the Bill of Rights

Questions 60 and 61 are based on the following graph.

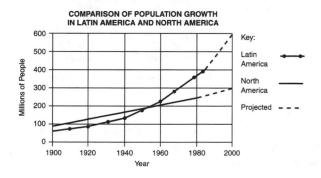

COMPARISON OF POPULATION GROWTH
IN LATIN AMERICA AND NORTH AMERICA

60. Based on the information in the graph, which is a valid conclusion about the populations of Latin America and North America?

    (1) There has always been a large difference in the population growth of Latin America and North America.

    (2) By the year 2000, the population of Latin America is expected to be approximately twice that of North America.

    (3) In 1900, the number of people in Latin America was equal to the number of people in North America.

    (4) In the early 1980s, the difference in population between the two regions was about 300 million.

    (5) The rate of population growth of Latin America has been steadier than that of North America.

61. Which best accounts for the situation shown in the graph?

    (1) decline in the standard of living in North America

    (2) growing trade surplus of most Latin American nations

    (3) improved nutrition and medical care in Latin America

    (4) increased death rate in North America due to contagious diseases

    (5) increase in democracy in Latin America

<u>Questions 62 and 63</u> are based on the following cartoon.

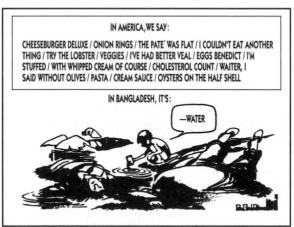

IN AMERICA, WE SAY:

CHEESEBURGER DELUXE / ONION RINGS / THE PATE´ WAS FLAT / I COULDN'T EAT ANOTHER THING / TRY THE LOBSTER / VEGGIES / I'VE HAD BETTER VEAL / EGGS BENEDICT / I'M STUFFED / WITH WHIPPED CREAM OF COURSE / CHOLESTEROL COUNT / WAITER, I SAID WITHOUT OLIVES / PASTA / CREAM SAUCE / OYSTERS ON THE HALF SHELL

IN BANGLADESH, IT'S:

—WATER

Source: The Times Union, July 1991

62. What is the main idea of the cartoon?

    (1) The people of developing nations have refused to ask for aid.

    (2) Relief workers have died trying to help suffering people in developing nations.

(3) Industrialized nations have prevented starvation in developing nations.

(4) People in some developing nations lack the basic necessities, while people in other nations have more than they need.

(5) Prosperous nations are concerned with the problems of developing nations.

63. The cartoon implies that
(1) Industrialized nations should help developing nations.
(2) People in some countries are doomed to a life of poverty.
(3) The problems of developing nations are no concern of America.
(4) Americans exploit developing nations.
(5) Some countries are overpopulated.

64. "I believe that it must be the policy of the United States to support free peoples who are resisting attempted subjugation by armed minorities or by outside pressures. I believe that we must assist free peoples to work out their own destinies in their own way. I believe that our help should be primarily through economic and financial aid...."

—Harry S. Truman

The recommendation made in this quotation resulted from a perception that the United States needed to
(1) oppose Communist expansion just after World War II
(2) prepare for World War I
(3) fight Nazi aggression in 1941
(4) justify the withdrawal of United States forces from Korea
(5) return to a policy of isolationism

END OF EXAMINATION

TEST 3: SCIENCE

Directions

Alloted Time: 95 minutes

The Science test consists of 66 multiple-choice questions intended to measure the general concepts in science. The questions are based on short readings that often include a graph, chart, or figure. Study the information given and then answer the question(s) following it. Refer to the information as often as necessary in answering the questions.

You will have 95 minutes to answer the questions. Work carefully, but do not spend too much time on any one question. Be sure you answer every question. You will not be penalized for incorrect answers.

To record your answers, mark the numbered space on the answer sheet beside the number that corresponds to the question in the test.

FOR EXAMPLE:

Which of the following is the smallest unit?
(1) solution   ① ② ● ④ ⑤
(2) element
(3) atom
(4) compound
(5) mixture

The correct answer is "atom"; therefore, space 3 would be marked on the answer sheet.

Questions 1 to 4 refer to the following article.

Scientists have different explanations of how evolution occurred, but they all agree that all living things evolved from other living things. Paleontologists have justified this conclusion from their studies of fossil remains. There is also evidence from other branches of science that there have been changes in organisms, and that these changes are still going on.

While archaeologists have been digging through the remains of ancient civilizations, adding their bit to knowledge, the origin of human beings has been the subject of study for the anthropologist. Anthropologists specialize in their areas of research. One may study the history of a language, while another investigates the various types of pottery that are unearthed. Physical anthropology is involved with the anatomy of various vertebrates. Of particular interest to physical anthropologists are primates, that is, the group of mammals that includes humans, apes, monkeys, and chimpanzees. With the aid of fossil records, comparisons can be made between the structures of animals from the past and present forms.

1. Which of the following terms includes all the others?
   (1) human
   (2) primate
   (3) monkey
   (4) ape
   (5) chimpanzee

2. Evolution is the biological process by which
   (1) fossils are produced in rocks
   (?) the anatomy of vertebrates is compared
   (3) ancient human life is studied
   (4) new kinds of living things arise
   (5) chimpanzees give rise to humans

3. Which of the following gives the most direct evidence that different forms of life existed in the past?
   (1) organic chemistry
   (2) fossils
   (3) comparative anatomy
   (4) archeology
   (5) laboratory experiments

4. Which of the following discoveries would suggest that the human species is still evolving?
   (1) The human brain is much larger than the brain of a gorilla.
   (2) In early stages of development, human embryos have a large tail.
   (3) There is a strong similarity between the chemistry of humans and that of chimpanzees.
   (4) The armor of medieval knights is too small for today's average man.
   (5) Tractors have replaced horses for farm work.

Questions 5 to 8 are based on the following diagrams.

 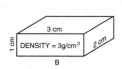 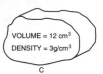

These diagrams, not drawn to scale, represent three samples of the same substance, each having a different size and shape. The following formulas are involved:

Volume = length × height × width

$$\text{Density} = \frac{\text{mass}}{\text{volume}}$$

5. What is the density of sample A?
    (1) 0.33 g/cm³
    (2) 2.0 g/cm³
    (3) 3.0 g/cm³
    (4) 4.0 g/cm³
    (5) 8.0 g/cm³

6. If sample B were split in half, what would be the density of each piece?
    (1) 1.0 g/cm³
    (2) 1.5 g/cm³
    (3) 3.0 g/cm³
    (4) 6.0 g/cm³
    (5) 8.0 g/cm³

7. Which graph best represents the relationship between the mass and the volume of the substance?

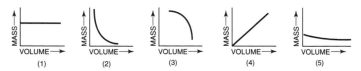

8. Which order of letters ranks the samples correctly by volume from largest to smallest?
    (1) A, B, C
    (2) A, C, B
    (3) B, C, A
    (4) C, B, A
    (5) C, A, B

9. An island may form when material expelled by an undersea volcano gradually builds up and rises above the surface of the water. This has happened in numerous places in the Pacific Ocean. Over time, however, another island may begin to form some distance from the first. It is possible that chains of islands, such as the Hawaiian Islands, were formed in this way. One reason for this may be that

(1) the volcano moves along the bottom of the ocean

(2) the plates of earth and rock that cover the interior of planet Earth are slowly moving, taking the islands with them

(3) when the first island was finished, some leftover lava started another island

(4) volcanoes erupted in places where islands were going to be formed

(5) volcanic eruptions have had nothing to do with the formation of islands

10. The depth of a body of water can be measured by a method called sonar. Sonar is an acronym for *SO*und *NA*vigation *R*anging, and the method works on the same principle as radar. Sound waves (sonar beams) are aimed at the ocean floor, and the times when they bounce back are recorded. Since we know that the speed of sound in water is approximately 4,800 feet per second, the depth of the ocean can be determined by measuring how long it takes a beam to bounce off the ocean floor and return to the ship.

How far, in feet, would a sonar beam travel in 2½ seconds?

(1) 14,400

(2) 9,500

(3) 2,400

(4) 4,850

(5) 12,000

Questions 11 to 13 refer to the following article.

The ancient Greeks found that pieces of a certain iron ore attract or repel each other. These were early examples of natural magnets, and the effect that the Greeks observed is called magnetism. Like the planet Earth, which is itself a giant magnet, these smaller magnets have a north and a south pole. Like poles repel each other, while opposite poles attract.

Magnets are in common use today and can be found on almost any refrigerator. Some are shaped like a rod or bar; in others the rod is bent into a horseshoe shape.

Wrapping a piece of metal, such as a nail, with wire can produce another kind of magnet, an electromagnet. When electricity is run through the wire, you get a magnetic field.

11. Magnets have many uses. Some are small enough to be used in the motor of a hair dryer, while others are large enough to lift enormous amounts of scrap metal that may once have been a car or truck. Since this kind of magnet can be turned on and off, it is probably
   (1) an electromagnet
   (2) a natural magnet
   (3) a magnetic ore
   (4) a horseshoe magnet
   (5) magnetite

12. The fact that the needle of a compass always points north is proof that
   (1) the point of the compass must be a north pole
   (2) many materials that occur in nature have a strong magnetic attraction
   (3) a compass is an important part of any navigator's equipment
   (4) Earth is itself a magnet and can exert a magnetic force
   (5) magnets have been used since ancient times

13. Lodestone is an ore used by ancient Chinese to make compasses. This use was possible only because lodestone was
   (1) very common in China
   (2) a neutral material capable of being magnetized
   (3) capable of being made into electromagnets
   (4) paramagnetic
   (5) a natural magnet

Questions 14 to 16 refer to the following article.

In one kind of internal-combustion engine, a mixture of gasoline and air is compressed in a cylinder and then ignited by a spark from a spark plug. The German engineer Rudolf Diesel developed another type of engine that works without spark plugs. The intake stroke of this engine admits only air, which is strongly compressed in a cylinder, causing it to heat to a very high temperature. Heavy fuels, such as oil, are then injected into this hot, compressed air and are exploded by the heat.

Because diesel engines need such a strong compression stroke, they are heavy and require the strength of a thick-walled compression chamber to function. However, they get more energy out of the less expensive fuel they burn because they can operate at a much higher temperature than a gasoline engine.

14. What is true of the diesel engine but not of the gasoline engine?
   (1) It needs no air supply.
   (2) It has no cylinders.
   (3) It has no spark plugs.
   (4) It uses less expensive types of gasoline.
   (5) It has no pistons.

15. Why are diesel engines used on locomotives?
   (1) They can get more heat energy from a less expensive fuel.
   (2) Coal-burning engines pollute the air.
   (3) It is difficult to store large quantities of gasoline safely in the locomotive.
   (4) Electric power is not easily available in remote, rural areas.
   (5) Diesel fuel is available in remote, rural areas.

16. Why aren't diesel engines used in airplanes?
   (1) Diesel engines are heavy engines.
   (2) Diesel oil is very explosive.
   (3) Airplanes do not need the power of diesel engines.
   (4) Housing the cylinders would take up too much space.
   (5) Diesel oil produces more pollutants than other fuels.

Questions 17 to 19 refer to the following article.

All nations agree that cooperative efforts are needed in research to study and predict earthquakes. In July 1956 the first World Conference on Earthquake Engineering was held in Tokyo. Its purpose was to share information about the prediction of earthquakes and methods of constructing buildings and bridges that can withstand the shocks.

What causes earthquakes? The crust of the Earth is a broken mosaic of pieces, bounded by deep cracks called faults. When forces deep inside the Earth move these pieces, tremendous shock waves start from the faults. Shock waves in the crust, from whatever source, can be detected by seismographs all over the world. If the earthquake occurs beneath the ocean, it produces an enormous wave, called a tsunami, that can do much damage when it arrives at a shore.

17. What is the most frequent cause of major earthquakes?
    (1) movements within the Earth
    (2) folding
    (3) landslides
    (4) submarine currents
    (5) tsunamis

18. How can earthquake destruction be minimized?
    (1) more frequent use of seismographs
    (2) better construction of buildings
    (3) quicker methods of evacuation
    (4) early detection and warning
    (5) better control of tsunamis

19. Nuclear explosions can be detected by seismographs because they
    (1) cause tsunamis
    (2) occur on geologic faults
    (3) cause earthquakes
    (4) produce shock waves in the crust
    (5) compress the rock

Questions 20 to 23 refer to the following article.

All matter is made up of atoms. Atoms contain protons, which have positive charges; electrons, which have negative charges; and neutrons, which are neither positively nor negatively charged. Since the atom has the same number of protons and electrons, the atom as a whole is neutral.

The center of the atom, the nucleus, holds protons and neutrons, while the electrons move around in orbits called shells. Each shell has the capacity to hold a maximum number of electrons. The first shell can hold no more than two electrons, while the second shell is complete with eight electrons. The third shell can hold eighteen electrons, except when it happens to be the outer shell, in which case its capacity is only eight electrons. In some atoms, additional shells carry additional electrons.

An atom tends to complete the outer shell either by borrowing electrons, lending electrons, or sharing electrons. The number of electrons available for such action is called valence. For example, a valence of + 2 means an atom has two electrons to lend. An atom with a valence of −1 needs one electron to complete its outer ring. The borrowing, lending, and sharing of electrons gives rise to the formation of compounds.

The atomic mass of an atom is the sum of the total mass of its protons and neutrons. The proton has a mass of one atomic mass unit. The neutron also has a mass of one atomic mass unit, but the electron adds almost nothing to the mass of an atom and so does not have to be considered in calculating atomic mass. The atomic number tells you the number of protons in the atom.

20. The valence of calcium (Ca) is +2. The valence of chlorine (Cl) is –1. When these elements combine to form calcium chloride, the correct formula for this compound is

(1) $CaCl$

(2) Ca_2Cl

(3) $CaCl_2$

(4) Ca_2Cl_2

(5) Ca_4Cl_2

21. Lithium has an atomic mass of 7 and an atomic number of 3. How many neutrons are there in the lithium atom?

(1) none

(2) two

(3) three

(4) four

(5) ten

22. The atomic number of an atom is always equal to the total number of

(1) neutrons in the nucleus

(2) neutrons and protons in the atom

(3) protons and electrons in the atom

(4) electrons in the orbits

(5) protons in the nucleus

23. What is the valence of an element that has 11 protons?

(1) +11

(2) –11

(3) +8

(4) +1

(5) –1

Questions 24 to 29 refer to the following article.

Photosynthesis is a complex process involving many steps. Water in the soil is absorbed by the roots of a plant, rises through veins called xylem, and moves through the stems and into a leaf. Carbon dioxide, diffused from the air through the stomata and into the leaf, comes into contact with the water and dissolves. The solution of carbon dioxide in water then diffuses through the cell walls and into the cells. Organelles within the cell, called chloroplasts, contain chlorophyll, a green pigment that captures light energy from the sun and transforms it into chemical energy. This chemical energy acts to decompose the carbon dioxide and water. The products of this decomposition are recombined into new compounds, then into other compounds. These compounds become more and more complex until finally a sugar is produced. Oxygen is given off as a by-product of the photosynthetic process.

24. Which plant structure is directly involved in the making of sugar?
    (1) stoma
    (2) xylem
    (3) cell wall
    (4) plasma membrane
    (5) chloroplast

25. To carry on photosynthesis, the water of the soil must be transported to the leaf. Which structure conducts soil water to the leaf?
    (1) chlorophyll
    (2) stoma
    (3) xylem
    (4) phloem
    (5) chloroplasts

26. Why is chemical energy needed for photosynthesis?
    (1) to bring water to the leaf
    (2) to decompose chlorophyll
    (3) to decompose water
    (4) to change the form of light energy
    (5) to recombine the products of photosynthesis

27. Sugar is composed of carbon, hydrogen, and oxygen. In the process of photosynthesis, what is the source of these chemical elements?
    (1) carbon dioxide alone
    (2) water alone
    (3) either the carbon dioxide or the water
    (4) both the carbon dioxide and the water
    (5) neither the carbon dioxide nor the water

28. What is the function of chlorophyll in photosynthesis?

(1) serves as a source of carbohydrate
(2) produces carbon dioxide
(3) changes light energy to chemical energy
(4) supplies chemical energy
(5) provides the green color

29. Carbon dioxide enters a plant by way of the

(1) roots
(2) xylem
(3) plasma membrane
(4) stomata
(5) intercellular spaces

---

30. In photosynthesis, green plants produce the carbohydrates that become the energy supply of the plants and of the animals that eat them. Photosynthesis can take place only when the plants are in sunlight.

Which statement below is a summary of this process?

(1) Light and chemical energy are used for growth.
(2) Chemical energy is converted to light energy.
(3) Light energy is used for growth.
(4) Chemical energy is used for growth.
(5) Light energy is converted to chemical energy.

31. Green plants, in sunlight, absorb carbon dioxide to produce glucose, releasing oxygen in the process. Which of the following would be most likely to increase the rate at which this process goes on?

(1) Increase the amount of oxygen in the air.
(2) Add glucose to the soil.
(3) Move the plants into the shade.
(4) Reduce the amount of carbon dioxide in the air.
(5) Increase the amount of carbon dioxide in the air.

Questions 32 to 34 refer to the following article.

In the process of evolution, organisms undergo certain physical changes so that they are better adapted to survive in their environment. These changes help them to find and eat their food, attract mates, or perhaps defeat or confuse their enemies.

A bird's bill usually defines the type of food that the bird eats. Some hunting birds have sharp hooked bills. Other birds have slender bills to extract nectar from flowers. The interesting bill of the South American toucan is huge and brightly colored and can be as long as half the length of the the bird's body. This bill is useful in picking fruit.

32. What is the probable reason that African hornbills closely resemble the South American toucan, even though the two species are unrelated?
    (1) The resemblance is purely a coincidence.
    (2) There has been an interchange of genetic material between the two species of birds.
    (3) The two species of birds have evolved from a common ancestor.
    (4) Both species of birds are fruit eaters in tropical rain forests.
    (5) The toucans have migrated from Africa.

33. When the Industrial Revolution introduced great smoke-belching factories into England, a certain species of moth found itself threatened. These white moths lived on the bark of light-colored trees, where they were virtually invisible to predators. When smog from the factories turned everything in the area black with soot, the trunks of the trees were not immune. As time passed, the population of this moth dropped dramatically. The chief reason for the decline may have been that
    (1) because the white moths were now visible against the sooty bark, they were easier for birds to catch
    (2) the soot was poisonous to the moths
    (3) the soot killed off the moth's primary source of food
    (4) the soot destroyed the moth's eggs
    (5) the moths had to find other trees because the old ones were now too dark

34. Snakes are solitary creatures. With a few exceptions, they crawl off to live alone after they hatch. Occasionally a female snake will lay a trail of a special scent called a pheromone. The reason for laying this trail is that the only life process a snake cannot carry on alone is
    (1) respiration
    (2) hibernation
    (3) reproduction
    (4) regulation
    (5) locomotion

35. Potassium is receiving special attention as an important nutritional requirement. Potassium conducts an electric charge that is important in the transmission of nerve impulses and muscle contraction. Such foods as

bananas and dried apricots are rich in potassium. These foods are recommended for persons who lose potassium because their medication causes the loss of body water. Why might the heart malfunction because of loss of potassium?

(1) The heart needs banana and apricot
(2) The heart absorbs much potassium
(3) High blood pressure can be treated
(4) Low blood pressure can be treated
(5) Contraction of heart muscles requires potassium

36. Oxides of carbon, sulfur, and nitrogen, which occur in the stack gases of coal-burning plants, react with atmospheric water to form acids. The pollution caused by stack gases may be responsible for all the following forms of environmental damage EXCEPT

(1) physical deformity of developing fish
(2) corrosion of buildings
(3) death of many forest trees
(4) damage to human lungs
(5) sewage contamination of water supplies

37. The laws that control recombination of genes seem to be much the same for all sexually reproducing organisms. These laws are studied by statistical analysis of large numbers of offspring for several generations. Which of the following organisms would be most useful in experiments to study the laws of recombination of genes?

(1) bacteria
(2) human beings
(3) mice
(4) dogs
(5) oak trees

38. The early atmosphere of the Earth had no oxygen. It was first produced when bacteria developed the green pigment that made photosynthesis possible. In which of the following groups is the sequence in which the organisms appeared on Earth presented correctly?

(1) animals, green bacteria, nongreen bacteria
(2) green bacteria, animals, nongreen bacteria
(3) animals, nongreen bacteria, green bacteria
(4) nongreen bacteria, green bacteria, animals
(5) nongreen bacteria, animals, green bacteria

39. The graph below shows the changes in the populations of wolves and moose in a northern forest for a period of 6 years. What is the most reasonable explanation of the facts shown?

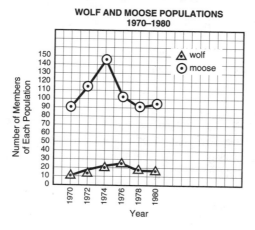

WOLF AND MOOSE POPULATIONS
1970–1980

(1) Moose produce more offspring when there are few wolves.
(2) When there are many moose, there are more recreational hunters.
(3) Wolves produce more offspring when there are many moose.
(4) Both wolf and moose populations vary according to the weather conditions.
(5) Wolf populations have no relationship to the availability of moose.

Question 40 is based on the following diagram.

40. When sediments are deposited in the ocean, new layers form on top of preexisting layers. The sediments may eventually turn into fossil bearing rocks. What might a geologist conclude about fossils found in the rock layers shown in the diagram above?
(1) All the fossils are of the same age.

(2) The relative ages of the fossils cannot be determined.

(3) The fossils in rock layer *D* are older than those in layer *A*.

(4) The fossils in rock layer *B* are older than those in layer *C*.

(5) The fossils in rock layer *A* are older than those in layer *B*.

---

41. The AIDS virus is transmitted from an infected person by direct introduction of his or her blood or other body fluids into the body of another person. An individual can contract AIDS by any of the following means EXCEPT

(1) breathing the air expelled by a person with the disease

(2) sexual intercourse with an infected person

(3) using a hypodermic needle that had been used by someone with the disease

(4) receiving a blood transfusion from an infected person

(5) passage of the virus from a pregnant woman into the fetus she is carrying

42. Some corn plants may have genes that make them immune to the poisonous effects of herbicides. These genes can arise spontaneously by mutation, and will then be passed on to future generations. What might a plant breeder do to develop a line of corn that would not be killed by herbicides?

(1) Apply herbicides to cause mutations.

(2) Prevent mutations by careful control of environmental conditions.

(3) Find immune plants by applying herbicides and breeding the survivors.

(4) Withhold all fertilizers and breed the plants that survive.

(5) Withhold all herbicides and breed whichever plants mutate.

43. Since World War II, new varieties of rice have been developed that produce two or three times as much grain when they are grown with heavy doses of chemical fertilizers. A farmer should decide NOT to use these varieties if

(1) he or she is accustomed to growing more familiar varieties of rice

(2) he or she is cultivating only a small plot

(3) his or her farm is in an unusually wet climate

(4) there is no way he or she can obtain the seed of the new varieties

(5) the fertilizer needed costs more than the value of the extra grain

44. Why do you feel cool when you get out of the surf on a dry day?

(1) The water takes heat from your body as it evaporates from your wet skin.

(2) Evaporation produces heat.

(3) Condensation cools the body.

(4) The air is cooler than the surf water.

(5) Sea breezes make you feel cooler.

Questions 45 to 49 refer to the following article.

Today some plants are cloned to produce millions of offspring from a small piece of the original plant. Plant cloning is possible because each plant cell contains a complete blueprint, in the form of chromosomes, for reproducing itself. After a piece of the plant is placed in a growth medium, special plant growth hormones, called auxins and cytokinin, are added to stimulate the production of new plants. The new plants are genetically identical to the original plant and to each other.

The process and equipment for cloning are more expensive than those used for other forms of vegetative propagation. The advantage of cloning is that large numbers of plants are produced in a short period of time. For example, a million plants of a new variety can be cloned in about six months. This process is very useful for developing strains of disease resistant crops or plants that not only can survive in a difficult climate but also will produce a large harvest.

45. For which reason is cloning used to reproduce plants?

(1) Plants with a large degree of genetic variability are produced.

(2) Plants are produced more cheaply than by other vegetative methods.

(3) Plants are produced by the sexual process, resulting in seeds.

(4) A large number of plants are produced in a short period of time.

(5) Plants with large degrees of variation are produced.

46. It is possible to clone plants that are identical to their parent plants because

(1) scientists have developed blueprints to make so many different plants

(2) every plant cell is the same

(3) chromosomes carry blueprints from the parent plant

(4) hormones are used to induce plants to reproduce

(5) plants are easy to grow under the correct conditions

47. Which statement describes the hormones auxin and cytokinin?

(1) They are forms of vegetative propagation.

(2) They can develop into a zygote.
(3) They stimulate the production of new plants.
(4) They inhibit the production of new plants.
(5) They are forms of asexual reproduction.

48. How is cloning defined?
(1) a form of sexual reproduction
(2) a form of vegetative propagation
(3) an inorganic hormone
(4) an inorganic component of the growing medium
(5) an auxin

49. An important difference between plants produced by cloning and plants grown from seed is that
(1) cloned plants are healthier
(2) cloned plants are identical to the parent plant
(3) plants grown from seed are identical to the parent plant
(4) plants grown from seed are better adapted to the conditions in which the plants are grown
(5) cloned plants do not need as much care

---

50. If particles are to be considered soluble, they must dissolve in water. In this case, the resulting solution will be clear. Sometimes, however, some of the substance will settle out of the solution, leaving a residue on the bottom of the container.

Why do we find the instruction "Shake well before using" on the labels of some medicines?
(1) The liquid is a solution.
(2) The mixture is not a solution.
(3) The particles are the size of molecules.
(4) The particles are not visible.
(5) Light goes through the solution.

Questions 51 to 53 refer to the following article.

Compounds known as bases are bitter to the taste and have a slippery feel. Acids taste sour. Litmus paper is used to determine whether a substance is acidic or basic; the paper turns blue in a base and red in an acid. If exactly correct quantities of an acid and a base are combined, they react chemically to produce a salt, which is neither acidic nor basic.

51. All of the following are acids EXCEPT
(1) oranges
(2) vinegar
(3) sour cream
(4) apples
(5) butter

52. Which of the following would turn litmus paper blue?
(1) alcohol
(2) soap
(3) grapefruit
(4) pure water
(5) cola

53. Either a base such as ammonia or an acid such as vinegar can clean accumulated dirt from glass. Knowing this, a housekeeper makes a mixture of ammonia and vinegar to clean windows. How will this work?
(1) There is no way to predict how well the mixture will work.
(2) The mixture will work better than either substance alone.
(3) The ammonia will still be effective, but the vinegar will not improve the material.
(4) The vinegar will still be effective, but the ammonia will not improve the material.
(5) The mixture will probably not work well at all.

---

54. Which of the following general rules is the best explanation of the way an ice cube cools a drink?
(1) Cold moves to objects of higher temperature.
(2) Heat moves to objects of higher density.
(3) Heat moves to objects of lower density.
(4) Cold moves to objects of lower temperature.
(5) Heat moves to objects of lower temperature.

Questions 55 to 58 are based on the following passage and diagram.

When air rises, it expands, and this change makes it cool down. Conversely, when air sinks, it is compressed and becomes warmer. As air cools down, its relative humidity rises; when the relative humidity reaches 100%, moisture condenses out of the air.

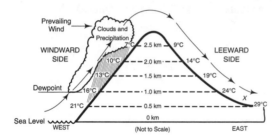

The diagram shows the prevailing wind directions and air temperatures at different elevations on both sides of a mountain.

55. What is the approximate air temperature at the top of the mountain?
(1) 12°C
(2) 10°C
(3) 0°C
(4) 7°C
(5) 4°C

56. On which side of the mountain and at what elevation is the relative humidity probably 100%?
(1) on the windward side at 0.5 km
(2) on the windward side at 2.5 km
(3) on the leeward side at 1.0 km
(4) on the leeward side at 2.5 km
(5) on the leeward side at 1.5 km

57. How does the temperature of the air change as the air rises on the windward side of the mountain between sea level and 0.5 kilometer?
(1) The air is warming owing to compression of the air.
(2) The air is warming owing to expansion of the air.
(3) The air is cooling owing to compression of the air.
(4) The air is cooling owing to expansion of the air.
(5) The air is warmed and cooled owing to expansion of the air.

58. Which feature is probably located at the base of the mountain on the leeward side (location X)?
(1) a dry, desertlike region
(2) a jungle
(3) a glacier
(4) a large lake
(5) a river

59. Human activities produce or add all these pollutants EXCEPT
   (1) sound
   (2) pollen
   (3) radiation
   (4) smoke
   (5) carbon oxides

Questions 60 and 61 are based on the following passage and diagram.

The block marked *A* is being pulled uphill at constant speed by the falling weight. Since the speed is constant, the force pulling the block uphill must be equal in magnitude to the force holding it back. This opposing force is called friction.

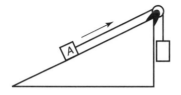

60. How would the situation change if a larger weight were used?
   (1) Nothing would be different.
   (2) Both the block and the weight would accelerate instead of going at a constant speed.
   (3) Both the block and the weight would be going at a higher constant speed.
   (4) The weight would accelerate, but the block would still travel at constant speed.
   (5) Both the block and the weight would slow down.

61. While you are probably most familiar with animals that have an internal skeleton, called an endoskeleton, certain organisms have their skeletons on the outside of their bodies. This exoskeleton is an excellent means of support and protection, but as the animal grows, its skeleton does not. Because of this, the exoskeleton has to be shed or molted now and then.

Animals with an exoskeleton are called invertebrates. Of the animals listed below, which one is *not* an invertebrate?
   (1) lobster
   (2) turtle
   (3) snail
   (4) horseshoe crab
   (5) spider

Questions 62 to 66 refer to the following information.

An experiment was performed to find out whether there are any circumstances in which an abnormal type of fruit fly has a selective advantage over the normal kind. Two culture bottles were prepared, using the same kind of food, and were kept next to each other for the entire period of the experiment. Bottle *A* had a small strip of flypaper suspended from its stopper; *B* did not. Four kinds of flies were introduced into each bottle: 10 males and 10 females each of wingless and normal fruit flies.

62. Which of the following is an important control in this experiment?
(1) the use of both males and females
(2) placing the flypaper in one bottle only
(3) using the same kind of food in both bottles
(4) putting both kinds of flies in each bottle
(5) taking care that the bottles are well stoppered

63. What is the hypothesis being tested?
(1) Male fruit flies have a better survival rate than females.
(2) Flies with wings have a better survival rate than those without.
(3) There are circumstances in which winglessness confers an advantage in survival.
(4) Wingless flies have a better survival rate than those with wings.
(5) All kinds of flies are equally likely to survive.

64. The experiment started with equal numbers of the four kinds of flies in each jar. This is
(1) an irrelevant fact
(2) a detail of experimental design
(3) an assumption
(4) a general law of nature
(5) an experimental finding

65. It is known that winglessness in fruit flies sometimes arises by mutation. In the context of this experiment, this is
(1) an assumption
(2) a general law of nature
(3) a hypothesis
(4) a statement of the problem
(5) an irrelevant fact

66. What general principle of nature would be explained by finding that most of the flies with wings died on the flypaper?

(1) Flypaper is an effective means of control of insects.

(2) Fruit flies exist in nature in many different forms.

(3) Evolution favors the forms with the best survival values.

(4) The survival value of a trait depends on the environment in which the organism lives.

(5) Processes in natural ecosystems cannot be simulated in the laboratory.

END OF EXAMINATION

TEST 4: INTERPRETING LITERATURE AND THE ARTS

Directions

Alloted Time: 65 minutes

The Interpreting Literature and the Arts test consists of excerpts from classical and popular literature and articles about literature or the arts. Each excerpt is followed by multiple-choice questions about the reading material.

Read each excerpt first and then answer the questions following it. Refer to the reading material as often as necessary in answering the questions.

Each excerpt is preceded by a "purpose question." The purpose question gives a reason for reading the material. Use these purpose questions to help focus your reading. You are not required to answer these purpose questions. They are given only to help you concentrate on the ideas presented in the reading materials.

You should spend no more than 65 minutes answering the questions. Work carefully, but do not spend too much time on any one question. Be sure you answer every question. You will not be penalized for incorrect answers.

To record your answers, mark the numbered space on the answer sheet beside the number that corresponds to the question in the test.

FOR EXAMPLE:

It was Susan's dream machine. The metallic blue paint gleamed, and the sporty wheels were highly polished. Under the hood, the engine was no less carefully cleaned. Inside, flashy lights illuminated the instruments on the dashboard, and the seats were covered in rich leather upholstery.

The subject ("It") of this excerpt is most likely

(1) an airplane   ① ② ● ④ ⑤
(2) a stereo system
(3) an automobile
(4) a boat
(5) a motorcycle

The correct answer is "an automobile"; therefore, answer space 3 would be marked on the answer sheet.

Questions 1 to 5 refer to the following excerpt from a work of prose nonfiction.

WHAT WAS MARY WHITE'S LAST HOUR LIKE?

The last hour of Mary White's life was typical of its happiness. She came home from a day's work at school, topped off by a hard grind with the copy on the high school annual, and felt that a ride would refresh her. She climbed into her khakis, chattering to her mother about the work she was doing, and

(5) hurried to get her horse and be out on the dirt roads for the country air and the radiant green fields of the spring. As she rode through the town at an easy gallop, she kept waving at passersby. She knew everyone in town. For a decade the little figure with the long pigtail and the red hair ribbon had been familiar on the streets of Emporia, and she got in the way of speaking to

(10) those who nodded at her. She passed the Kerrs, walking the horse, in front of the Normal Library, and waved at them; passed another friend a few hundred feet farther on, and waved at her. The horse was walking, and as she turned into North Merchant Street, she took off her cowboy hat, and the horse swung into a lope. She passed the Tripletts and waved her cowboy hat at

(15) them, still moving gaily north on Merchant Street. A Gazette carrier passed— a high school boy friend—and she waved at him, but with her bridle hand; the horse veered quickly, plunged into the parking lot where a low-hanging limb faced her, and while she still looked back waving, the blow came. But she did not fall from the horse; she slipped off, dazed a bit, staggered, and

(20) fell in a faint. She never quite recovered consciousness.

—W.A. White

1. The passage gives details that create a picture of
    (1) a sad death
    (2) a bookish lady
    (3) an active girl
    (4) a boy-crazy kid
    (5) a pathetic child

2. Mary White was
    (1) small of stature
    (2) big-boned
    (3) tall
    (4) husky
    (5) pretty

3. The picture contains such details as
    (1) jeans, a green ribbon, a pigtail
    (2) riding clothes, sombrero, plait
    (3) overalls, cowboy hat, short hair
    (4) khakis, cowboy hat, red hair ribbon
    (5) bridle, saddle, spurs

4. The death of Mary White can be said to have been caused indirectly by her
    (1) poor horsemanship
    (2) small size
    (3) fast riding
    (4) friendliness
    (5) failure to take proper precautions

5. The main purpose of the author is to
    (1) report the tragic end of a happy life
    (2) stress that it was an accident that killed Mary White
    (3) inform us of the mistake she made in waving with the wrong hand
    (4) show Mary White's bravery in not falling from the horse
    (5) emphasize the unexpectedness of the fatal blow

Questions 6 to 10 refer to the following excerpt from a work of prose fiction.

WHAT CAN A BEREAVED FATHER DO?

Iona sees a hall porter with some sacking, and decides to talk to him.

"Friend, what sort of time is it?" he asks.

"Past nine. What are you standing here for? Move on."

Iona moves on a few steps, doubles up, and abandons himself to his grief. He gives a tug at the reins; he can bear it no longer. "The stables," he thinks, and the little horse, as if it understood, starts off at a trot.

One of the cabdrivers around the stove half gets up, grunts sleepily, and stretches toward a bucket of water.

"Do you want a drink?" Iona asks him.

"Don't I want a drink!"

"That's so? Your good health! But listen, mate—you know, my son is dead...Did you hear? This week, in the hospital...It's a long story."

Iona looks to see what effect his words have, but sees none—the young man is fast asleep again. Just as much as the young one wants to drink, the old man wants to talk. Is It nothing to tell?

"I'll go and look after my horse," thinks Iona; "there's always time to sleep. No fear of that!"

When he is alone, he dares not think of his son; he can speak about him to anyone, but to think of him, and picture him to himself, is unbearably painful.

"That's how it is, my old horse. There's no more Kuzma Ionitch. Now let's say, you had a foal, you were this foal's mother, and suddenly, let's say, that foal went out and left you to live after him. It would be sad, wouldn't it?"

The little horse munches, listens, and breathes over its master's hand...

Iona's feelings are too much for him, and he tells the little horse the whole story.

6. In this story it is ironic that
   (1) the cabdriver wants a drink
   (2) the hall porter tells Iona to move on
   (3) Iona tells his story to his horse
   (4) Iona has run out of food for his horse
   (5) the horse had a foal

7. Iona goes to take care of his horse. He does so most probably to
   (1) have something to do
   (2) protest the high cost of feed
   (3) show his great love for his horse
   (4) prove that he does not resent the cabdriver's action
   (5) remove his feelings of guilt

8. The setting for this story is probably a 19th-century
   (1) American city
   (2) eastern European city
   (3) northern European farm
   (4) American small town
   (5) English city

9. The author's purpose in using the present tense is most probably to
   (1) make the story seem modern
   (2) increase the length of the story
   (3) heighten the reader's sense of immediacy
   (4) write the story as consciously as possible
   (5) reinforce the first-person point of view

10. Iona's situation is brought home to the reader when he
   (1) asks the hall porter for the time
   (2) asks the cabdriver for a drink
   (3) talks to himself
   (4) fights off sleep
   (5) compares himself to a foal's mother

Questions 11 to 15 refer to the following excerpt from a work
of prose fiction.

HOW DID A MOTHER AND A SON REACT TO A TRAGEDY?

After living nearly two years in Cairo, I had brought my son Guy to
enter the University of Ghana in Accra. Guy was seventeen and quick. I
was thirty-three and determined. We were Black Americans in West
Africa, where for the first time in our lives the color of our skin was
(5) accepted as correct and normal. The future was plump with promise. For
two days Guy and I laughed. On the third day, Guy, on a pleasure outing,
was injured in an automobile accident. One arm and one leg were
fractured and his neck was broken.

July and August stretched out like fat men yawning after a sumptuous
(10) dinner. They had every right to gloat, for they had eaten me up. Gobbled
me down. Consumed my spirit, not in a wild rush, but slowly, with the
obscene patience of certain victors. I became a shadow walking in the
white hot streets, and a dark spectre in the hospital.

Trying utterly, I could not match Guy's stoicism. He lay calm, in a
(15) prison of plaster from which only his face and one leg and arm were
visible. His assurances that he would heal and be better than new drove
me into a faithless silence.

Admittedly, Guy lived with the knowledge that an unexpected sneeze
could force the fractured vertebrae against his spinal cord, and he would
(20) be paralyzed or die immediately, but he had only an infatuation with life.
He hadn't lived long enough to fall in love with this brutally delicious
experience. He could lightly waft away to another place, if there really
was another place, where his youthful innocence would assure him
wings, a harp, and an absence of nostalgic yearning. My wretchedness
(25) reminded me that, on the other hand, I would be rudderless. We had
been each other's home and center for seventeen years. He could die if
he wanted to and go off to wherever dead folks go, but I, I would be left
without a home.

—Maya Angelou

11. The narrator notes that there are differences between herself
and Guy in both age and
(1) education
(2) temperament
(3) intelligence
(4) agility
(5) devotion

12. Which literary device is used in line 9?
(1) understatement
(2) hyperbole
(3) simile
(4) onomatopoeia
(5) metaphor

13. The word *they*, as used in line 10, is intended to mean the
(1) certain victors
(2) days of July and August
(3) fat men
(4) narrator's thoughts
(5) West Africans

14. The narrator portrays the delicate nature of her son's life with the words
(1) "seventeen and quick"
(2) "dark spectre"
(3) "hadn't lived long"
(4) "lightly waft away"
(5) "infatuation with life"

15. What does the imagery in lines 12 and 13 convey about the narrator's situation?
  (1) Her sudden helplessness seemed unreal.
  (2) Her physical health had deteriorated.
  (3) She was a Black American walking freely in a once white-only area.
  (4) She was undefeated by the adversity of life.
  (5) She was uncertain about her future.

Questions 16 to 20 refer to the following poem.

WHAT IS IT LIKE WHEN ELECTRIC POLES REPLACE TREES?

On their sides, resembling fallen timbers without rough
Barks—a hundred feet apart—lie power poles.
Just yesterday, this road was edged
With eucalyptus; in aisles
Between rows of trees, seats for the aged.
Now tree odors hover in the air, residues of life.
The poles are erected. The frigid,
Passionless verticals
Strive
To fill the socket-shaped holes
Left by trees. Identical, cement-wedged
Below, parasitically fastened to live wires above,
Tree imposters, never to be budged
From a telegraphic owl's
Knowitallness, they stand—rigid!
Sad children, wishing to climb, scan the miles
And miles of uninterrupted electric forests for
leaves.

16. Which phrase best expresses the ideas of this poem?
  (1) the new trees
  (2) the promising verticals
  (3) improving the landscape
  (4) on climbing trees
  (5) tree odors

17. The poet seems to resent the power poles'
  (1) rough barks
  (2) new odors
  (3) lifelessness

    (4) expensiveness
    (5) electric charge

18. In this poem, the children are sad because
    (1) the poles are too slippery to climb
    (2) the poles are too rigid to climb
    (3) they have been forbidden to climb the poles
    (4) the poles have replaced the trees
    (5) they have grown to love the owls

19. The poet's point of view is expressed by the use of such phrases as
    (1) fallen timbers
    (2) power poles
    (3) passionless verticals
    (4) socket-shaped holes
    (5) live wires

20. An example of a poetic figure of speech is found in the words
    (1) tree odors
    (2) cement-wedged
    (3) tree imposters
    (4) sad children
    (5) scan the miles

Questions 21 to 25 refer to the following poem.

WHAT IS THE REACTION OF A TEACHER
TO HIS STUDENT'S DEATH?

I remember the neckcurls, limp and damp
    as tendrils;
And her quick look, a sidelong pickerel
    smile;
(5) And how, once startled into talk, the light
    syllables leaped for her,
And she balanced in the delight of her
    thought,
A wren, happy, tail into the wind,
(10) Her song trembling the twigs and small
    branches.
The shade sang with her;
The leaves, their whispers turned to kissing;

And the mold sang in the bleached valleys
(15)   under the rose.
Oh, when she was sad, she cast herself
down into such a pure depth,
Even a father could not find her:
Scraping her cheek against straw;
(20) Stirring the clearest water.
My sparrow, you are not here,
Waiting like a fern, making a spiny shadow.
The sides of wet stones cannot console me,
Nor the moss, wound with the last light.

(25) If only I could nudge you from this sleep,
My maimed darling, my skittery pigeon.
Over this damp grave I speak the words of
my love:
I, with no rights in this matter,
(30) Neither father nor lover.

—Theodore Roethke, *"Elegy for Jane"*

21. The poet wrote this poem mainly to
(1) describe Jane
(2) criticize Jane
(3) mourn Jane
(4) remember Jane
(5) forget Jane

22. The poet's feeling for Jane, as indicated in the poem, is one of
(1) awe
(2) reverence
(3) regret
(4) nostalgia
(5) love

23. To what does the poet repeatedly compare Jane?
(1) a flower
(2) a shooting star
(3) a bird
(4) a small pet
(5) a lovely song

24. The change that takes place in the poem starting on line 21
is that the poet
(1) becomes resigned
(2) recollects further details
(3) compares himself to a father
(4) talks directly to the dead student
(5) becomes more angry at his loss

25. The poem is powerful in its impact on the reader because
the poet feels he
(1) is like a father to Jane
(?) is like a lover to Jane
(3) is like a teacher to Jane
(4) has no right to write the poem
(5) is responsible for her tragedy

Questions 26 to 30 refer to the following excerpt from a play.

HOW DOES THE FAMILY RESPOND TO LINDNER'S OFFER?

WALTER: I mean—I have worked as a chauffeur most of my life—and
          my wife here, she does domestic work in people's kitchens.
          So does my mother, I mean—we are plain people . . .

LINDNER: Yes, Mr. Younger—

WALTER: [*Really like a small boy, looking down at his shoes and then
          up at the man*] And—uh—well, my father, well, he was a
          laborer most of his life.

LINDNER: [*Absolutely confused*] Uh, yes—

WALTER: [*Looking down at his toes once again*] My father almost
          beat a man to death once because this man called him a
          bad name or something, you know what I mean?

LINDNER: No, I'm afraid I don't.

WALTER: [*Finally straightening up*] Well, what I means is that we
          come from people who had a lot of pride. I mean—we are
          very proud people. And that's my sister over there and
          she's going to be a doctor—and we are very proud—

LINDNER: Well—I am sure that is very nice, but—

WALTER: [*Starting to cry and facing the man eye to eye*] What I am
          telling you is that we called you over here to tell you that
          we are very proud and that this is—this is my son, who
          makes the sixth generation of our family in this country,
          and that we have all thought about your offer and we have

decided to move into our house because my father—my
father—he earned it. [MAMA *has her eyes closed and is
rocking back and forth as though she were in church, with
her head nodding the amen yes*] We don't want to make no
trouble for nobody or fight no causes—but we will try to be
good neighbors. That's all we got to say. [*He looks the man
absolutely in the eyes*] We don't want your money. [*He
turns and walks away from the man*]

LINDNER: [*Looking around at all of them*] I take it then that you have
              decided to occupy.

BENEATHA: That's what the man said.

LINDNER: [*To* MAMA *in her reverie*] Then I would like to appeal to
              you, Mrs. Younger. You are older and wiser and understand
              things better I am sure...

MAMA: [*Rising*] I am afraid you don't understand. My son said we
              was going to move and there ain't nothing left for me to
              say. [*Shaking her head with double meaning*] You know
              how these young folks is nowadays, mister. Can't do a
              thing with 'em. Good-bye.

LINDNER: [*Folding up his materials*] Well—if you are that final about
              it... There is nothing left for me to say. [*He finishes. He is
              almost ignored by the family who are concentrating on*
              WALTER LEE. *At the door* LINDNER *halts and looks around*]
              I sure hope you people know what you're doing. [*He shakes
              his head and exits*]

—Lorraine Hansberry, *A Raisin in the Sun*

26. The story Walter tells about his father almost beating a man
    to death for calling him a name is
    (1) an anecdote
    (2) a lie
    (3) a warning
    (4) a dream
    (5) an allusion

27. From this point on, the family will
    (1) stay in the ghetto
    (2) try for a new life
    (3) sell their house
    (4) retreat to the South
    (5) fight for causes

28. After this incident, the head of the house will be
(1) Travis
(2) Mama
(3) Walter
(4) Ruth
(5) Beneatha

29. Mr. Lindner
(1) understands the Youngers
(2) despises the Youngers
(3) is sympathetic to the Youngers
(4) is tolerant of the Youngers
(5) disagrees with the Youngers

30. The word that best describes Walter's family is
(1) plain
(2) vicious
(3) proud
(4) trouble-making
(5) uncooperative

Questions 31 to 35 refer to the following passage.

HOW DOES AN INDIAN CHIEF REMEMBER HIS CHILDHOOD?
I have acted in the movies and in Wild West shows, and served as an
interpreter between the Indian and the White man. I have met presidents
and kings, writers, scientists, and artists. I have had much joy and
received many honors, but I have never forgotten my wild, free childhood
when I lived in a tepee and heard the calling of the coyotes under the
stars . . . when the night winds, the sun, and everything else in our
primitive world reflected the wisdom and benevolence of the Great Spirit.
I remember seeing my mother bending over an open fire toasting buffalo
meat, and my father returning at night with an antelope on his shoulder. I
remember playing with the other children on the banks of a clean river,
and I shall never forget when my grandfather taught me how to make a
bow and arrow from hard wood and flint, and a fishhook from the rib of a
field mouse. I am not sentimental but memories haunt me as I review
scenes from those days before I was old enough to understand that all
Indian things would pass away.
The average American child of today would enjoy the privileges I had
out there on the unspoiled prairie one hundred years ago. I was usually

awake in time to see the sun rise. If the weather was warm, I went down to the river that flowed near our village and dipped water out of it with my hands for a drink, then plunged into it. The river came down out of the hills, ferrying leaves, blossoms, and driftwood. Fish could be seen in the pools formed near the rapids over which it rippled. Birds nested and flew among the banks, and occasionally I would see a coon or a fox in the brush. Hawks circled overhead, searching the ground for mice or other small animals for their breakfast, or to feed the young in their nests. There were never enough hours in a day to exhaust the pleasure of observing every living creature—from the orb spider spinning his magic and all but invisible web to the bald eagles on their bulky nests atop the tallest trees, teaching fledglings how to eject safely.

—Memoirs of Chief Red Fox

31. The mood of the selection is one of
 (1) nostalgia
 (2) bitterness
 (3) resignation
 (4) envy
 (5) anticipation

32. One of the most important of the chief's memories is that of
 (1) Wild West shows
 (2) many honors
 (3) meeting presidents and kings
 (4) family members
 (5) coyotes

33. The writer's primitive world was characterized by
 (1) evidence of the Great Spirit
 (2) fishhooks
 (3) bow and arrow
 (4) the call of the coyotes
 (5) night winds

34. The writer's love of nature led him to
 (1) observe it closely
 (2) benefit from its warmth
 (3) collect specimens
 (4) search for small animals
 (5) sleep late

35. Nature a hundred years ago was preferable to nature today because it was more

(1) varied
(2) wild
(3) magical
(4) friendly
(5) unspoiled

Questions 36 to 40 refer to the following commentary on the plays *Romeo and Juliet* and *West Side Story.*

HOW DO *ROMEO AND JULIET* AND *WEST SIDE STORY* COMPARE?

What glorious verse falls from the lips of Shakespeare's boys and girls! True, there is a rollicking jazzy vigor in such songs of *West Side Story* as the one of Officer Krupke, but it pales alongside the pyrotechnical display of Mercurio's Queen Mab speech. There is
(5) tenderness in "Maria," but how relatively tongue-tied is the twentieth-century hero alongside the boy who cried, "He jests at scars that never felt a wound." "Hold my hand and we're halfway there," say Maria and Tony to each other, and the understatement touches us. But "Gallop apace, you fiery-footed steeds" and the lines that follow glow with a glory
(10) that never diminishes. The comparisons of language could be multiplied, and always, of course, Shakespeare is bound to win.

Without its great poetry *Romeo and Juliet* would not be a major tragedy. Possibly it is not, in any case; for as has frequently been remarked, Shakespeare's hero and heroine are a little too slender to carry
(15) the full weight of tragic grandeur. Their plight is more pathetic than tragic. If this is true of them, it is equally true of Tony and Maria: for them, too, pathos rather than tragedy. But there is tragedy implicit in the environmental situation of the contemporary couple, and this must not be overlooked or underestimated. Essentially, however, what we see is that
(20) all four young people strive to consummate the happiness at the threshold on which they stand and which they have tasted so briefly. All four are deprived of the opportunity to do so, the Renaissance couple by the caprice of fate, today's youngsters by the prejudice and hatred engendered around them. All four are courageous and lovable. All four
(25) arouse our compassion, even though they may not shake us with Aristotelian fear.

Poets and playwrights will continue to write of youthful lovers whom fate drives into and out of each other's lives. The spectacle will always trouble and move us.

36. The author of the selection implies that

   (1) the songs of *West Side Story* lack strength

   (2) the language of *West Side Story* leaves us cold

   (3) the language of *Romeo and Juliet* lacks the vigor of that of *West Side Story*

   (4) the poetry of *Romeo and Juliet* will prevail

   (5) the speech of *West Side Story* can compete with the verse of *Romeo and Juliet*

37. In comparing the language of *Romeo and Juliet* with that of *West Side Story* the author

   (1) takes no position

   (2) likes each equally

   (3) favors that of *Romeo and Juliet*

   (4) favors that of *West Side Story*

   (5) downplays the differences

38. Both plays share a common weakness. That weakness is

   (1) the stature of their heroes and heroines

   (2) the absence of deep emotion

   (3) their dramatic construction

   (4) the lack of substance of their themes

   (5) the lack of linguistic power

39. The couples in the two plays share all of the following EXCEPT

   (1) a pathetic situation

   (2) lack of opportunity to achieve happiness

   (3) courage

   (4) inability to instill fear in the reader

   (5) inability to arouse pity in the reader

40. The couples in the two plays differ in the nature of

   (1) their plight

   (2) their ultimate fate

   (3) the cause of their tragic situation

   (4) their attractiveness

   (5) their love for one another

Questions 41 to 45 refer to the following article on art.

WHAT IS THE MESSAGE OF CHAGALL'S WORK?

"Your colors sing!" Chagall's teacher, Leon Bakst, had told him.
Indeed, Chagall slapped on colors in bold, solid patches, often
contrasting them with striking effects. His burning reds, juicy greens and
the magic "Chagall blue" give an almost sensual gratification. Yet when I
(5) once asked, "How do you get your blues?" he replied with a typical pixie
twinkle, "I buy them in a shop. They come in tubes."

When he entered his 60s, the painter's inventiveness began to run
dry. He had become, in the words of one critic, "his own most faithful
imitator." At this crucial point, inspiration struck. Chagall turned to
(10) stained glass. He spent days examining the gemlike windows in France's
great medieval cathedrals, where plain bits of colored glass were turned
into jewels by the sun. In 1957 he made two small windows, depicting
angels, for a chapel in Savoy. The next year he met one of France's
foremost stained-glass makers, Charles Marq. Chagall began spending up
(15) to 12 hours a day at the Marq workshop in the cathedral town of Reims.

Chagall's stained-glass creations, a staggering total of 11,000 square
feet, include windows for churches, a cynagogue in Jerusalem, and the
General Assembly Building of the U.N. in New York. But when Chagall
was approached in 1972 to do three windows in Reims's 13th-century
(20) cathedral, where more than 20 French kings were crowned, he was
alarmed. "I adorn a national shrine? Unthinkable." Finally he complied,
once more refusing pay.

On entering the dim Gothic nave of Reims Cathedral today, the first
thing you perceive in the distance is the sapphire gleam of Chagall's
(25) stained-glass window, depicting, on the left, the sacrifice of Abraham
and, on the right, Christ on the cross. In joining Old and New Testaments
into a harmonious whole, Chagall reflected his own deep faith in the all-
embracing message of Scripture—mankind's ascent through suffering to
salvation.

41. The author writes approvingly of which of the following traits in
Chagall's character?
(1) his sensuality
(2) his arrogance
(3) his imitativeness
(4) his impish humor
(5) his materialism

42. The article is most concerned with Chagall's
    (1) paintings
    (2) pastels
    (3) murals
    (4) drawings
    (5) stained glass

43. In his paintings, Chagall used
    (1) contrasting colors
    (2) soft solid colors
    (3) Chagall reds
    (4) gemlike radiances
    (5) sapphire gleams

44. According to the article, Chagall believed deeply in
    (1) French kings
    (2) national shrines
    (3) mankind's salvation
    (4) the Old Testament only
    (5) the New Testament only

45. Chagall turned to the medium of stained glass because
    (1) it was more profitable
    (2) he met Charles Marq
    (3) he was invited to work in the Reims Cathedral
    (4) he had come to imitate his own work
    (5) he got magic blues

END OF EXAMINATION

TEST 5: MATHEMATICS

Directions

Alloted Time: 90 minutes

The Mathematics test consists of 56 multiple-choice questions intended to measure general mathematics skills and problem-solving ability. The questions are based on short readings that often include a graph, chart, or figure.

You should spend no more than 90 minutes answering the questions. Work carefully, but do not spend too much time on any one question. Be sure you answer every question. You will not be penalized for incorrect answers.

Formulas you may need are given below. Only some of the questions will require you to use a formula. Not all the formulas given will be needed. Some questions contain more information than you will need to solve the problem. Other questions do not give enough information to solve the problem. If the question does not give enough information to solve the problem, the correct answer is "Not enough information is given."

The use of calculators is not allowed.

To record your answers, mark the numbered space on the answer sheet beside the number that corresponds to the question in the test.

EXAMPLE:

If a grocery bill totaling $15.75 is paid with a $20.00 bill, how much change should be returned?

(1) $5.26   ① ② ● ④ ⑤
(2) $4.75
(3) $4.25
(4) $3.75
(5) $3.25

The correct answer is "$4.25"; therefore, answer space 3 would be marked on the answer sheet.

FORMULAS

Description	Formula
AREA (*A*) of a:	
square	$A = s^2$; where s = side
rectangle	$A = lw$; where l = length, w = width
parallelogram	$A = bh$; where b = base, h = height
triangle	$A = \frac{1}{2}bh$; where b = base, h = height
circle	$A = \pi r^2$; where π = 3.14, r = radius
PERIMETER (*P*) of a:	
square	$P = 4s$; where s = side
rectangle	$P = 2l + 2w$; where l = length, w = width
triangle	$P = a + b + c$; where a, b, and c are the sides
circumference (*C*) of a circle	$C = \pi d$; where π = 3.14, d = diameter

FORMULAS continued

Description	Formula
VOLUME (V) of a: cube rectangular container cylinder	$V = s^3$; where s = side $V = lwh$; where l = length, w = width, h = height $V = \pi r^2 h$; where π = 3.14, r = radius, h = height
Pythagorean relationship distance (d) between two points in a plane slope of a line (m)	$c^2 = a^2 + b^2$; where c = hypotenuse, a and b are legs, of a right triangle $d = \sqrt{(x_2 - x_1)^2 + (y_2 - y_1)^2}$; where (x_1,y_1) and (x_2,y_2) are two points in a plane $m = \dfrac{y_2 - y_1}{x_2, y_1}$; where (x_1,y_1) and (x_2, y_2) are two points in a plane
mean median	$\text{mean} = \dfrac{x_1 + x_2 + \ldots + x_n}{n}$; where the x's are the values for which a mean is desired, and n = number of values in the series median = the point in an ordered set of numbers at which half of the numbers are above and half of the numbers are below this value
simple interest (i) distance (d) as function of rate and time total cost (c)	$i = prt$; where p = principal, r = rate, t = time $d = rt$; where r = rate, t = time $c = nr$; where n = number of units, r = cost per unit

1. On 5 successive days a deliveryman listed his mileage as follows: 135, 162, 98, 117, 216. If his truck averages 14 miles for each gallon of gas used, how many gallons of gas did he use during these 5 days?
   (1) 42
   (2) 52

(3) 115
(4) 147
(5) 153

2. Parking meters in Springfield read: "12 minutes for 5¢. Maximum deposit 50¢." What is the maximum time, in hours, that a driver may be legally parked at one of these meters?
    (1) 1
    (2) 1.2
    (3) 12
    (4) 2
    (5) Not enough information is given.

Question 3 is based on the following figure.

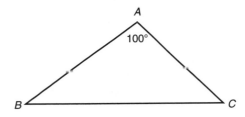

3. If *AB* = *AC* and m ∠*A* = 100°, what is the measure of ∠*B*?
    (1) 40°
    (2) 45°
    (3) 50°
    (4) 60°
    (5) 80°

---

4. The ABC Department Store had a special sale on shirts. One group sold at $15 per shirt, and another group sold at $18 per shirt. If 432 shirts were sold at $15 each and 368 shirts were sold at $18 each, the number of dollars taken in at the shirt sale may be represented as
    (1) 800(15 + 18)
    (2) (15)(368) + (18)(432)
    (3) (15)(800) + (18)(800)
    (4) 33(432 + 68)
    (5) (15)(432) + (368)(18)

5. A hockey team won X games, lost Y games, and tied Z games. What fractional part of the games played were won?

(1) $\dfrac{X}{X + Y + Z}$

(2) $\dfrac{X}{XYZ}$

(3) $\dfrac{X}{XY}$

(4) $\dfrac{X}{X + Y}$

(5) $\dfrac{X}{X - Y - Z}$

6. One-half the students at Madison High School walk to school. One-fourth of the rest go to school by bicycle. What part of the school population travels by some other means?

(1) 1/8
(2) 3/8
(3) 3/4
(4) 1/4
(5) Not enough information is given.

7. Which of the following is a solution of the inequality $2x > 9$?

(1) 0
(2) 2
(3) 3
(4) 4
(5) 5

8. Which of the following units would be most appropriate to measure the distance between New York and San Francisco?

(1) meter
(2) kilometer
(3) kilogram
(4) liter
(5) centimeter

9. A flagpole casts a shadow 16 feet long. At the same time, a pole 9 feet high casts a shadow 6 feet long. What is the height, in feet, of the flagpole?

(1) 18
(2) 19
(3) 20

(4) 24
(5) Not enough information is given.

10. Martin has a piece of lumber 9 feet 8 inches long. He wishes to cut it into 4 equal lengths. How far from the edge should he make the first cut?
    (1) 2.5 ft.
    (2) 2 ft. 5 in.
    (3) 2.9 ft.
    (4) 29 ft.
    (5) 116 in.

11. A purse contains 6 nickels, 5 dimes, and 8 quarters. If one coin is drawn at random from the purse, what is the probability that the coin drawn is a dime?
    (1) 5/19
    (2) 5/14
    (3) 5/8
    (4) 5/6
    (5) 19/5

12. The leaders in the Peninsula Golf Tournament finished with scores of 272, 284, 287, 274, 275, 283, 278, 276, and 281. What is the median of these scores?
    (1) 273
    (2) 274
    (3) 276
    (4) 278
    (5) 280

13. The cost of a dozen ballpoint pens and 8 pencils is $4.60. If the cost of the pens is 3 for $0.97, what is the cost, in cents, of 1 pencil?
    (1) 6
    (2) 8
    (3) 8.5
    (4) 9
    (5) 9.5

14. The scale on a map is 1 inch = 150 miles. The cities of Benton and Dover are $3\frac{1}{2}$ inches apart on this map. What is the actual distance, in miles, between Benton and Dover?

(1) 525
(2) 545
(3) 580
(4) 625
(5) Not enough information is given.

Question 15 is based on the following figure.

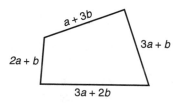

15. What is the perimeter of the figure?
(1) $8a + 5b$
(2) $9a + 7b$
(3) $7a + 5b$
(4) $6a + 6b$
(5) $8a + 6b$

Question 16 is based on the following number line.

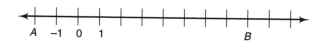

16. On the number line, what is the coordinate of the midpoint of $\overline{AB}$?
(1) −11
(2) 0
(3) 2
(4) 3
(5) 8

17. The Men's Shop advertised a spring sale. David Morris was especially interested in the following sale items.

ties: 3 for $23
shirts: 3 for $43
slacks: $32.75 per pair
jackets: $58.45 each
David bought 6 ties, 3 shirts, 2 pairs of slacks, and 1 jacket. What was his bill?
(1) $157.20
(2) $180.20
(3) $189.95
(4) $202.95
(5) $212.95

18. In which of the following lists are the numbers written in order from greatest to smallest?
(1) 0.80, 19%, 0.080, 1/2, 3/5
(2) 0.80, 1/2, 0.080, 3/5, 19%
(3) 0.80, 3/5, 1/2, 19%, 0.080
(4) 1/2, 0.80, 3/5, 19%, 0.080
(5) 3/5, 1/2, 19%, 0.080, 0.80

19. If an airplane completes its flight of 1,364 miles in 5 hours and 30 minutes, what is its average speed, in miles per hour?
(1) 240
(2) 244
(3) 248
(4) 250
(5) 260

20. The distance between two heavenly bodies is 85,000,000,000 miles. This number, written in scientific notation, is
(1) 8.5×10^{-10}
(2) 8.5×10^{10}
(3) 85×10^{9}
(4) 0.85×10^{-9}
(5) 850×10^{7}

21. What is the value of $3ab - x^2y$ if $a = 4$, $b = 5$, $y = 3$, and $x = 2$?
(1) 18
(2) 24
(3) 48
(4) 54
(5) 72

Questions 22 and 23 are based on the following graph.

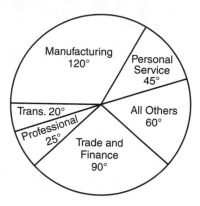

This circle graph shows how 180,000 wage earners in a certain city earned their livings during a given period.

22. The number of persons engaged in transportation in the city during this period was
   (1) 3,600
   (2) 9,000
   (3) 10,000
   (4) 18,000
   (5) 36,000

23. If the number of persons in trade and finance is represented by M, then the number in manufacturing is represented as
   (1) $M \div 3$
   (2) $M + 3$
   (3) $30M$
   (4) $4M \div 3$
   (5) Not enough information is given.

Question 24 is based on the following figure.

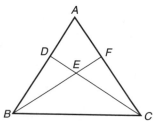

24. If $\overline{BF}$ bisects $\angle ABC$, $\overline{CD}$ bisects $\angle ACB$, $m\angle ABC = 68°$, and $m\angle ACB = 72°$, then $m\angle BEC =$
- (1) 90°
- (2) 98°
- (3) 100°
- (4) 110°
- (5) 120°

---

25. Bill has $5 more than Jack, and Jack has $3 less than Frank. If Frank has $30, how much money does Bill have?
- (1) $30
- (2) $27
- (3) $32
- (4) $36
- (5) Not enough information is given.

26. John Davis weighed 192 pounds. His doctor put him on a diet, which enabled him to lose at least 4 pounds per month. What was John's weight after 6 months on the diet?
- (1) 160 lb.
- (2) 165 lb.
- (3) 167 lb.
- (4) 168 lb.
- (5) Not enough information is given.

27. Mr. Ames bought a bond for $10,000. The bond yields interest at $8\frac{1}{2}\%$ annually. If the interest is paid every 6 months, how much is each interest payment?
- (1) $400
- (2) $425
- (3) $475
- (4) $500
- (5) $850

28. An aquarium is in the form of a rectangular solid. The aquarium is 3 feet long, 1 foot 8 inches wide, and 1 foot 6 inches high. What is the volume, in cubic feet, of the aquarium?
- (1) 6.16
- (2) 6.4
- (3) 7.5

(4) 7.875
(5) 8.64

29. The ratio of men to women at a professional meeting was 9:2. If there were 12 women at the meeting, how many men were at the meeting?
(1) 33
(2) 44
(3) 54
(4) 66
(5) Not enough information is given.

30. What is the slope of the line that passes through point A (2,1) and point B (4,7)?

(1) 1/3
(2) 2/3
(3) 3/2
(4) 2
(5) 3

31. In a basketball game Bill scored three times as many points as Jim. Together they scored 56 points. How many points did Bill score?
(1) 14
(2) 28
(3) 42
(4) 48
(5) Not enough information is given.

Question 32 is based on the following graph.

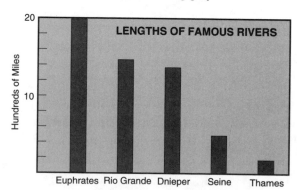

32. The graph shows the lengths of some famous rivers correct
to the nearest hundred miles.

Which one of the following statements is correct?
(1) The Thames is more than one-half as long as the Seine.
(2) The Dnieper is 1,200 miles long.
(3) The Euphrates is about 250 miles longer than the Rio Grande.
(4) The Rio Grande is about 1,000 miles longer than the Seine.
(5) The Thames is about 100 miles long.

Question 33 is based on the following graph.

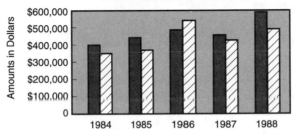

RECEIPTS AND EXPENDITURES

33. The graph shows receipts and expenses for the years indicated. The
receipts are designated by shaded bars and the expenses by striped bars.

The year in which receipts exceeded expenses by $100,000 was
(1) 1984
(2) 1985
(3) 1986
(4) 1987
(5) 1988

---

34. If 1 pencil costs y cents, then 6 pencils will cost, in cents,
(1) $6y$

(2) $\dfrac{y}{6}$

(3) $\dfrac{6}{y}$

(4) $y + 6$

(5) $\dfrac{y}{2}$

35. Mr. Martin earns $12 per hour. One week Mr. Martin worked 42 hours; the following week he worked 37 hours. Which of the following indicates the number of dollars Mr. Martin earned for the 2 weeks?

(1) $12 \times 2 + 37$
(2) $12 \times 42 + 42 \times 37$
(3) $12 \times 37 + 42$
(4) $12 + 42 \times 37$
(5) $12(42 + 37)$

36. The enrollment of a college is distributed as follows:

      360 freshmen
      300 sophomores
      280 juniors
      260 seniors

The freshman class makes up what percent of the total enrollment?

(1) 18%
(2) 20%
(3) 25%
(4) 30%
(5) Not enough information is given.

Question 37 is based on the following figure.

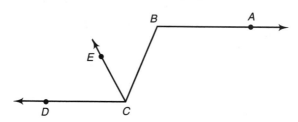

37. In the figure $\overleftrightarrow{AB}$ II $\overleftrightarrow{CD}$, $\overrightarrow{CE}$ bisects $\angle BCD$, and m$\angle ABC = 112°$. Find m$\angle ECD$.

(1) 45°
(2) 50°
(3) 56°
(4) 60°
(5) Not enough information is given.

38. Mrs. Garvin buys a bolt of cloth 22 feet 4 inches in length. She cuts the bolt into four equal pieces to make drapes. What is the length of each piece?

(1) 5 ft.
(2) 5 ft. 7 in.
(3) 5 ft. 9 in.
(4) 6 ft. 7 in.
(5) Not enough information is given.

Questions 39 and 40 are based on the following graph.

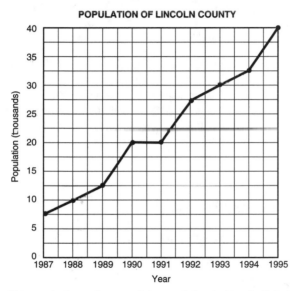

The graph shows the growth in population in Lincoln County between the years 1987 and 1995.

39. What was the population of Lincoln County in the year 1992?

(1) 20,000
(2) 25,000
(3) 26,000
(4) 27,500
(5) 30,000

40. The population of Lincoln County did not change between the years

(1) 1988 and 1989
(2) 1989 and 1990
(3) 1990 and 1991
(4) 1991 and 1992
(5) 1992 and 1993

---

41. A box is in the form of a rectangular solid with a square base of side x units in length and a height of 8 units. The volume of the box is 392 cubic units. Which of the following equations may be used to find the value of x?
(1) $x^2 = 392$
(2) $8x = 392$
(3) $8x^3 = 392$
(4) $8x^2 = 392$
(5) $8 + x^2 = 392$

42. There were three candidates at a school board election. Mrs. Clay received twice as many votes as Mr. Dunn, and Mr. Arnold received 66 votes more than Mr. Dunn. How many votes did Mrs. Clay receive?
(1) 209
(2) 275
(3) 320
(4) 402
(5) Not enough information is given.

Question 43 is based on the following figure.

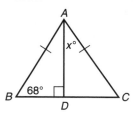

43. If $\overline{AB} = AC$, $\overline{AD} \perp \overline{BC}$, and m$\angle B = 68°$, what is the value of x?
(1) 12°
(2) 22°
(3) 32°
(4) 44°
(5) 68°

44. A hiker walks 12 miles due north. Then he turns and walks 16 miles due east. At this point, how many miles is the hiker from his starting point?
  (1) 12
  (2) 16
  (3) 18
  (4) 20
  (5) Not enough information is given.

45. The square root of 30 is between which of the following pairs of numbers?
  (1) 3 and 4
  (2) 4 and 5
  (3) 5 and 6
  (4) 6 and 7
  (5) 15 and 16

Question 46 is based on the following figure.

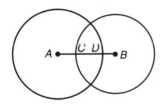

46. The radius of circle A measures 20 inches, and the radius of circle B measures 8 inches. If $CD = 6$ inches, find AB, in inches.
  (1) 22
  (2) 24
  (3) 25
  (4) 28
  (5) Not enough information is given.

Question 47 is based on the following figure.

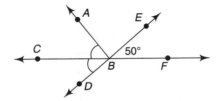

47. $\overleftrightarrow{CF}$ and $\overleftrightarrow{ED}$ intersect at B, m$\angle EBF = 50°$ and $\overrightarrow{CB}$ bisects $\angle ABD$. Find m$\angle ABC$.

(1) 30°
(2) 32°
(3) 40°
(4) 50°
(5) 60°

---

48. A woman buys *n* pounds of sugar at *c* cents a pound. She gives the clerk a $1.00 bill. The change she receives, in cents, is
(1) $nc - 100$
(2) $n + c - 100$
(3) $100 - (n + c)$
(4) $100 - nc$
(5) Not enough information is given.

49. Of a high school graduating class, 85% planned to go to college. If 170 graduates planned to go to college, how many students were in the graduating class?
(1) 200
(2) 250
(3) 340
(4) 400
(5) 500

Question 50 is based on the following figure.

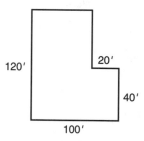

50. Mr. Denby planned to build a house on the plot of ground shown. What is the area, in square feet, of this plot of ground?
(1) 10,000
(2) 10,400
(3) 10,800
(4) 12,000
(5) 104,000

51. If $x = 10$, each of the following is true EXCEPT
    (1) $3x + 1 > 12$
    (2) $2x - 3 < 25$
    (3) $x^2 + 1 > x^2 - 1$
    (4) $4x - 1 = 39$
    (5) $2x - 7 < 7 - 2x$

52. In a right triangle the measure of one acute angle is 4 times as great as the measure of the other acute angle. What is the measure of the larger acute angle?
    (1) $18°$
    (2) $36°$
    (3) $40°$
    (4) $65°$
    (5) $72°$

53. The cost of borrowing a book from a circulating library is $0.50 for the first 3 days and $0.15 per day thereafter. A formula for finding the cost (C), in cents, of borrowing a book for n days ($n \geq 3$) is
    (1) $C - 50 + 15n$
    (2) $C = 50 + 15(n + 3)$
    (3) $C = 50(n - 3) + 15n$
    (4) $C = 50 + 15(n - 3)$
    (5) $C = 50(n + 3) + 15n$

Questions 54 and 55 are based on the following information.

In the figure below line $\overrightarrow{PQ}$ is parallel to line $\overrightarrow{RS}$.

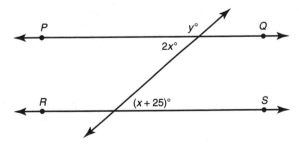

54. What is the value of x?
    (1) 15
    (2) 20
    (3) 25

(4) 30

(5) 35

55. What is the value of y?

(1) 130°

(2) 135°

(3) 140°

(4) 145°

(5) Not enough information is given.

---

56. Given the equation $x^2 - x - 12 = 0$, which of the following give(s) a complete solution of the equation?

(1) 4 only

(2) −4 only

(3) 3 and 4

(4) −3 and 4

(5) −4 and 3

END OF EXAMINATION

ANSWER KEYS, SUMMARIES OF RESULTS, AND SELF-APPRAISAL CHARTS

TEST 1: WRITING SKILLS, PART I

I. CHECK YOUR ANSWERS, using the following answer key:

1. **2**	12. **1**	23. **5**	34. **4**	45. **5**
2. **3**	13. **5**	24. **3**	35. **3**	46. **2**
3. **3**	14. **2**	25. **5**	36. **2**	47. **5**
4. **1**	15. **2**	26. **5**	37. **4**	48. **1**
5. **4**	16. **3**	27. **4**	38. **2**	49. **4**
6. **5**	17. **5**	28. **1**	39. **5**	50. **1**
7. **2**	18. **3**	29. **2**	40. **5**	51. **2**
8. **3**	19. **4**	30. **1**	41. **1**	52. **4**
9. **5**	20. **3**	31. **5**	42. **4**	53. **5**
10. **4**	21. **2**	32. **1**	43. **3**	54. **1**
11. **5**	22. **5**	33. **2**	44. **1**	55. **4**

II. SCORE YOURSELF:

Number correct:

Excellent _____
50–55

Good _____
44–49

Fair _____
36–43

III. EVALUATE YOUR SCORE: Did you get at least 38 correct answers? If not, you need more practice for the Writing Skills, Part I test. In any event, you can improve your performance to Excellent or Good by analyzing your errors.

IV. ANALYZE YOUR ERRORS: To determine your areas of weakness, list the number of correct answers you had under each of the following categories (which correspond to the content areas of the Writing Skills, Part I test), and compare your score with the average scores specified in the right-hand column. Review the answer analysis section beginning on page 347 for each of the questions you got wrong, and give yourself more practice in your weak areas with the appropriate material in Unit II before attempting Practice Examination One.

CONTENT AREAS	ITEMS	YOUR SCORE	AVERAGE SCORE
Sentence Structure	3, 5, 12, 16, 25, 29, 32, 34, 38, 40, 44, 49, 53, 55	_____	10
Usage	1, 8, 19, 20, 24, 52, 54	_____	5
Spelling	7, 10, 15, 18, 27–28, 43, 46, 48, 50	_____	7
Punctuation	2, 4, 14, 21, 26, 30, 33, 35–37, 41–42, 51	_____	9
Capitalization	4	_____	1
No correction	6, 9, 11, 13, 17, 22–23, 31, 39, 45, 47	_____	8
	Total	_____	

TEST 2: SOCIAL STUDIES

I. CHECK YOUR ANSWERS, using the following answer key:

1. **1**	14. **4**	27. **1**	40. **5**	53. **1**
2. **4**	15. **1**	28. **2**	41. **5**	54. **3**
3. **4**	16. **3**	29. **2**	42. **2**	55. **5**
4. **5**	17. **2**	30. **5**	43. **1**	56. **5**
5. **2**	18. **2**	31. **3**	44. **1**	57. **1**
6. **5**	19. **4**	32. **4**	45. **5**	58. **2**
7. **4**	20. **4**	33. **1**	46. **4**	59. **1**
8. **2**	21. **1**	34. **2**	47. **1**	60. **2**
9. **4**	22. **2**	35. **2**	48. **4**	61. **3**
10. **4**	23. **1**	36. **1**	49. **1**	62. **4**
11. **1**	24. **4**	37. **3**	50. **3**	63. **1**
12. **3**	25. **2**	38. **1**	51. **2**	64. **1**
13. **1**	26. **3**	39. **2**	52. **5**	

II. SCORE YOURSELF:

Number correct:

Excellent	_____
	57–64
Good	_____
	51–56
Fair	_____
	45–50

III. EVALUATE YOUR SCORE: Did you get at least 45 correct answers? If not, you need more practice for the Social Studies test. In any event, you can improve your performance to Excellent or Good by analyzing your errors.

II. ANALYZE YOUR ERRORS: To determine your specific weaknesses, list the number of correct answers you had under each of the following categories (which correspond to the content areas of the Social Studies test), and compare your score with the average scores specified in the right-hand column. Review the answer analysis section beginning on page 351 for each of the questions you got wrong, and give yourself more practice in your weak area with the appropriate material in Unit IV (including the "Glossary of Social Studies Terms") before attempting Practice Examination One.

CONTENT AREAS	ITEMS	YOUR SCORE	AVERAGE SCORE
Political Science	1–3, 12, 41–44, 56, 59	_____	8
Economics	4–6, 9, 13–14, 17–19, 21–22, 24, 32–33, 48, 52–54	_____	13
History	15–16, 20, 25, 34–38, 50–51, 57–58, 62–64	_____	12
Geography	7–8, 10–11, 26–28, 39–40, 60–61	_____	9
Behavioral Science	23, 29–31, 45–47, 49, 55	_____	6
	Total	_____	

TEST 3: SCIENCE

I. CHECK YOUR ANSWERS, using the following answer key:

1.	2	15.	1	29.	4	43.	5	57.	4
2.	4	16.	1	30.	5	44.	1	58.	1
3.	2	17.	1	31.	5	45.	4	59.	2
4.	4	18.	2	32.	4	46.	3	60.	2
5.	3	19.	4	33.	1	47.	3	61.	2
6.	3	20.	3	34.	3	48.	2	62.	3
7.	4	21.	4	35.	5	49.	2	63.	3
8.	5	22.	5	36.	5	50.	2	64.	2
9.	2	23.	4	37.	3	51.	5	65.	5
10.	5	24.	5	38.	4	52.	2	66.	4
11.	1	25.	3	39.	3	53.	5		
12.	4	26.	3	40.	3	54.	5		
13.	5	27.	4	41.	1	55.	5		
14.	3	28.	3	42.	3	56.	2		

II. SCORE YOURSELF:

Number correct:

Excellent   _____
                     60–66

Good   _____
                     49–59

Fair   _____
                     40–48

III. EVALUATE YOUR SCORE: Did you get at least 40 correct answers? If not, you need more practice for the Science test. In any event, you can improve your performance to Excellent or Good by analyzing your errors.

IV. ANALYZE YOUR ERRORS: To determine your specific weaknesses, encircle the number of each question that you got wrong. This will reveal the specific science area that needs emphasis in planning your study program. After studying the answer analysis section beginning on page 356 for each of the questions you got wrong, list the terms that you feel need further explanation and study them in the "Glossary of Scientific Terms." Then give yourself more practice in your weak areas with the appropriate material in Unit V before attempting Practice Examination One.

CONTENT AREAS	ITEMS	YOUR SCORE	AVERAGE SCORE
Biology	1–4, 24–39, 41–43, 45–49, 59, 61–66	_____	24
Earth Science	9–13, 17–19, 40, 44, 55–58	_____	7
Chemistry	20–23, 44, 50–52	_____	6
Physics	5–8, 14–16, 53–54, 60	_____	7
	Total	_____	

TEST 4: INTERPRETING LITERATURE AND THE ARTS

I. CHECK YOUR ANSWERS, using the following answer key:

1. **3**	10. **5**	19. **3**	28. **3**	37. **3**
2. **1**	11. **2**	20. **3**	29. **5**	38. **1**
3. **4**	12. **3**	21. **3**	30. **3**	39. **4**
4. **4**	13. **2**	22. **5**	31. **1**	40. **3**
5. **1**	14. **4**	23. **3**	32. **4**	41. **4**
6. **3**	15. **1**	24. **4**	33. **1**	42. **5**
7. **1**	16. **1**	25. **4**	34. **1**	43. **1**
8. **2**	17. **3**	26. **3**	35. **5**	44. **3**
9. **3**	18. **4**	27. **2**	36. **4**	45. **4**

II. SCORE YOURSELF:

Number correct:

Excellent _____
41–45

Good _____
36–40

Fair _____
31–35

III. EVALUATE YOUR SCORE: Did you get at least 31 correct answers? If not, you need more practice for the test on Interpreting Literature and the Arts. In any event, you can improve your performance to Excellent or Good by analyzing your errors.

IV. ANALYZE YOUR ERRORS: To determine your specific weaknesses, first list the number of correct answers you had under each of the following categories and compare your score with the average scores specified in the right-hand column. After studying the answer analysis section beginning on page 361 for each of the questions you got wrong, study the material in the section Basic Reading Skills and the section Reading Prose, Poetry, and Drama in Unit VI as well as the "Glossary of Literary Terms" to strengthen your weak areas before attempting Practice Examination One.

READING SKILLS	ITEMS	YOUR SCORE	AVERAGE SCORE
Locating the Main Idea	5, 16, 21, 44	_____	3
Finding Details	2, 3, 12, 18, 23–24, 32–33, 38–45	_____	11
Inferring Meaning	13–15, 19–20, 22, 34–35	_____	5
Making Inferences	1, 4, 7, 10, 25, 36–37	_____	5
Determining Tone and Mood	6, 9, 17, 26–27, 31	_____	4
Inferring Character	11, 28–30	_____	3
Inferring Setting	8	_____	1
	Total	_____	

Now, to see how your scores in the content areas of Interpreting Literature and the Arts test compare with the average scores in the right-hand column, list your score for each of the following:

CONTENT AREAS	ITEMS	YOUR SCORE	AVERAGE SCORE
Popular Literature	6–10, 16–35	_____	17
Classical Literature	1–5, 11–15	_____	7
Commentary	36–45	_____	7
	Total	_____	

LITERARY FORMS	ITEMS	YOUR SCORE	AVERAGE SCORE
Prose Fiction	6–15	_____	7
Prose Nonfiction	1–5, 31–35	_____	7
Prose Nonfiction (Commentary)	36–45	_____	7
Poetry	16–25	_____	7
Drama	26–30	_____	3
	Total	_____	

Note: While Commentary on the Arts is a content area in itself, the commentary, as written, is in the form of prose nonfiction.

TEST 5: MATHEMATICS

I. CHECK YOUR ANSWERS, using the following answer key:

1.	**2**	13.	**4**	25.	**3**	37.	**3**	49.	**1**
2.	**4**	14.	**1**	26.	**5**	38.	**2**	50.	**2**
3.	**1**	15.	**2**	27.	**2**	39.	**4**	51.	**5**
4.	**5**	16.	**4**	28.	**3**	40.	**3**	52.	**5**
5.	**1**	17.	**5**	29.	**3**	41.	**4**	53.	**4**
6.	**2**	18.	**3**	30.	**5**	42.	**5**	54.	**3**
7.	**5**	19.	**3**	31.	**3**	43.	**2**	55.	**1**
8.	**2**	20.	**2**	32.	**4**	44.	**4**	56.	**4**
9.	**4**	21.	**3**	33.	**5**	45.	**3**		
10.	**2**	22.	**3**	34.	**1**	46.	**1**		
11.	**1**	23.	**4**	35.	**5**	47.	**4**		
12.	**4**	24.	**4**	36.	**4**	48.	**4**		

II. SCORE YOURSELF:

Number correct:

Excellent	_____
	41–45
Good	_____
	36–40
Fair	_____
	31–35

III. EVALUATE YOUR SCORE: Did you get at least 38 correct answers? If not, you need more practice for the Mathematics test. In any event, you can improve your performance to Excellent or Good by analyzing your errors.

IV. ANALYZE YOUR ERRORS: To determine your specific weakness, list the number of correct answers you had under each of the following skill areas, and compare your score with the average scores specified in the right-hand column. After studying the answer analysis section beginning on page 363 for each of the questions you got wrong, give yourself more practice in your weak areas with the appropriate material in Chapter 7 before attempting Practice Examination One.

CONTENT AREAS	ITEMS	YOUR SCORE	AVERAGE SCORE
Arithmetic	1–2, 4, 6, 8, 10–14, 16–20, 22–23, 25–27, 32–33, 35–36, 38–40, 45	_____	18
Algebra	5, 7, 15, 21, 28–29, 31, 34, 41–42, 48–49, 51–53, 55–56	_____	11
Geometry	3, 9, 24, 30, 37, 43–44, 46–47, 50, 54	_____	7
	Total	_____	

YOUR TOTAL GED SCORE

The Writing Skills Test   _____

The Social Studies Test   _____

The Science Test   _____

The Interpreting Literature
and the Arts Test   _____

The Mathematics Test   _____

                    Total   _____

ANSWER ANALYSIS

TEST 1: WRITING SKILLS, PART I

1. **2** There is an error in usage. The subject of the sentence is *combination*, which is singular. A singular verb, *makes*, is required for agreement.

2. **3** The error is in punctuation. A comma is needed to set off an introductory phrase.

3. **3** There is a sentence fragment beginning with *seldom*. This is corrected by removing the period and joining the fragment to the rest of the sentence.

4. **1** There is an error in capitalization. Seasons are *not* capitalized.

5. **4** The run-on sentence can be corrected by subordinating the second idea to the first. *Some...vegetables* can be frozen...while *other vegetables can be stored...in a cool area.*

6. **5** No correction is necessary.

7. **2** The correct spelling is *exercise*.

8. **3** The usage error is in the shift in person in two pronouns that refer to the same person. The second-person pronoun *your* in the introductory clause requires a continuation of the second person, *you,* in the main clause.

9. **5** No change is necessary.

10. **4** The correct spelling is *assistance*.

11. **5** No correction is necessary.

12. **1** The original is correct. Two sentences are needed.

13. **5** No correction is necessary.

14. **2** A comma is required to set off items in a series.

15. **2** *Equipment* is the correct spelling.

16. **3** The meaning of the sentence requires *may be served*.

17. **5** No correction is necessary.

18. **3** The correct spelling is *their* rather than *they're*, which is a contraction of *they are*.

19. **4** There is an error in usage. Parallel structure requires the use of infinitives: *to develop, to increase, to learn* (rather than *learning*).

20. **3** The sentence requires the use of *there are* rather than *they are (they're). They are a number of...steps* doesn't make sense.

21. **2** A comma is required after the introductory clause "While...protection."

22. **5** No correction is necessary.

23. **5** No correction is necessary.

24. **3** The future tense should be used for an action taking place in the future, that is, when you take the car in.
25. **5** Two sentences are necessary to correct the run-on sentence. To accomplish this, a period after *order* and a capitalized *That* are needed.
26. **5** No correction is necessary.
27. **4** The correct spelling is *determined*.
28. **1** The correct spelling is *receive*.
29. **2** The rewritten sentence should read "A buying decision is affected by total dollars...."
30. **1** A comma is needed to set off items in a series.
31. **5** No correction is necessary.
32. **1** The original way is the best among the choices offered.
33. **2** Commas are used to set off words or phrases that interrupt the normal word order of the sentence.
34. **4** The relative pronoun *that* avoids the unnecessary use of the words *such programs*.
35. **3** A semicolon is used to separate independent clauses in a sentence.
36. **2** A comma is used after an introductory clause.
37. **4** An apostrophe must be added after the plural noun *shoppers'* to show possession.
38. **2** Making "You are going to move" the subject of the verb *is* eliminates the need for "That statement" and effectively combines the two sentences.
39. **5** No correction is necessary
40. **5** *Or* is correct because "another way" to state the fact is given.
41. **1** A comma is used after an introductory phrase.
42. **4** A comma is used to set off items in a series.
43. **3** The correct spelling is *fulfillment*.
44. **1** The original is correct because *or* connects two independent clauses (*has come through* is understood after *an opportunity to move to a better climate*).
45. **5** No correction is necessary.
46. **2** The correct spelling is *familiar*.
47. **5** No correction is necessary.
48. **1** The correct spelling is *available*.
49. **4** Rewriting the sentence with *The next phase* as the subject requires a singular verb, *is*, in the present tense.
50. **1** The correct spelling is *stationary* when the reference is to a nonmoving object.

51. **2** A phrase inserted in a sentence is set off by commas. Here the second comma should be inserted after *tip*.
52. **4** The subject, *timing*, is singular and the verb *controls* must agree in number with the subject.
53. **5** This is necessary to correct the run-on sentence.
54. **1** An adverb, *nearly*, is necessary when the word modified is an adjective.
55. **4** The sentences can be combined by using an adjective clause, beginning with *which include*, to describe the noun *game fish*.

TEST 1: WRITING SKILLS, PART II
SAMPLE ESSAYS

For involvement

> *Americans who believe, as I do, that we should intervene in the problems of the world cite a number of reasons for their view.*
>
> *The world, they claim, has been made so small by modern technology that countries are interrelated. Thanks to television, we are present when wars break out anywhere in the world. Leaders of foreign nations can communicate directly with us through radio and television. Foreign correspondents bring foreign affairs to our doorstep daily. What happens in Europe, Asia, Africa, and Latin America affects us directly.*
>
> *Since our foreign markets are essential to us, if we help other nations, we help ourselves. Trading partners throughout the world are essential to our economy since many of our largest corporations are multinational.*
>
> *Stable governments abroad are in our own best interest. If we support democracies, they are likely to support us if conflict breaks out.*
>
> *There is also the American tradition of helping the less fortunate. After World War 11, the United States helped rebuild Europe to everyone's benefit. We have been in the forefront of such programs as CARE and the Peace Corps. Many Americans have adopted children living in poor nations. We should continue this tradition of national outreach.*
>
> *These are the reasons why the United States should remain involved in world affairs.*

Summary of reasons <u>for</u> involvement:

1. In our time, the entire world is interrelated.
2. The world has been made small by technology.
3. By helping other nations and their economies, we help our own.
4. Promoting stable foreign governments is in our own best interest.
5. Helping the less fortunate is an American tradition.

Against involvement

Many Americans believe, as I do, that we should not be involved with other nations' problems. They feel that we should help ourselves first. The needs of our own homeless, poor, and unemployed should receive priority. Our resources should be used for domestic purposes before we help foreign nations.

Also, foreign aid often does not reach the people who need it most. Food and medical supplies fall into the hands of the military and others who profit from their distribution. Many foreign nations are under the rule of dictatorships, and aid is used to enrich the people in power and to keep them in office.

The United States contributes over a billion dollars to such organizations as the United Nations and NATO and over 15 billion dollars in aid to foreign military programs, including the cost of maintaining 1.5 million military personnel abroad. Thus we shoulder a disproportionate amount of the foreign aid burden. Nations in Europe and Asia should contribute their fair share.

Many Americans feel that they are overtaxed in order to pay for the millions in aid that is sent abroad.

For these reasons, we should solve our own problems before taking on the world's.

Summary of reasons <u>against</u> involvement:

1. We should solve our own domestic problems first.
2. Foreign aid does not reach the people who need it.
3. In some instances, foreign aid keeps dictatorships in power.
4. The United States pays a disproportionate amount of foreign aid and contributes more military personnel than other nations.
5. American citizens are overtaxed at present and should not have to bear the additional taxes needed for foreign involvement.

TEST 2: SOCIAL STUDIES

1. **1** The last paragraph of the passage states clearly that the governor's veto power is not used sparingly, and that more than one out of four bills fails to receive approval.

2. **4** The second paragraph of the selection deals with the "30 day" rule. The first sentence of this paragraph states that all bills passed within the last ten days of the legislative session are covered by this rule.

3. **4** The first sentence of the first paragraph states that the governor has the power to veto single items of the budget bill. This is an authority not possessed by the president of the United States.

4. **5** Nearly all of the selection deals with a plan of action for use before tho consumer buys. See the second sentence and also the first words of the third paragraph.

5. **2** The consumer is advised to get all promises in writing.

6. **5** It is specifically mentioned that pro rata (or partial) return of moneys and credit toward a replacement may be part of a warranty.

7. **4** By 2030, increasing numbers of Americans will reach the age that makes them eligible for Social Security benefits.

8. **2** A large increase in the birth rate would cause the average age to become lower since the many babies added to the population would counteract the older Americans.

9. **4** Persons concerned with the natural environment fear that an emphasis on greater production and consumption will mean further pollution of the air (by factory smokestacks and apartment house incinerators) and of rivers, lakes, and streams (by industrial wastes and sewage disposal); and increased problems of solid waste disposal and rising noise levels.

10. **4** There is no movement toward a solution to the energy problem as long as the two cyclists representing energy and environment keep pedaling in different directions.

11. **1** A fivefold increase in the price of imported crude oil from 1973 to 1980 severely affected the U.S. economy and forced a search for alternative domestic sources of energy, despite possible immediate negative effects on the environment.

12. **3** This is directly related to the big change from isolationism to internationalism in U.S. foreign policy. From 1920 to 1940 we had no political or military ties to non-American countries, and we never joined the League of Nations. Since World War II, which ended in 1945, the United States has pursued policies of collective security. President F. D. Roosevelt called for the United Nations, of which we are a charter member. President Truman committed U.S. aid to

Europe through the Marshall Plan, the Truman Doctrine, and NATO. Subsequent presidents have continued economic aid to Asia and Africa, military assistance to Middle East and Asian nations, and commitments to Korea and Vietnam. President Kennedy started the Peace Corps, and President Nixon tried to negotiate peace in Vietnam and in Israel. Each of the other choices involves areas in which the Congress, the Supreme Court, and the states have been more influential than the president.

13. **1** The passage stresses the ability of the United States to compete with other countries in a free market.

14. **4** In the final paragraph, President Kennedy mentioned the need for bipartisan support (by both houses of Congress) for his trade legislation.

15. **1** The Gettysburg Address was delivered in 1863. Fourscore and seven years earlier—that is, 87 years earlier—the Declaration of Independence had been signed. It declared the liberty of the thirteen colonies and stated that all men are created equal.

16. **3** The speech was delivered at the Gettsyburg cemetery. In the second paragraph, Lincoln states that this is the purpose of the occasion.

17. **2** Lacking land for agriculture, Nation *A* will use its abundant labor, capital, and management skills to develop industry. The resulting products can be sold to domestic and foreign markets.

18. **2** In the 1800s, Great Britain led the world in manufactures and resembled Nation *A* in factors of production.

19. **4** Nation *B*, with its natural resources and labor, must encourage new industries by protectionist tariffs and by tax concessions to attract capital investment.

20. **4** The purpose of the Truman Doctrine, as opposed to President Monroe's policy of noninterference, was to support the governments of Greece and Turkey against direct and indirect Communist aggression. In 1947 Greece was in especially weakened condition following Nazi occupation during World War II, and was under attack by Communist guerrilla bands.

21. **1** From '60 to '65, the increase was 29.3% minus 18.6%, or 10.7%, greater than for any other interval.

22. **2** Between '70 and '80, the percentage of women working part time remained unchanged at 35.1%.

23. **1** The Chinese of the Middle Kingdom and the ancient Greeks held the belief that their cultures were superior to those of any other group. The word *barbarian* comes from the term used by the Greeks of antiquity to describe foreigners who did not speak Greek.

24. **4** A recession takes place in the economy when purchasing, saving, and business profits go down. The result is an increase in unemployment and a period of reduced economic activity—a recession.

25. **2** Social Darwinism became popular in the second half of the 19th century. It applied Darwin's theory of natural selection to people and nations, attempting thereby to justify the widening gap between the rich and the poor in the United States.

26. **3** The focus of the paragraph is the "problems we face in conserving natural resources."

27. **1** "The pressures of human growth" are identified in the passage as being "acute."

28. **2** The author recognizes the problems realistically and does not minimize them.

29. **2** The purpose of this speech by President Lyndon Johnson was to help troubled young people lead productive lives. In dealing with delinquent and potentially delinquent youth, he was concerned first about preventing them from getting into trouble; then, if they did, in helping them to become useful citizens. These ideas are stated in the first two paragraphs.

30. **5** President Johnson states that he recommends the Juvenile Delinquency Prevention Act of 1967.

31. **3** Family counseling is recommended because so many delinquents "live in broken families, burdened with...problems."

32. **4** Economic controls tried by government have been unable to slow down or catch up with the greased pig of runaway price inflation.

33. **1** Higher interest rates discourage bank loans by business owners and consumers, thereby decreasing the amount of money in circulation and reducing the rate of inflation.

34. **2** Humanists stressed human concerns rather than problems of the next world.

35. **2** The writer states that the frontier experience was the unique element in the development of American culture and values.

36. **1** American social development on the frontier is noted in the first sentence of the passage.

37. **3** Such new opportunities as space exploration and computerization are an important part of contemporary American society.

38. **1** A primary source is an eyewitness account of an event, such as a description in a diary, or an artifact constructed in a specific time period.

39. **2** The data support the conclusion that Belize and Costa Rica are meeting the water needs of their urban populations. In 1980 and

1988, all of the urban population of both nations had access to piped water.

40. **5** The bars for urban population and urban population with access to piped water in 1988 are almost the same height for all countries except Guatemala and El Salvador. The disparity is greatest, however, for Guatemala, where over a million urban-dwelling people have no access to piped water.

41. **5** Lobbyists are representatives of special-interest groups who attempt to influence congressmen by providing information, preparing bills, and testifying at hearings.

42. **2** (*B*) Lobbyists sometimes use undesirable ways of influencing legislation by giving gifts and campaign contributions. The laws they sponsor may not benefit the general public.

43. **1** (*A*) Thousands of bills in many areas are introduced during each session of Congress. These must be handled by standing committees who try to bring expertise to each subject.

44. **1** Out of concern for their own reelection, legislators (the Boy Scouts in the cartoon) introduce consumer protection bills during an election year.

45. **5** Parents, teachers, and age peers are mentioned in the two classes of socializing agents.

46. **4** In the last sentence, all of the reasons are mentioned except the *number* of peers. The group is mentioned as being of increasing importance.

47. **1** The passage, in the second sentence, refers to the great influence of the family.

48. **4** Speaker *A* is talking about a world made smaller by modern technology. Speaker *B* agrees and adds that the problems of any area now become the problems of all humankind. Both feel that, as the world becomes one community, interdependence is a factor in world survival.

49. **1** Ethnocentrism is the view that one's own culture is superior to all others. Speaker *C* is calling for the appreciation of other people's value systems and ways of life.

50. **3** The extermination of over six million people, nearly all Jews, by the Nazi regime in Germany is called the Holocaust.

51. **2** The Nuremberg Trials after World War II, conducted by the Allies against Germany and Japan, established the principle that individuals are responsible to a higher law than that of individual nations. Acts against humanity could not be defended on the grounds of having to follow orders from a superior.

52. **5** A supply-side economist would welcome cutbacks in government

spending to eliminate deficits. An action by the president that sought to cut spending would be supported by a supply-side economist.

53. **1** Mercantilism advocates tariffs to protect local industries from foreign competition.

54. **3** A company is bought out by its employees. This action would be in the direction of the Marxist belief that the means of production should be controlled by the workers.

55. **5** Basketball is a part of U.S. culture that has been adopted by the Russians through the process of cultural diffusion.

56. **5** Thoreau urged his followers to refuse to obey unjust laws, and he himself disobeyed laws that he considered unjust; in other words, he practiced civil disobedience.

57. **1** The Immigration Act of 1965 established occupation as a basic factor in selecting immigrants according to current needs, particularly in technology.

58. **2** Both the immigration policy suggested in the cartoon and the U.S. immigration policy in the 1920s show a preference for certain groups, be they specific nationalities (as in the 1920s) or programmers and electrical engineers (as in the cartoon).

59. **1** President Nixon refused to turn the Watergate tapes over to Congress until the Supreme Court told him that his continued refusal would be an unconstitutional act. This check by the judiciary on the powers of the executive branch of government is an illustration of the system of checks and balances.

60. **2** The graph shows a projected Latin American population of about 600 million people by the year 2000, as opposed to an estimated 300 million for North America (the United States and Canada).

61. **3** Improved nutrition and medical care help account for an increase in the growth rate of the Latin American population.

62. **4** The cartoon shows that people in underdeveloped nations lack basic necessities, whereas people in developed nations have more than they need. The point is made by showing a child in Bangladesh, one of the poorest, most overpopulated nations, who is unable to find drinkable water while an American can choose from an abundance and variety of food.

63. **1** The stark contrast in diet for Americans and Bangladeshi is designed by the cartoonist to arouse our pity for the underfed and to motivate us to do something about the situation.

64. **1** This quotation from a speech on March 12, 1947, has come to be known as the Truman Doctrine. Truman asked for and got $400 million in economic and financial aid to Greece and Turkey to help them resist the "outside pressures" of communism.

TEST 3: SCIENCE

1. **2** Human, monkey, ape, and chimpanzee all belong to the primate group of mammals.

2. **4** Evolution is a process in all of life, not just humans or chimpanzees. Fossils and anatomy provide some of the evidence for evolution.

3. **2** Fossils are the remains of actual living things of the past, so they give the most direct evidence that different forms of life existed.

4. **4** The discovery that today's men are different in size from those of only a few hundred years ago suggests that evolution has not stopped.

5. **3** Use the formula:

$$\text{Density} = \frac{\text{mass}}{\text{volume}}$$

$$\frac{24 \text{ g}}{8 \text{ cm}^3} = 3 \text{ g} / \text{cm}^3$$

6. **3** The diagram indicates that the density of sample B is 3 g/cm³. If the sample were split in half, the density would remain the same. The density of a sample is the ratio of its mass to its volume. When the sample is cut in half, both the mass and the volume of the sample are also reduced by half. As a result, the density remains the same.

7. **4** The mass and volume for different samples of a given substance are directly proportional. This relationship is illustrated by graph 4, which shows a direct relationship between mass and volume. As mass increases, volume increases proportionally.

8. **5** To answer this question, the volumes of samples A and B must first be calculated.

   Volume = length × width × height

   For A: Volume =
   2 cm × 2 cm × 2 cm = 8 cm³
   For B: Volume =
   3 cm × 2 cm × 1 cm = 6 cm³
   The volume for sample C is given as 12 cm³. Sample C therefore has the largest volume, and sample B has the smallest volume.

9. **2** According to the theory of continental drift and plate tectonics, the surface of the Earth is moving. The undersea volcanic vent, however, opens deep into the center of the Earth and is stable. One theory about the formation of the Hawaiian Islands suggests that a section of the Earth moves over the volcanic vent, which spews forth enough

material to form an island; then, as a new section of Earth moves over the vent, another island is formed.

10. **5** $2.5 \times 4,800$ ft./sec. = 12,000 ft.

11. **1** An electromagnet is the only type of magnet that can be turned on and off.

12. **4** That Earth is a magnet is proved by the fact that the planet can exert a magnetic force.

13. **5** Lodestone is a well-known natural magnet.

14. **3** In diesel engines the tight-fitting pistons compress air and thus cause the temperature to rise above the kindling temperature of the heavy fuels used. This serves the same purpose as the spark plugs in the gasoline engine.

15. **1** Locomotives can easily carry the heavy diesel engine and thus take advantage of using a less expensive fuel.

16. **1** Because of the strong compression stroke, diesel engines are very heavy and therefore not suitable for airplanes.

17. **1** Earthquakes are the result of the movement of rock masses below the Earth's surface, resulting in breaking rock layers and displacement (fault) of segments of the layer at the breaking point. The folding of rock layers results from the action of lesser forces acting over a longer period of time. The forces produced by landslides are too small to create an earthquake.

18. **2** The 1989 earthquake in San Francisco killed many people because older buildings and roadways were not built to withstand such a severe shock. The more modern buildings stood.

19. **4** It is shock waves in the crust that a seismograph detects, whether they are produced by earthquakes or by nuclear explosions.

20. **3** A calcium atom with a valence of +2 has two electrons in its outer ring. Chlorine with a valence of −1 needs one electron to complete its outer ring. Two chlorine atoms can combine with one atom of calcium to form calcium chloride ($CaCl_2$).

21. **4** Atomic mass (number of protons plus number of neutrons) minus atomic number (number of protons) equals number of neutrons. For lithium, $7 - 3 = 4$.

22. **5** The atomic number is equal to the number of protons.

23. **4** This element, sodium, which has 11 protons, must have 11 electrons in its shells. The first shell holds 2, and the second shell holds 8, leaving 1 electron in its outer shell. Since it can lend this electron to another atom, it has a valence of +1.

24. **5** Many parts of the plant are involved, but it is in the chloroplasts that the actual chemical process takes place.

25. **3** Water from the soil is conducted through the xylem.

26. **3** Chemical energy is needed to split water into H^+ (combined in the glucose) and O_2.

27. **4** Hydrogen and carbon dioxide are successively built up into sugars.

28. **3** Chlorophyll in the chloroplasts of the cells transforms the energy of light into chemical energy.

29. **4** The stomata are openings through which carbon dioxide enters the leaf.

30. **5** The energy that enters the plant is in the form of light; the output is the chemical energy stored in the carbohydrates. The passage says nothing about growth.

31. **5** Since carbon dioxide is used in photosynthesis, increasing the supply would speed up the process.

32. **4** The birds have come to resemble each other because they have evolved to adapt to the same lifestyle. Choices 2, 3, and 5 contradict the statement that the birds are unrelated.

33. **1** According to the information, the white moths were invisible to predators against the light-colored bark. When the trees were darkened by soot, however, the moths were very easy to see.

34. **3** The only life process that a snake cannot perform alone is reproduction.

35. **5** Since the heart is a muscle with nerves that conduct impulses, potassium is an important nutrient. Many prescription drugs that heart patients take have a tendency to remove excess water. Dissolved potassium is thus lost.

36. **5** Stack gases combine with atmospheric water to produce acid rain, which can damage embryos, buildings, trees, and lungs.

37. **3** Mice have many offspring, with a short time between generations. Choice 1 is wrong because bacteria do not reproduce sexually. Choices 2 and 4 are wrong because dogs and humans, while of great practical interest, are not as prolific as mice. Oak trees are extremely prolific, but they have to grow for many years before they produce acorns.

38. **4** The passage implies that green bacteria evolved from nongreen forms, which must have been on earth first. Animal life requires oxygen, so it must have come after the green bacteria changed the atmosphere.

39. **3** The wolf population peaked a year after the peak of the moose population, so many wolves must have been born when the moose population was at its highest.

40. **3** The fossils in rock layer *D* are older than those in layer *A*. Fossils are found in sedimentary rocks. Sedimentary rocks are formed as layer upon layer of material is deposited. The oldest sediment layer *D* was laid down first and appears at the bottom. The youngest layer is at the top.

41. **1** Breathing air is not a form of direct transmission of body fluids. In sexual intercourse, each person has intimate contact with the body fluids of the other, so Choice 2 is wrong. Choices 3, 4 and 5 all involve transmission of blood from person to person.

42. **3** The breeder's problem is to locate the immune plants, which will be those that survive when herbicides are applied.

43. **5** Choice 1 is wrong; a farmer might follow this practice, but it is not what he *should* do. Choice 4 is wrong because you are asked the basis on which he should decide. There is no reason to suspect that Choices 2 and 3 are relevant.

44. **1** When evaporation occurs, heat is required to change a liquid (here, water) to a gas. Evaporation is a cooling process.

45. **4** Cloning is used to produce a large number of plants in a short period of time. According to the passage, one million plants can be cloned in about 6 months.

46. **3** According to the passage, each cell contains chromosomes, a complete blueprint for reproducing itself.

47. **3** The hormones auxin and cytokinin stimulate the production of new plants. Hormones are substances that regulate the growth and reproduction of organisms.

48. **2** Cloning is defined as a form of vegetative propagation. Vegetative propagation is a form of asexual reproduction; that is, only one parent is required.

49. **2** Sexual reproduction processes mix the heredities of the two parents, and produce offspring different from both. In cloning and other vegetative methods, there is no change in the genotype.

50. **2** The medicine is a suspension, not a solution. All incorrect choices are characteristic of solutions.

51. **5** All other choices have a sour taste, so they are acid.

52. **2** The slippery feel of soap indicates that it is a base.

53. **5** Mixing an acid and a base would produce a product that is neither.

54. **5** Heat is a form of energy that moves spontaneously from regions of higher temperatures to lower. Cold is not a thing; the word here is used as an adjective.

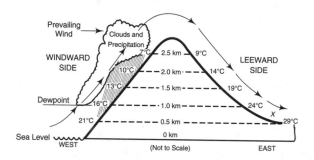

55. **5** On the west side of the mountain, the temperature is dropping 3°C for each 0.5 km. At 2.5 km the temperature is 7°C. At the top it is 3° less, or 4°C. The same results would be obtained by using data from the east side of the mountain, where the temperature is dropping 5°C for each 0.5 km.

56. **2** When precipitation occurs, the relative humidity is 100%. In the diagram, precipitation is occurring on the windward side of the mountain at an elevation of 2.5 km.

57. **4** As the air rises, it expands. When it expands, it cools. You may have noticed that the air rushing out of a tire feels cool. This is because the air is expanding.

58. **1** As the air descends on the leeward side of the mountain, it becomes warmer. As a result, there will rarely be precipitation there. The lack of precipitation will produce an arid region. The deserts in the southwestern part of the United States are located on the leeward sides of mountain ranges.

59. **2** Some plants release pollen to the atmosphere. Human activity does not greatly affect the amount of pollen in the atmosphere. Substances are usually considered pollutants when they are added to the environment by human activity. Any portion of the environment can become polluted, including the atmosphere, the hydrosphere, or the lithosphere. The environment is said to be polluted when more of some substance is added than would normally be present. If, for example, large amounts of waste are dumped into a river, the water becomes polluted. Fish and other living organisms in the river may die if the pollution level becomes too great.

60. **2** The block and the weight are tied together, so they must always have the same speed. If the force moving the block becomes larger than the friction, the block must accelerate.

61. **2** Although a turtle has a hard outer shell similar to an exoskeleton, it also has an internal skeleton and is classified as a vertebrate.

62. **3** If the experiment is to test the effect of the flypaper, there must be no other difference between the two bottles; all properties that are the same in both are controls.

63. **3** The investigator is clearly using flypaper in the bottle because it will trap flies that can fly, but not the others.

64. **2** The experimenter must decide in advance what to put in the bottles in order that the outcome will give a meaningful answer to the question.

65. **5** The source of winglessness has nothing to do with the experimental problem.

66. **4** In most circumstances in nature, it must be expected that wings are useful. This experiment sets up an artificial environment in which the survival values are reversed. Some such environment might well exist in nature.

TEST 4: INTERPRETING LITERATURE AND THE ARTS

1. **3** Mary's activities included school work, volunteer editorial work, and riding.

2. **1** Mary is referred to as a "little figure."

3. **4** All three are mentioned: she wore khakis and a red hair ribbon, and waved her cowboy hat.

4. **4** Because she waved to a friend with the wrong hand, the horse veered.

5. **1** The topic sentence refers to Mary White's last hour as being typical of her happiness.

6. **3** Only an animal is awake to listen to Iona.

7. **1** Iona feels he must do something since he can always sleep later.

8. **2** The name of Iona's son, Kuzma Ionitch, is a clue to an eastern European setting.

9. **3** The present tense gives a feeling that the events described are happening now.

10. **5** Iona asks the horse to put herself in the position of a foal's mother who loses her foal.

11. **2** Guy is "quick," and the narrator is "determined." There is a contrast also, in their reactions to the accident and the possibility of death.

12. **3** A simile is a direct comparison that uses the word *like* or *as*.

13. **2** The pronoun *they* refers to the subjects of the preceding sentence, July and August.

14. **4** If the narrator's son were to die, he would "lightly waft" or float away.

15. **1** The narrator became a shadow and a spectre, a ghost, both of which are intangible or unreal.

16. **1** The power poles are replacing the eucalyptus and thus are, in a sense, new trees.

17. **3** The poet calls the power poles "frigid" and "passionless."

18. **4** The children realize they cannot climb the "new trees" and miss the old ones.

19. **3** The poet considers the electric poles incapable of feeling ("passionless verticals") since they are not like trees, which are members of the Plant Kingdom and draw life from the earth.

20. **3** "Tree imposters" is a metaphor in which the poles are compared to false-pretending people.

21. **3** Line 25 states that the poet cannot be consoled. He wishes he could wake Jane from "this sleep"—death.

22. **5** In line 28, he speaks of "my love."

23. **3** Jane is referred to as "a wren," "my sparrow," and "my skittery pigeon."

24. **4** The poet goes from "she" to "her" to "you."

25. **4** In line 29, he indicates he has "no rights in this matter."

26. **3** Walter indirectly indicates that Lindner can expect the same treatment if Lindner insults him.

27. **2** It can be inferred that a better home will be part of a new life.

28. **3** Mama says, "My son said we was going to move," so Walter will be the head of the house.

29. **5** As he leaves, Lindner shakes his head in disagreement.

30. **3** Walter says, "We are very proud people."

31. **1** The author repeats "I remember" and says he has "never forgotten" and "shall never forget."

32. **4** The chief remembers his mother cooking, his father returning from hunting, his grandfather teaching him.

33. **1** The writer says his world reflected the wisdom and benevolence of the Great Spirit.

34. **1** The author writes, "There were never enough hours in a day to exhaust the pleasure of observing every living creature."

35. **5** The author describes the privileges he had on the "unspoiled prairie one hundred years ago."

36. **4** The author says that, in comparisons of language, Shakespeare is bound to win.

37. **3** The author says, among other unfavorable comparisons, that the songs of West Side Story pale next to the speech of Mercutio.

38. **1** The passage states that Romeo and Juliet "arc a little too slender" to carry the play and this is "equally true of Tony and Maria."

39. **4** The passage observes that the heroes and heroines do "not shake us with...fear."

40. **3** Romeo and Juliet suffer from "the caprice of fate," while Tony and Maria suffer from prejudice and hatred.

41. **4** The author reports that Chagall plays down the "almost sensual gratification" of his colors with a "typical pixie twinkle."

42. **5** Only the first paragraph is concerned with painting. The rest of the article deals with stained glass.

43. **1** The article states that Chagall "slapped on colors . . ., often contrasting them."

44. **3** The conclusion of the article stresses Chagall's faith in mankind's ascent through suffering to salvation.

45. **4** A critic is quoted as saying that Chagall became "his own most faithful imitator."

TEST 5: MATHEMATICS

1. **2** First find the total mileage.

   135 + 162 + 98 + 117 + 216 = 728 mi.

   Divide the total mileage (728) by the number of miles covered for each gallon of gas used (14) to find the number of gallons of gas needed.
   728 ÷ 14 = 52 gal.

2. **4** Since 5¢ will pay for 12 min. $0.50 will pay for 10 × 12 = 120 min. 120 min. = 2 hr.

3. **1** If $AB = AC$, then $\angle ABC$ is an isosceles triangle and base angles B and C have equal measures: $m\angle B = m\angle C$.

    Let $x = m\angle B = m\angle C$.

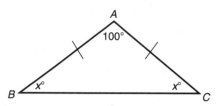

The sum of the measures of the angles of a triangle is 180°, so

$$
\begin{array}{rcl}
x + x + 100 & = & 180 \\
2x + 100 & = & 180 \\
2x & = & 180 - 100 = 80 \\
x & = & 40
\end{array}
$$

4. **5** Since 432 shirts were sold at $15 each, the number of dollars taken in was 15 × 432.

    Since 368 shirts were sold at $18 each, the number of dollars taken in was 18 × 368.

    The total amount taken in was 15 × 432 + 18 × 368, which may be written as (15)(432) + (368)(18).

5. **1** The total number of games played was $X + Y + Z$.

    The number of games won was X.

    The fractional part of the games won was $\dfrac{X}{X + Y + Z}$

6. **2** 1/2 of the pupils walk to school.

    1/4 of the other 1/2 = 1/4 × 1/2 = 1/8 use bicycles.

    1/2 + 1/8 = 4/8 + 1/8 = 5/8 of the pupils either walk or use bicycles.

    Therefore, 1 − 5/8 = 3/8 use other means.

7. **5** Since $2x > 9$, then $x > 9/2, = 4\frac{1}{2}$.

    The only choice that is greater than $4\frac{1}{2}$ is 5.

    An alternative method is to replace x by each of the choices given. The only choice that makes the inequality true is $x = 5$.

8. **2** Only three of the choices are units of distance: centimeter, meter, and kilometer. Of these, the kilometer is the largest, and is the only one that is appropriate for measuring the distance between cities. Note that 1 km is approximately 5/8 mi.

9. **4** Let x = height of flagpole. The two poles and their shadows can be
represented by two triangles.

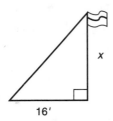 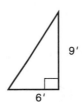

Since the triangles are similar, the lengths of corresponding sides
are in proportion.

Set up the proportion:

$$\frac{h \text{ (flagpole)}}{h \text{ (pole)}} = \frac{l \text{ (flagpole shadow)}}{l \text{ (pole shadow)}}$$

$$\frac{x}{9} = \frac{16}{6}$$

$$6x = 9 \times 16 = 144$$

$$x = \frac{144}{6} = 24$$

10. **2** 1 ft. = 12 in.

9 ft. 8 in. = 9 × 12 + 8 = 116 in.

116 ÷ 4 = 29 in. = 2 ft. 5 in.

11. **1** The purse contains 6 + 5 + 8 = 19 coins, 5 of which are dimes.

Therefore, the probability of drawing a dime is $\frac{5}{19}$.

12. **4** When an odd number of scores are arranged in increasing order, the
median is the middle number. In this case, there are 9 numbers, so
the median is the fifth number.

272, 274, 275, 276, 278, 281, 283, 284, 287

median

13. **4** The pens cost 3 for $0.97.

Cost of 1 dozen pens = 4($0.97) = $3.88.

Cost of 8 pencils = $4.60 − 3.88 = $0.72.

Cost of 1 pencil = $0.72 ÷ 8 = 9 cents.

14. **1** Since 1 in. on the map represents 150 mi., 3 in. represents
3(150) = 450 mi., and 1/2 in. represents $\frac{1}{2}$(150) = 75 mi.
Then $3\frac{1}{2}$ in. represents 450 + 75 = 525 mi.

15. **2** To find the perimeter of the figure, find the sum of the lengths of the four sides:

$$2a + b + a + 3b + 3a + b + 3a + 2b = 9a + 7b.$$

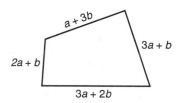

16. **4** The distance between point A and point B is 10 units. Thus, the midpoint of $\overline{AB}$ is located at 5 units to the right of point A.
The coordinate of the midpoint of $\overline{AB}$ is 3.

17. **5** Since 3 ties sold for $23, 6 ties cost 2($23) = $46.
3 shirts cost $43.
Since slacks sold for $32.75 per pair, 2 pairs of slacks cost 2($32.75) = $65.50.
1 jacket cost for $58.45.
$46 + $43 + $65.50 + $58.45 = $212.95

18. **3** Write all the numbers as decimals, so that it is easier to arrange the numbers in order of size.
19% = 0.19, $\frac{1}{2}$ = 0.50, and $\frac{3}{5}$ = 60.
The correct order from greatest to smallest is
0.80, 0.60, 0.50, 0.19, 0.080
or 0.80, $\frac{3}{5}$, $\frac{1}{2}$, 19%, 0.080
The correct choice is (3).

19. **3** To find the average speed, in miles per hour, divide the distance, in miles, by the time, in hours. Since 5 hr. and 30
min. is $5\frac{1}{2}$, or 5.5 hr., divide 1,364 by
5.5: 1364 ÷ 5.5 = 248.

20. **2** To write a number in scientific notation, write it as the product of a number between 1 and 10 and a power of 10. In this case, the number between 1 and 10 is 8.5. In going from 8.5 to 85,000,000,000, you move the decimal point 10 places to the right. Therefore $85,000,000,000 = 8.5 \times 10^{10}$.

21. **3** $3ab - x2y = 3(4)(5) - (2)(2)(3)$
$$= 60 \quad - 12 = 48$$

22. **3** The sum of the measures of the angles around the center of the circle is 360°. The fraction that represents the part of the total number of workers engaged in transportation is

$$\frac{20}{360} = \frac{1}{8}.$$
$$\frac{1}{18} \text{ of } 180,000 = \frac{180,000}{18} = 10,000$$

23. **4** M = number of persons in trade and finance
Let x = number of persons in manufacturing
Set up a proportion:
$$\frac{90}{M} = \frac{120}{x}$$
$$90x = 120M$$
$$x = \frac{120M}{90} = \frac{4M}{3}$$

24. **4** Since m∠ABC = 68° and $\overline{BF}$ bisects ∠ABC, then m∠EBC = 1/2 (68) = 34°.
Since m∠ACB = 72° and $\overline{CD}$ bisects ∠ACB, then m∠ECB = 1/2 (72) = 36°.

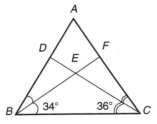

Since the sum of the measure of the angles of a triangle is 180°,
m∠EBC + m∠ECB + m∠BEC = 180°
$$34 + 36 + m∠BEC = 180°$$
$$70 + m∠BEC = 180°$$
$$m∠BEC = 180 - 70 = 110°$$

25. **3** Frank has $30.
       Jack has $30 − $3 = $27.
       Bill has $27 + $5 = $32.

26. **5** You know that John Davis lost *at least* 4 lb. each month. But he may have lost much more. Not enough information is given to determine his exact weight after the 6-month period.

27. **2** The annual interest on $10,000 at
       $8\frac{1}{2}$% is $10,000 × 0.085 = $850. Thus, every 6 months Mr. Ames receives 1/2 of $850 = $425.

28. **3** Since the aquarium is in the shape of a rectangular solid, its volume is given by the formula $V = lwh$. To find the volume in cubic feet, express each of l, w, and h in feet.

    Length, l, is 3 ft.

    Width, w = 1 ft. 8 in. = $1\frac{2}{3}$ ft. = $\frac{5}{3}$ ft.

    Height, h, is 1 ft. 6 in. = $1\frac{1}{2}$ ft. = $\frac{3}{2}$ ft.

    $V = 3 \times \frac{5}{3} \times \frac{3}{2} = \frac{15}{2}$ = 7.5 cu. ft.

29. **3** Let $9x$ = number of men at the meeting, and $2x$ = number of women at the meeting.
       Since $2x = 12$, $x = 6$.
       Then $9x = 9(6) = 54$.

30. **5** Slope of $\overleftrightarrow{AB}$

    $= \dfrac{\text{change in y-coordinates}}{\text{change in x-coordinates}}$

    Slope of $\overleftrightarrow{AB} = \dfrac{7-1}{4-2} = \dfrac{6}{2} = 3$

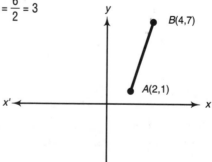

31. **3** Let x = number of points scored by Jim, and
$3x$ = number of points scored by Bill.
$$x + 3x = 56$$
$$4x = 56$$
$$x = 56 \div 4 = 14$$
$$3x = 3(14) = 42$$

32. **4** Note that each subdivision line on the vertical axis represents 200 mi. The Rio Grande is about 1,500 mi. long, and the Seine is about 500 mi. long. Therefore, the Rio Grande is about 1,000 mi. longer than the Seine.

33. **5** In 1988, the receipts were $600,000 and the expenses were $500,000. In 1988, receipts exceeded expenses by $100,000.

34. **1** Six pencils will cost 6 times as much as 1 pencil. Since y is the cost of 1 pencil, the cost of 6 pencils is 6 times $y = 6y$.

35. **5** In 2 weeks Mr. Martin worked a total of $(42 + 37)$ hr. and earned $12 for each hour. Therefore, the total number of dollars he earned was $12(42 + 37)$.

36. **4** The total enrollment is
$$360 + 300 + 280 + 260 = 1,200$$
The part of the total enrollment that represents the freshmen is
$$\frac{360}{1,200} = \frac{36}{120} = \frac{3}{10} = 30\%.$$

37. **3** Since pairs of alternate interior angles of parallel lines have equal measures, $m\angle BCD = m\angle ABC$. Thus $m\angle BCD = 112°$.
$$m\angle ECD = \frac{1}{2} m\angle BCD$$
$$= \frac{1}{2}(112°) = 56°$$

38. **2** 22 ft. 4 in. = 22(12) + 4 = 268 in.
$$268 \div 4 = 67 \text{ in. per piece}$$
$$\frac{67}{12} = 5\frac{7}{12}$$
Each piece is 5 ft. 7 in. in length.

39. **4** According to the graph, the population in 1992 was midway between 25,000 and 30,000.
25,000 + 30,000 = 55,000
55,000 ÷ 2 = 27,500

40. **3** According to the graph, the population in 1990 was 20,000 and in 1991 it was also 20,000. There was no change in population between 1990 and 1991.

41. **4** Use the formula $V = lwh$ to represent the volume of the rectangular solid.

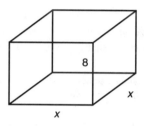

$V = x \cdot x \cdot 8 = 8x^2$
$8x^2 = 392$

42. **5** Since the total number of votes cast is not given, an equation to solve the problem cannot be set up.

43. **2** If $AB = AC$, $m\angle C = m\angle B = 68°$.
Since $\overline{AD} \perp \overline{BF}$, $m\angle ADC = 90°$.

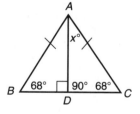

Since the sum of the measures of the angles of a triangle is 180°:
$68 + 90 + m\angle x = 180$
$158 + m\angle x = 180$
$m\angle x = 180 - 158 = 22°$

44. **4** In the right triangle use the Pythagorean theorem.

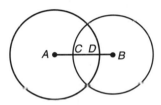

$$x^2 = (12)^2 + (16)^2$$
$$= 144 + 256 = 400$$
$$x = \div \sqrt{400} = 20$$

45. **3** Since $5^2 = 25$ and $6^2 = 36$, $\sqrt{30}$ is between 5 and 6.

46. **1** AD = radius of large circle = 20 in.
BC = radius of small circle = 8 in.

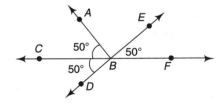

$CD = 6$
$DB = BC - CD = 8 - 6 = 2$
$AB = AD + DB = 20 + 2 = 22$ in.

47. **4** $m\angle EBF = m\angle CBD = 50°$ since vertical angles have equal measures.

Since $\overleftrightarrow{CB}$ bisects $\angle ABD$, $m\angle ABC = m\angle CBD$.
Thus, $m\angle ABC = 50°$.

48. **4** To find the cost of n lb. of sugar at c cents per pound,
multiply n by c to obtain nc.
To find the change received subtract nc cents from 100 cents.
The result is $100 - nc$.

49. **1** Let x = number of students in the graduating class.
    0.85x plan to go to college

    0.85x = 170, so x = 170 ÷ 0.85

$$0.85 \overline{)170.00} \quad \begin{array}{c} 200 \end{array}$$

50. **2** Divide the given figure into two rectangles by drawing a dotted line.

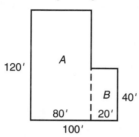

Width of rectangle A = 100 − 20 = 80
Length of rectangle A = 120
Area of rectangle A = (80)(120) = 9,600 sq. ft.
Area of rectangle B = 40 × 20 = 800 sq. ft.
Area of figure = 9,600 + 800 = 10,400 sq. ft.

51. **5** Check each inequality or equation in turn.
    (1) 3(10) + 1 > 12, 30 + 1 > 12. True
    (2) 2(10) − 3 < 25, 20 − 3 < 25. True
    (3) 10^2 + 1 > 10^2 − 1,
        100 + 1 > 100 − 1. True
    (4) 4(10) − 1 = 39, 40 − 1 = 39. True
    (5) 2(10) − 7 > 7 − 2(10),
        20 − 7 < 7 − 20. Not true
    The correct choice is (5).

52. **5** Let x = measure of smaller acute angle, and 4x = measure of larger
    acute angle.

$$\begin{aligned}
x + 4x &= 90° \\
5x &= 90° \\
x &= 90 ÷ 5 = 18° \\
4x &= 4(18) = 72°
\end{aligned}$$

53. **4** The borrower pays 50 cents for the first 3 days plus 15 cents for each of the $(n-3)$ days after the third day.
Thus, the correct formula is $C = 50 + 15(n-3)$.

54. **3** Since PQ is parallel to RS, alternate interior angles are equal: $2x = x + 25$. Subtracting x from each side yields $x = 25$.

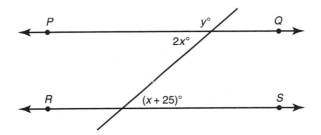

55. **1** The diagram shows that $2x + y = 180°$. In question 55 it was determined that $x = 25°$. Then $180 = 2(25) + y = 50 + y$, so $y = 130°$.

56. **4** Factor the left-hand side of
$$x^2 - x - 12 = 0:$$
$$(x-4)(x+3) = 0,$$
$$x - 4 = 0 \quad \textbf{or} \quad x + 3 = 0$$
$$x = 4 \quad \textbf{or} \qquad x = -3$$